D1191087

DAVID L. PHILLIPS is Director of the Program on Peace-building and Human Rights at Columbia University's Institute for the Study of Human Rights. He has worked as a senior advisor to the United Nations Secretariat and as a foreign affairs expert and senior advisor to the US Department of State. He has held positions as a visiting scholar at Harvard University's Center for Middle East Studies, Executive Director of Columbia University's International Conflict Resolution Program, Director of the Program on Conflict Prevention and Peace-building at the American University, Associate Professor at New York University's Department of Politics, and Professor at the Diplomatic Academy of Vienna. He has also been a Senior Fellow and Deputy Director of the Council on Foreign Relations' Center for Preventive Action, Senior Fellow at the Atlantic Council of the United States, Senior Fellow at the Center for Strategic and International Studies, Director of the European Centre for Common Ground, Project Director at the International Peace Research Institute of Oslo, President of the Congressional Human Rights Foundation, and Executive Director of the Elie Wiesel Foundation. His previous publications include *An Uncertain Ally: Turkey under Erdogan's Dictatorship*; *The Kurdish Spring: A New Map of the Middle East*; *From Bullets to Ballots: Violent Muslim Movements in Transition*; *Losing Iraq: Inside the Postwar Reconstruction Fiasco* and *Unsilencing the Past: Track Two Diplomacy and Turkish–Armenian Reconciliation*. He has also authored many policy reports and writes regularly for publications including the *New York Times*, *Wall Street Journal*, *Financial Times*, *International Herald Tribune*, and *Foreign Affairs*.

"This excellent work by David Phillips has broadened the canvas of failed American policy by exposing the darkest period of our national honor in this new century. *The Great Betrayal* accurately portrays how our government treacherously delivered to Iran, the Iraqi Kurds, our only pro-American ally in a region of Iranian dominance. In October 2017 the US President promised to get tough on Iran and to roll back their influence in the region. Immediately following that announcement, the administration stood paralyzed as the Iraqi Army, commanded by Iran's leading general, Qasem Soleimani and supported by both Iranian and Hezbollah militias, overwhelmed the Kurdish Peshmerga in Kirkuk. Consequently, our nation's cowardly policy has allowed Iran to extend their dominance from Tehran to the Mediterranean, a reach they have not achieved since the Medo-Persian Empire. Furthermore, it signals to both friends and enemies that America can no longer be considered a trusted and dependable ally. This book should be required reading for all government officials!"

Jay Garner, Lt General (ret), US Army

"*The Great Betrayal* is well-researched and written about the tragedy that has befallen the Kurdish people. The only real friend of the United States and the West, they fought and died with US forces fighting ISIS, yet, when they were attacked, both in Iraqi Kurdistan and in Afrin, the US declared, 'we don't take sides', thus emboldening the Shi'ite militias and the Jihadists in Syria. A must-read for anyone interested in Middle East geopolitics."

Najmaldin Karim, Governor of Kirkuk

"*The Great Betrayal* tells how the Trump administration sided with Iran's top general and a terrorist convicted of blowing up an American embassy against the Iraqi Kurds, America's most loyal ally in the fight against ISIS. Like so much of Donald Trump's presidency, this story—well told by long-time Iraq expert David Phillips—wouldn't be believable if it weren't also true."

Peter W. Galbraith, first US Ambassador to Croatia
from 1993 to 1998 and author of *The End of Iraq*

"This is not a work of detachment—David Phillips makes that clear from the outset. But one does not have to agree with all his premises (I do not) to find great value in this book. Phillips has compiled an extraordinary amount of research that he weaves into his well-written narrative. It will be of great value to policy-makers, pundits and historians alike—as well as to general readers seeking a better understanding of a complicated situation. As for the Kurds, spread among four countries that unite in opposition to an independent nation, they objectify the hard truth noted by Ernest Gellner many years ago: in this world, there are more nationalisms than nations."

Ryan C. Crocker, former US Ambassador to Iraq (2007–2009)

"A must-read for those who want to understand why the Kurds play such a key role in the future of the Middle East."

Bernard Kouchner,
French Minister of Foreign and European Affairs 2007–10

THE
GREAT
BETRAYAL

HOW AMERICA ABANDONED THE KURDS AND LOST THE MIDDLE EAST

DAVID L. PHILLIPS

I.B. TAURIS
LONDON · NEW YORK

Published in 2019 by
I.B.Tauris & Co. Ltd
London • New York
www.ibtauris.com

Copyright © 2019 David L. Phillips

The right of David L. Phillips to be identified as the author of this work has been
asserted by him in accordance with the Copyright, Designs and Patents Act 1988.

All rights reserved. Except for brief quotations in a review, this book, or any part
thereof, may not be reproduced, stored in or introduced into a retrieval system, or
transmitted, in any form or by any means, electronic, mechanical, photocopying,
recording or otherwise, without the prior written permission of the publisher.

Every attempt has been made to gain permission for the use of the images
in this book. Any omissions will be rectified in future editions.

References to websites were correct at the time of writing.

ISBN: 978 1 78831 397 1
eISBN: 978 1 78672 576 9
ePDF: 978 1 78673 576 8

A full CIP record for this book is available from the British Library
A full CIP record is available from the Library of Congress

Library of Congress Catalog Card Number: available

Text design and typesetting by Tetragon, London
Printed and bound in Great Britain

To my recently deceased father, Lawrence S. Phillips,
who was a champion of social justice.

This book is also dedicated to breaking the cycle of betrayal
and abuse that has afflicted the Kurdish people.

CONTENTS

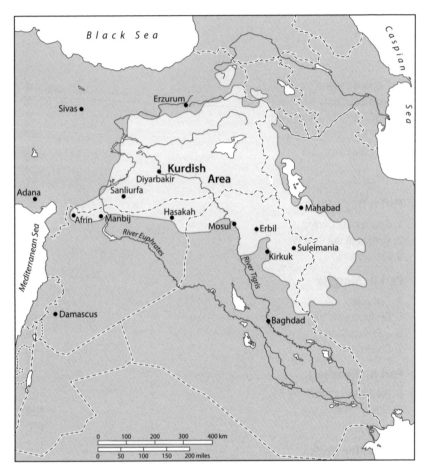

Map of Kurdistan

LIST OF ILLUSTRATIONS

ACKNOWLEDGMENTS

With thanks to Alexis Crews, my research assistant, and Joanna Godfrey, my editor. Special thanks to my daughters, Tara and Maya, for tolerating my writing at the kitchen table.

ABBREVIATIONS AND ACRONYMS

AQI	Al-Qaeda in Iraq
BSF	Border Security Force
CENTO	Central Treaty Organization
CJD	Coalition for Justice and Democracy
COIN	counter-insurgency strategy
CPA	Coalition Provisional Authority
FDI	foreign direct investment
FSA	Free Syrian Army
FTO	foreign terrorist organization
GOI	Government of Iraq
ICTS	Iraqi Counter-Terrorism Services
IDF	Israeli Defense Forces
IDP	internally displaced person
IED	improvised explosive device
IHEC	Independent High Electoral Commission (of Iraq)
IHERC	Independent High Elections and Referendum Commission (Kurdistan)
INC	Iraqi National Congress
IRGC	Iranian Revolutionary Guard Corps
ISF	Iraqi Security Forces
ISIS	Islamic State in Iraq and Syria
JCC	Joint Crisis Coordination Center
JCPOA	Joint Cooperative Plan of Action
KDP	Kurdistan Democratic Party
KDPI	Kurdistan Democratic Party of Iran
KDPS	Kurdistan Democratic Party of Syria
KIHEC	Kurdistan Independent High Electoral Commission
KNC	Kurdish National Council
KRG	Kurdistan Regional Government
KRI	Kurdistan Region of Iraq

KRM	Kurdish Referendum Movement
KRSC	Kurdistan Region Security Council
KTJ	Society for the Ascension of Kurdistan
MIT	National Intelligence Agency (Turkey)
MRAP	Mine-Resistant Ambush-Protected (Vehicle)
NATO	North Atlantic Treaty Organization
OAPEC	Organization of Arab Petroleum Exporting Countries
OCHA	(UN) Office for the Coordination of Humanitarian Affairs
OPCW	Organization for the Prohibition of Chemical Weapons
OPEC	Organization of Petroleum Exporting Countries
PAK	Parti Azadi Kurdistan
PJAK	Party for a Free Life in Kurdistan
PKK	Kurdistan Workers' Party
PMU	Popular Mobilization Unit
PSA	production-sharing agreement
PUK	Patriotic Union of Kurdistan
PYD	Democratic Union Party
SCO	Shanghai Cooperation Organization
SDF	Syrian Democratic Forces
SEATO	Southeast Asia Treaty Organization
SFRC	Senate Foreign Relations Committee
SGBV	sexual and gender-based violence
SOFA	Status of Forces Agreement
SOMO	State Oil Marketing Organization (Iraq)
TAL	Transitional Administrative Law
TGNA	Turkish Grand National Assembly
UNHCR	United Nations High Commissioner for Refugees
UNSC	United Nations Security Council
WFP	World Food Program
WHO	World Health Organization
WMD	weapons of mass destruction
YPG	People's Protection Units

GLOSSARY OF PERSONALITIES

Heider al-Abadi served as Prime Minister of Iraq from 2014 to 2018.

Madeleine Albright served as US Secretary of State from 1997 to 2001.

Hussein bin Ali, Sharif of Mecca, was a Hashemite Arab leader who led the Arab revolt against the Ottoman Empire.

Hadi Al-Ameri is the former Iraqi minister of transportation and the head of the Badr Organization, which was the military wing of the Supreme Islamic Iraqi Council. He heads the Fatih political movement.

Bashar al-Assad is the 19th and current President of Syria, who has held office since 2000. He concurrently serves as the commander in chief of the Syrian Armed Forces.

Hafez al-Assad is the father of Bashar al-Assad. Hafez served as President of Syria from 1971 to 2000.

Mustafa Kemal Atatürk founded the Republic of Turkey in 1923.

Masoud Barzani is the son of Mulla Mustafa Barzani and was President of the Kurdistan Regional Government (KRG) from 2005 to 2017. He remains the President of the Kurdistan Democratic Party (KDP).

Masrour Barzani is the son of Masoud Barzani and the Chancellor of the Kurdistan Regional Security Council.

Mulla Mustafa Barzani was chosen to lead the KDP in 1946. He died in 1979.

Nechirvan Barzani is the nephew of Masoud Barzani. He has served as the Prime Minister of the KRG since March 2012 and from March 2006 to August 2009.

John Bolton currently serves as President Trump's National Security Advisor (2018 to present). He served as George H.W. Bush's United States Ambassador to the United Nations from 2005 to 2006.

Paul Bremer III served as the Administration of the Coalition Provisional Authority of Iraq from 2003 to 2004.

George H.W. Bush served as the 41st President of the United States from 2001 to 2008.

George W. Bush served as 43rd President of the United States. He launched military actions in Iraq and Afghanistan.

Dick Cheney served as Vice President of the United States from 2001 to 2009 and Secretary of Defense during the Gulf War from 1989 to 1993.

Winston Churchill served as Prime Minister of Great Britain from 1940 to 1945 and again from 1951 to 1955. He was Britain's Secretary of State for the Colonies from 1921 to 1922.

Hillary Clinton served as US Secretary of State from 2009 to 2012. Secretary Clinton unsuccessfully ran for President of the United States in 2016.

Ryan Crocker is a former career ambassador within the United States Foreign Service who served as US Ambassador to Iraq, Afghanistan, Pakistan, Syria, Kuwait and Lebanon.

Selahattin Demirtas is a Kurdish leader in Turkey who has served as member of the parliament since 2007.

Recep Tayyip Erdoğan was a founder of Turkey's Justice and Development Party and has served as Prime Minister or President from 2003 to the present.

Peter W. Galbraith is an American author, academic, commentator, politician, policy advisor and former US diplomat who helped uncover Saddam Hussein's gassing of the Kurds.

Antonio Guterres is the current UN Secretary General, elected in 2017.

François Hollande served as President of France from 2012 to 2017.

Fuad Hussein is chief of staff to the KRG Presidency.

Saddam Hussein served as President of Iraq from 1979 until April 2003. He was tried and convicted by an Iraqi court for crimes against humanity and hanged in 2006.

Najmaldin Karim is a neurosurgeon from Maryland who was elected the Governor of Kirkuk in 2011.

Sierwan Karim is the son of Najmaldin Karim and the head of the governor's security team.

Zozan Karim is the wife of Najmaldin Karim and daughter of the famous Peshmerga General Abdul Rahman Qazi, who served with Mulla Mustafa Barzani.

Ayatollah Ali Hosseini Khamenei is a marja and the second and current Supreme Leader of Iran, in office since 1989. He was previously President of Iran from 1981 to 1989.

Ayatollah Ruhollah Khomeini is the former Supreme Leader of Iran who led the 1979 Iranian Revolution.

Henry Kissinger served as both President Nixon's and President Ford's National

Security Advisor and United States Secretary of State during the years 1969 to 1977.

Bernard Kouchner is a French politician and physician who co-founded Médecins Sans Frontières and Médecins du Monde. He was France Foreign Minister from 2007 to 2010.

Nouri al-Maliki served as Iraq's Prime Minister from 2006 to 2014. He is Secretary General of the Islamic Dawa Party and a Vice President of Iraq.

Fuad Masum is a veteran Patriotic Union of Kurdistan (PUK) politician who became President of Iraq in 2014.

James N. Mattis is currently the US Secretary of Defense. He was formerly head of US Central Command.

Brett H. McGurk is currently the US Special Presidential Envoy for the Global Coalition to the Islamic State in Iraq and Syria (ISIS).

Qazi Muhammad was an Iranian Kurdish separatist leader who founded the Democratic Party of Iranian Kurdistan and headed the Republic of Mahabad.

Abu Mahdi al-Muhandis is head of Kata'ib Hezbollah and Deputy Commander of the Iraqi Popular Mobilization Forces.

Hassan Nasrallah is the third and current Secretary General of Hezbollah in Lebanon.

Benjamin Netanyahu is the current Prime Minister of Israel, serving from 1996 to 1999 and again from 2009 to the present.

Barack Obama was the 44th President of the United States from 2009 to 2017.

Reza Shah Pahlavi became the Shah of Iran on 15 December 1925. He abdicated on 16 September 1941 following the Anglo-Soviet invasion.

Shimon Peres served as the President of Israel and the Prime Minister of Israel. He passed away in September 2016.

David Petraeus is a retired United States Army general and the former Director of the Central Intelligence Agency (CIA) from 2011 to 2012.

François Georges-Picot was a French diplomat and lawyer who negotiated the dismemberment of the Ottoman Empire with his British counterpart, Mark Sykes.

Colin Powell served as National Security Advisor from 1987 to 1989, Chairman of the Joint Chiefs of Staff from 1989 to 1993, and US Secretary of State from 2001 to 2005.

Vladimir Putin is the current President of the Russian Federation, who was re-elected in May 2018. He has served as both the Prime Minister of Russia and President of Russia since 1999.

Bayan Sami Abdul Rahman has served as KRG Representative to the US since 2015.

Hassan Rouhani became the President of Iran in 2013.

Donald H. Rumsfeld served as Secretary of Defense from 1975 to 1977 under Gerald Ford, and again from 2001 to 2006 under George W. Bush.

Muqtada al-Sadr is founder of the Mahdi Army and head of the Sa'iroun political alliance.

Rakan Said is a Sunni Arab from Hawija who was appointed as Governor of Kirkuk, replacing Karim.

Barham Salih served as Prime Minister of the KRG from 2009 to 2012 and as deputy prime minister of Iraq from 2004 to 2009. He founded the Coalition for Democracy and Justice in 2017.

Mohammad bin Salman is Saudi Arabia's Crown Prince who also serves as the First Deputy Prime Minister, President of the Council for Economic and Development Affairs and Minister of Defense. He was appointed Crown Prince in June 2017.

Norman Schwarzkopf was the Commander of Operation Desert Storm, which liberated Kuwait in early 1991.

Brent Scowcroft is the former US National Security Advisor for President Ford from 1975 to 1977, and for President George H.W. Bush from 1989 to 1993.

Douglas A. Silliman has served as US Ambassador to Iraq since September 2016.

Ayatollah Ali al-Sistani is an Iranian Shi'ite Marja based in Najaf.

Karim Sinjari is the current KRG Interior Minister, first appointed in 2006.

Qasem Soleimani has served as Commander of the Iranian Revolutionary Guard Corps (IRGC) Quds Forces since 1998.

Mark Sykes was a British army officer and diplomat who negotiated the dismemberment of the Ottoman Empire with his French counterpart, François Georges-Picot.

Araz Talabani is a businessman and brother of Lahur Talabani.

Bafel Talabani is the older son of Jalal Talabani and became head of Zanyari, the PUK's intelligence unit, in 2004.

Hero Talabani was married to Jalal Talabani until his death in 2017. She is the mother of Qubad and Bafel Talabani.

Jalal Talabani was the founder of the PUK and served as President of Iraq from 2006 to 2014. He passed away in 2017.

Lahur Talabani, known as Sheikh Jash Lahur, is currently head of the Zanyari. He is brother of Araz and cousin to Bafel. Lahur is well connected with Iran's Quds forces as well as Iraq's Hashd al Shabi militias.

Qubad Talabani is the youngest son of Jalal Talabani, and served as KRG representative to the United States and then as deputy prime minister from 2005 to the present.

Rex Tillerson served as US Secretary of State from 2017 to 2018. He was formerly the CEO of Exxon Mobil.

Donald J. Trump was elected as the United States' 45th President in November 2016.

Woodrow Wilson was the 28th President of the United States who served from 1913 to 1921. He championed the right to self-determination in his "Fourteen Points Speech."

Mohammad Javad Zarif is currently serving as Iran's Foreign Minister. He was the Permanent Representative of Iran to the United Nations from 2002 to 2007.

FOREWORD

The birth of what is generally called the modern world has not been kind to the Kurdish people. When the last of the global empires collided during World War I and ultimately killed themselves at Gallipoli, on the banks of the Tigris and in the gas-filled trenches of Western Europe, some people found new opportunities. When the victors of the Great War took out their maps, rulers and pencils to carve up the spoils, new states and kingdoms were drawn up out of thin air. For the Middle East, it was an especially jarring and radical transformation. The region, with its ancient civilizations and numerous ethnic and religious groups, was suddenly chopped into unfamiliar states with borders that paid little respect to long-established traditions. New lines in the sand divided language groups, tribes and even families. Over the course of just a few years, the maps of the Middle East were literally redrawn. The countries we know today as Iraq, Syria, Lebanon and Jordan never existed before World War I. They were the bright ideas of European leaders—encouraged by local potentates—who thought that the deeply religious and largely undeveloped region would be easier to manage if it were divided into neat little political entities with pliant monarchs, ministers, generals and presidents. But as the new flags and currencies were sewn and minted, the fate of the Kurdish people—an ethnic and linguistic group that has long lived in Upper and Lower Mesopotamia—never appears to have been given any serious consideration.

Instead of getting a new country of their own, the Kurds, who number roughly 35 million today, found themselves divided over four nations: Turkey, Iraq, Syria and Iran. The divisions made the Kurds powerless and easy to neglect. In fact, one of the biggest dangers to the newly crafted Middle East was, and remains, that the Kurds would somehow pull themselves together like dollops of mercury on a plate, destroying the European-imposed borders keeping them apart. If the Kurds could unite, they'd fundamentally break the Middle East drawn up after World War I. Opposition to Kurdish unity is one of the few issues the regimes in Turkey, Iraq, Syria and Iran have all managed to agree on. Not surprisingly, not one of them wants to give up a piece of their land so the Kurds, left out of the big carve-up a century ago, can get their slice today.

It was like this for decades. The Kurds were a divided afterthought, seldom—if ever—talked about on the world stage until the United States charged into the Middle East like an angry bull in a china shop. Then, everything changed in a flash and the Kurds emerged from the background to take a role on the American center stage. After 9/11, President George W. Bush invaded Iraq and toppled Saddam Hussein even though the country and its leader had nothing to do with the terrorist atrocities in the United States. But the Iraq war did far more than just unseat the brutal regime in Baghdad. It unleashed an epidemic of religious violence between Sunni and Shi'ite Muslims, called into question the very idea of a unified Iraq, and broke the mold set in sand and oil after World War I. After the US invasion, the map of the Middle East was once again being redrawn. The Kurds saw an opportunity in the chaos that swirled around US troops who tried to contain a religious civil war that their presence was fueling. They saw an opportunity to make powerful friends. They saw a path to statehood. Kurds in Iraq welcomed occupying US forces with open arms. Some Kurdish shopkeepers in northern Iraqi cities even hung American flags in their windows. Many Kurds began to wonder if President Bush's dramatic, unexpected and forceful entry into the Middle East could deliver what they'd long been denied: a united Kurdish homeland, although Kurdish leaders remained divided over just how big and independent it should be.

Then everything changed again. A decade after the US invasion of Iraq, the Arab Spring and the Syrian civil war spread like wildfire, jumping from city to city, square to square, smartphone to smartphone. The uprisings once again challenged long-accepted concepts of who should rule the Middle East and what its borders should be. The Iraq war tore up the map once. Now just a decade later it was being torn up again: ISIS believed with fanatical clarity that the Middle East should have no borders at all, but be ruled instead as a puritanical Islamic caliphate. The entire Middle East, not just Iraq, was suddenly moldable and in flux. The Kurds, whose main political parties have long espoused secularism and women's rights over religious chauvinism, were ISIS's natural enemies. Furthermore, they saw the religious zealots as rivals, trying to create an Islamic State on land Kurds wanted for Kurdistan. For many Kurds, there was no choice at all.

They'd fight against ISIS, and in the process fight to lay a claim on their homeland.

After a century of division and neglect, the chips all seemed to be falling the Kurds' way. When the Americans destroyed Saddam Hussein's regime, the Kurds welcomed them in. When ISIS rampaged from Mosul to Raqqah, the Kurds fought hand in glove with US special forces. In return, Kurds expected grateful American governments to reward them and let them finally raise a Kurdish flag of independence. Instead, the Kurds still have no state and remain divided. Many believe their sacrifices have not been repaid. They accuse the Americans of twenty-first-century betrayal.

RICHARD ENGEL
NBC News

INTRODUCTION

Kurds are the largest group of stateless people in the world. More than 35 million Kurds live in contiguous territory across Iraq (South Kurdistan), Syria (West Kurdistan), Turkey (North Kurdistan) and Iran (East Kurdistan). Kurds are an ancient people and a distinct ethnic group, neither Arab nor Persian. However, Kurds are far from homogeneous. They are made up of many tribes who speak different dialects (Kurmanji and Sorani). Most are Sunni Muslim, although some are Shi'ite and Christian. There are a few Islamist Kurds, although almost all Kurds oppose the Islamic State (ISIS). The Kurdish character is defined by centuries of struggle against Arabs, Persians and Turks, and betrayal by western powers. Kurds have found solidarity in their community and sanctuary in their remote villages. According to an apt Kurdish adage, "Kurds have no friend but the mountains."

Kurdish national aspirations emerged during the Ottoman Empire's collapse, as European powers redrew the map of Europe and the Middle East after World War I. However, promises of self-determination and a referendum in the 1920 Treaty of Sèvres were nullified by the Treaty of Lausanne in 1923, which did not even mention the "Kurds" or the word "Kurdistan." The first betrayal occurred at this point after World War I when Kurds were denied a state of their own.

The 1975 Algiers Agreement was the second betrayal. Henry Kissinger, President Nixon's National Security Advisor, brokered the Algiers Agreement, resolving a border dispute between Iraq and Iran to the detriment of the Kurds. The Algiers Agreement also established a maritime boundary at the Shatt al-Arab waterway at the mouth of the Persian Gulf, ensuring safe passage of oil tankers from Basra in Iraq and Kargh Island in Iran to international markets. As part of the deal, Iran agreed to stop supporting Mulla Mustafa Barzani, which resulted in the collapse of the Kurdish resistance. The CIA treated the Kurds as pawns in the Cold War. Kissinger explained:

"Covert action is not missionary work."[1] He maintained, "America has no permanent friends or enemies, only interests."[2]

The third betrayal occurred days after the Gulf War ceasefire in 1991. US President George H.W. Bush urged the Kurds and the Shi'ites to rise up and overthrow Saddam Hussein. Emboldened by Bush's encouragement, Kurdish fighters—Peshmerga, "those who stand before death"—seized Kirkuk. They celebrated, firing guns in the air, honking horns and adorning their vehicles with the green, red and white Kurdistan flag, a symbol of their desire for independence. But the celebration was short-lived: the US forces stood aside when Saddam counterattacked with helicopter gunships, allowed under the terms of the ceasefire agreement between Iraq and the international community. Approximately 1.5 million Kurds fled to the mountains along Iraq's border with Turkey and Iran. Kurds who stayed behind were subject to arrest, torture and execution.

Between 2003 and 2012, the US spent $25 billion to bolster the Iraqi military and police.[3] However, Iraqi forces fled Mosul when just a few hundred Islamic State in Iraq and Syria (ISIS) fighters attacked on 3 June 2014. The Iraqi army abandoned an arsenal of heavy weapons to ISIS, leaving tanks and more than 2,000 armored Humvees behind, with keys in the ignition. Iraq teetered on the brink of collapse, with 30 percent of its territory under ISIS control. Kurdistan now faced a perfect storm of problems. It shared a 1,050-kilometer border with ISIS. More than one million refugees and internally displaced persons sought sanctuary in Kurdistan. World oil prices collapsed, and Baghdad suspended its constitutional commitment to share oil revenues, which emptied the coffers of the Kurdistan Regional Government (KRG), the self-governing body of Iraqi Kurds based in Erbil, northern Iraq. Kurdistan was on the verge of being overrun by ISIS until the US intervened.

Kurds viewed Iraq as a failed state and agitated for independence, but US officials implored KRG President Masoud Barzani to delay the opposed referendum. With his presidency coming to an end, Barzani held the vote on 25 September 2017. The "Yes" to independence passed overwhelmingly with 92.7 percent of the vote. Barzani emphasized that the referendum was not a declaration of independence but a starting point for negotiations with Iraq over the terms of a friendly divorce.

The fourth betrayal occurred in the fall of 2017. The US maintained a "Baghdad first" policy, coordinating weapons transfers "by, with and through" Baghdad. The Pentagon refused to provide heavy and offensive weapons to the

Peshmerga. State-of-the-art US weapons and equipment given to the Iraqi army were handed over to Shi'ite militias backed by Iran. Iraqi Special Forces, Shi'ite militias, Hezbollah fighters and the Iranian Revolutionary Guard Corps (IRCG) led by Quds Force Commander General Qasem Soleimani attacked Kirkuk on 16 October 2017. Kurdish leaders thought that US officials would mediate to diffuse the crisis, with consideration to the great sacrifices made by Peshmerga in the US-led fight against ISIS. Between 2014 and 2017, more than 1,700 Peshmerga were killed and more than 10,000 injured, as the Peshmerga liberated 30,000 square miles from ISIS.[4] On 16 October, Peshmerga who were affiliated with the Patriotic Union of Kurdistan (PUK) were influenced by Iran and disappeared from the battlefield as the Kurdish lines collapsed. Disunity among the Kurds was a major factor in their defeat.

The Trump administration's betrayal of the Peshmerga was followed by its betrayal of the Kurds in Syria. The People's Protection Units (YPG), Syrian Kurdish fighters, served as America's boots on the ground in the Battle for Raqqa, the "caliphate" of the Islamic State. After close cooperation with US Special Forces over two years, the Syrian Kurds expected protection and support from the US. However, Washington turned a blind eye when Turkey attacked Afrin, killing more than 1,000 YPG members and slaughtering hundreds of civilians. Many Kurds were beheaded and their bodies mutilated by Turkish-backed jihadists.

Kirkuk's former governor, Najmaldin Karim, has a long history of advocating for Kurdish national rights. He was the personal physician of Mulla Mustafa Barzani, who had supported Qazi Muhammad in the founding of the Mahabad Republic. Karim and Barzani left Iraqi Kurdistan when the Kurdistan revolution collapsed in 1975. They initially found refuge in Iran, and then came to the United States. Barzani was diagnosed with an advanced stage of lung cancer and received medical treatment at the Mayo Clinic. He died on 1 March 1976, soon after arriving in the United States. Karim stayed in the US to study neurosurgery at George Washington University and set up a medical practice in Maryland.

My work on Kurdish issues is closely tied to Karim, who became Kurdistan's leading advocate in Washington, DC. We met in 1988 when I headed the Congressional Human Rights Foundation. On 16 March 1988, during the final phase of the Iran–Iraq war, Iraqi forces used a toxic cocktail of sarin and mustard gas on civilians in Halabja. Karim showed me photos of men in traditional Kurdish garb, women in colorful robes with bright printed head scarves, and young children. Their faces were covered in deadly foam, agonized expressions frozen in death. Between February and September 1988 approximately 182,000 Kurds were killed, and millions displaced during the Al-Anfal Campaign.

After the Gulf War, in February 1992, Karim and I traveled through Turkey, entered Iraq at the Habur Crossing, and went to Kirkuk. Returning to Kirkuk after nearly 20 years was an emotional moment for Karim. At that time, Kirkuk was under the control of the Iraqi government. We skirted the Arab sections of the city, avoiding checkpoints armed by Iraq's security services to arrive at his family home in the Shorja neighborhood, a 100 percent Kurdish community on the outskirts of Kirkuk. We were greeted by Karim's father, Omar. As an imam and local religious leader, he dressed in a long black tunic with a matching black skullcap. The word "sheikh" in Kurdish does not mean a tribal chief as it does to Arabs. It refers to a man who is holy and venerated either on account of his birth or his pious life. Sheikh Omar was joined by Karim's mother, Najma, who wore a dark blue gown gathered at the waist with a small matching turban on her head, and poured tea from a traditional ornate tea set. One of Karim's brothers, Sardar, an engineer, also greeted us. The home was modest, except for its floor covering of Persian carpets. After about an hour, we put our shoes on and left. Karim was concerned that local intelligence units, "Mukhabarat," might learn of our visit and come for us. In the car heading north, Karim explained the historical and emotional significance of Kirkuk to Kurds. Saddam Hussein's Arabization program in the 1980s drove Kurds from their homes and changed Kirkuk's demographic balance. Kurds have always struggled and died for control of Kirkuk, which is claimed by other minorities such as the Turkmen. According to Jalal Talabani, Kirkuk is the Kurdish "Jerusalem."

Karim returned to America and did not visit Kurdistan again until after the Iraq War of 2003. He was elected a member of the Iraqi National Assembly from Kirkuk on 7 March 2010. He played an important role in Kurdistan's politics, maintaining good relations with the primary Kurdish parties—Barzani's Kurdistan Democratic Party (KDP), Talabany's PUK, and the Gorran "Change" movement. Karim was known in Baghdad as a Kurdish nationalist but respected as a straight shooter who advocated Kurdish interests in accordance with Iraq's 2005 constitution. Kurds were prepared to forego their dream of independence if Iraq was truly a democratic and federal republic. The constitution devolved power to Iraq's regions, established a role for Peshmerga in local security and allowed Kurdistan's ownership of future oil development. Article 140 of the constitution pledged a referendum to determine the status of Kirkuk by 31 December 2007. Karim was sworn in as Governor of Kirkuk on 3 April 2011. Despite the twenty-foot concrete blast walls surrounding his residence, Karim governed in an open and transparent fashion. He invited me to a meeting of the Kirkuk Governorate Council, which included Kurds, Arabs, Turkmen, Assyrians and others. His governing style was consultative and inclusive. Under Karim's leadership, Kirkuk experienced a renaissance. Electricity supplies were regularized, garbage was collected and security was established. Minority rights were protected and promoted. Karim ran for the Iraqi parliament heading the PUK list in 2014 and received the highest percentage of votes of any candidate in all of Iraq. Twenty-five percent of Iraqis who voted for the PUK were from non-Kurdish communities.[5]

Karim is a US citizen and strongly pro-American. He believes that Kurds and Americans share values as well as strategic interests. Since the Gulf War in 1991 when the US enforced a no-fly zone, Karim and his Kurdish compatriots have made the most of their opportunity to consolidate de facto independence. When Kirkuk collapsed after the 2017 referendum, Shi'ite militias hunted for Karim to capture or kill him. Karim went underground and found his way to safety in Erbil after a dramatic extraction. The Kurdish dream of independence had apparently shattered.

Defeating ISIS was the focus of US policy towards Iraq during the Obama administration. Destroying ISIS and limiting Iran's influence have been priorities for President Donald J. Trump. Both administrations have adopted a "Baghdad first" policy to prevent the Kurds from exercising their right to self-determination and to preserve Iraq's territorial integrity. But the US policy has had the opposite effect, undermining both goals. Iraq's Prime Minister Heider al-Abadi further polarized Sunnis who oppose the Shi'ite-led government in Baghdad; ISIS may be defeated, but it will be back. The Islamic State's next incarnation will have new leadership and a new name, but the network of aggrieved Sunnis will remain. Washington's approach has allowed Iran to gain the upper hand.

The Trump administration has focused on militarily defeating ISIS. In pursuit of this goal, it has either ignored Iran's involvement or colluded with Baghdad to punish the Kurds for conducting the independence referendum in September 2017. According to Senator John McCain, "Beyond our tactical successes in the fight against the Islamic State, the United States is still dangerously lacking a comprehensive strategy toward the rest of the Middle East in all of its complexity."[6] Anti-American elements have filled the gap created by the collapse of regional order and the diminished influence of the United States.

The Trump administration has underestimated the importance of soft power to drain the swamp of support for ISIS. It has failed to put in place a policy effectively promoting freedom and democracy as the best antidotes to Islamist extremism. Kurdistan is not perfect; far from it. Corruption and nepotism have had a corrosive effect on governance. Nonetheless, Kurdistan's democracy is more advanced than any Arab country in the Middle East. Iraqi Kurdistan can have a positive influence on Kurds in the region, as well as reform movements in frontline states.

While the US has an anti-ISIS strategy, it lacks a strategy for countering Iranian influence. The Trump administration has allowed Iran to achieve a critical objective—control of a corridor from Tehran to Baghdad, Damascus and Beirut that Iran uses to resupply Hezbollah and Hamas. The Trump administration announced its get-tough policy on Iran, then allowed it to subvert Iraq and orchestrate the takeover of Kirkuk. The US looks like a paper tiger for failing to match its actions to its words. Canceling the Iran nuclear deal is not a strategy for preventing a Shi'ite crescent from extending across the Persian Gulf to the Mediterranean.

Iran succeeded in sowing sectarian and ethnic discord inside Iraq by supporting Shi'ite militias and backing Arabs against Kurds. Iran pursues this same strategy where it is involved in other sectarian conflicts such as Syria, Yemen and Lebanon. After making an enormous contribution of troops and treasure, America's influence receded after Iraq's national elections on 12 May 2018. Washington's decision to sit on the sidelines during the Kirkuk crisis marked America's decline in Iraq and the region.

The Trump administration's passive approach contrasts with Russia's muscular support of Syria's President Bashar al-Assad, who is allied with Iran and Hezbollah. Russia's President Vladimir Putin re-established Russia as a regional power broker by demonstrating Russia's risk-taking and resilience. Traditional US allies are concerned about America's acquiescence to Iran and have taken note. Soon after Kirkuk, Saudi Arabia's King Salman visited Moscow. He and other world leaders have observed the gap between America's rhetoric and its actions and are hedging their bets against America's diminished role. Washington wants the Gulf States to fill the vacuum after

ISIS. However, they will gauge the US commitment to containing Iran and Syria before spending resources and political capital.

The Middle East is changing. Existing state structures are breaking down and new ones are emerging. Conflict between Iran and the Gulf States affects the entire region, exacerbating volatility and Islamist extremism. Even with the ISIS caliphate in Raqqa destroyed and Mosul liberated, Iraq and Syria are not yet functioning states. Kurds are an island of stability in both countries. They have proved to be the most effective fighters against ISIS, as well as remaining America's staunch allies. The Trump administration may want to reduce its role in the region, but America's continued involvement is critical to preventing a comeback by ISIS and stabilizing fragile states. The US needs to recognize its true friends rather than try to placate its adversaries. A leading member of the US House of Representatives Committee on Foreign Affairs stated: "The Kurds for many years have been our most courageous allies in the struggle against radical Islam. Our policy should be to support friends, not betray them. The US appears to be currying favor with an enemy by betraying a friend."[7]

Iraq and Syria are deformed twins with autocratic leaders under Iran's influence. In both countries the Kurds are a counterweight to abusive central governments, and Kurds have paid the price for America's strategically incoherent and morally inconsistent policy. Abandoning the YPG in Syria was flawed and short-sighted: flawed because the Kurds are proven and effective warriors; short-sighted because forsaking the Kurds cedes influence to Iran and its allies in Baghdad and Damascus. In addition to staining America's reputation, it was also a strategic mistake; Syrian Kurds found common cause with Assad and turned to Russia. The events in Kirkuk are a milestone of America's demise in Iraq and the broader Middle East. These pages describe America's persistent betrayal and abuse of the Kurds.

Part I

Tragic History

1 SOVEREIGNTY DENIED

> *"People and provinces are not to be bartered about from sovereignty to sovereignty as if they were chattels and pawns in a game, even the great game, now forever discredited."*

US PRESIDENT WOODROW WILSON[1]

Sykes–Picot

The Kurds aligned with the Allies against the Axis Powers in World War I. As countries gathered in Versailles to redraw the map of Europe and the Middle East, Kurds fought alongside the British to liberate Kirkuk from Ottoman control. Kurds wanted a state of their own. After World War I, the map of Europe and the Middle East was changing, with the demise of the Ottoman and Austro-Hungarian Empires. Ethno-national movements demanded legal status, claiming their right to self-determination rather than majoritarian rule.

Opposing worldviews sharpened at the Paris Peace Conference, where international representatives discussed the fate of vanquished empires. US President Woodrow Wilson emerged as the voice of small captive nations. The first salvo in this debate occurred with World War I still raging. Mark Sykes, a British officer, and François Georges-Picot, a French diplomat, held a series of meetings to determine the status of peoples who would be liberated in the Great War. The fate of the Kurds hung in the balance.

The Sykes–Picot Agreement—also known as "The Asia Minor Agreement"—was finalized on 16 May 1916. It drew a figurative line in the sand from the Persian border in the northeast to Mosul and Kirkuk, across the desert towards the Mediterranean, skirting the top of Palestine.[2] Sykes and Picot envisioned that lands north of the line would be a French zone and lands to the south would be controlled by the British. Sykes–Picot notionally assigned the Basra and Baghdad districts (vilayets) to Britain, and the Mosul vilayet to France. Sykes told Britain's Prime Minister H.H.

Asquith, "I should like to draw a line from the 'E' in Acre to the last 'K' in Kirkuk."[3]

The Sykes–Picot Agreement sanctioned a process to carve up territories, but the borders of new states in the Middle East ultimately bore little resemblance to the original Sykes–Picot map. The Sykes–Picot Agreement was not a formal treaty. It did, however, set the stage for establishing new nation states through a series of conferences and treaties over the next nine years. The root of conflict in the modern Middle East lies in the arbitrary way states were established during this period. As the primary protagonists, Britain and France pursued a policy of "divide and rule," installing local leaders as clients to do their bidding. Britain's assurances were especially duplicitous.

British officials offered Sharif Hussein bin Ali of Mecca an independent Arab state in greater Syria and Mesopotamia in exchange for help fighting the Ottoman army. Hussein and the Arab tribes joined the battle in June 1916. The Arab revolt was decisive, helping British forces capture Damascus, Mecca and Medina after a two-year siege. Kurdish fighters fought shoulder-to-shoulder with the British against the Ottomans. The Kirkuk garrison fell in May 1918, leading to the Ottoman surrender and the Mudros Armistice on 30 October 1918.

Both Arab and Kurdish leaders expected payback for their roles in the war. However, the Foreign Office made more promises that it could keep. Britain offered Hussein an Arab state spanning territories from Aleppo (modern-day Syria) to Yemen (on the Persian Gulf). British officials told the Kurds they could govern themselves and have a state of their own on lands in Mesopotamia and Anatolia (modern Iraq and Syria). Britain's Middle East policy raised unrealistic expectations, laying the ground for decades of distrust and conflict.

The Fourteen Points

Woodrow Wilson presented progressive ideas about democracy and self-determination for the subjugated peoples of the Austro-Hungarian and Ottoman Empires. His egalitarian worldview was a road map for peace-building in the waning months of World War I. Wilson enlisted a team of 150 advisors led by Edward M. House, who helped write his "Fourteen Points" speech, delivered on 8 January 1918. Wilson addressed a global audience, including the German government and the German people.

The speech was broadcast on radio and printed copies of the speech were air-dropped behind German lines. The Kurds were also listening closely. Point 5 called for

A free, open-minded, and absolutely impartial judgment of all colonial claims, based on strict observance of the principle that in determining all such questions of sovereignty and interests of the populations concerned must have equal weight with the equitable claims of government whose title is to be determined.[4]

For the Kurds, point 5 assured them that their national aspirations would be considered.

Point 12 indicated that "The Turkish portions of the present Ottoman Empire should be assured a secure sovereignty, but other nationalities which are now under Turkish rule should be assured an undoubted security of life and an absolutely unmolested opportunity for autonomous development."[5] Point 12 spoke directly to the Kurds, seeking separation from Ottoman rule.

Point 14 proposed the creation of a League of Nations to ensure "Political independence and territorial integrity [of] great and small states alike."[6] Point 14 provided an assurance that the Kurds would have a forum to petition for statehood.

Wilson believed that the enactment of his Fourteen Points would form the basis for a just and lasting peace. He expanded on his Fourteen Points speech in an address to a joint session of the US Congress on 11 February 1918.

First, that each part of the final settlement must be based upon the essential justice of that particular case and upon such adjustments as are most likely to bring a peace that will be permanent;

Second, people and provinces are not to be bartered about from sovereignty to sovereignty as if they were chattels and pawns in a game, even the great game, now forever discredited.

Third, every territorial settlement involved in this war must be made in the interest and for the benefit of the populations concerned, and not as a part of any mere adjustment or compromise of claims amongst rival states; and

Fourth, that all well-defined national aspirations shall be accorded the utmost satisfaction that can be accorded them without introducing new or perpetuating old elements of discord and antagonism that would be likely in time to break the peace of Europe and consequently of the world.[7]

Wilson was awarded the Nobel Peace Prize the following year. In bestowing its honor, the Nobel Committee heralded Wilson's commitment to "the principle of justice to all peoples and nationalities and their right to live on equal terms of liberty and safety with one another, whether they be weak or strong."[8]

World leaders met at Versailles to finalize details of the postwar world order. The Fourteen Points became the basis of the German armistice surrender. The Paris Peace Conference, which was actually held at Versailles, lasted six months from January to July 1919, with the discussions dominated by Britain, France and Italy. France's Prime Minister Georges Clemenceau hosted the conference. Britain and Italy were represented by their prime ministers, David Lloyd George and Vittorio Orlando. Russia had just gone through its revolution and the new Bolshevik government declined to attend. The defeated Central Powers—Germany, Austria–Hungary, Turkey and Bulgaria—were not invited.

The United States was the other member of the "Big Four." Through its contribution to the war effort and growing economy, the US had emerged as one of the world's great powers. Wilson staked out a theme for the Paris Peace Conference: the right to self-determination. He viewed the Conference as a forum for dialogue between ethnic-national groups and the Great Powers of Old Europe. Allies were surprised by Wilson's Fourteen Points, but lent their support. France formally endorsed the Fourteen Points on 1 November 1918. UK Foreign Secretary Arthur Balfour pledged support in exchange for America's endorsement of reparations in the text of the final armistice. German Chancellor Count von Hertling welcomed Wilson's Fourteen Points in conciliatory remarks to the Reichstag, but conditioned his support with a demand that the Paris Peace Conference consider the status of Alsace-Lorraine. Balfour scoffed at the notion of Alsace-Lorraine as a disputed territory between France and Germany.

Wilson headed the US delegation, but became ill with influenza soon after arriving in France. With Wilson's health waning, David Lloyd George shifted the focus of discussions from freedom and rights to accountability and reparations. Clemenceau focused on security guarantees and territories. Clemenceau also insisted on a guilt clause assigning full responsibility to

Germany for the war and enshrining the principle of reparations by Germany to the Allies. The Treaty of Versailles was finalized on 28 June and published on 21 October 1919. Article 231 of Versailles, the "War Guilt Clause," established Germany's responsibility for the War and demanded reparations. The Austro-Hungarian, Ottoman and Russian empires all collapsed. Versailles created nine new states emerging from the Austro-Hungarian Empire. They were Poland, Finland, Austria, Hungary, Czechoslovakia, Yugoslavia, Estonia, Latvia and Lithuania. As envisioned by Sykes–Picot, Versailles divided the former Ottoman territories into zones of influence. Britain took what is now Iraq, Kuwait, Jordan and Palestine. France received what is now Syria and Lebanon. Versailles failed to address the contentious issue of control over Mosul, leaving it for Britain and France to decide or for the League of Nations to address as a matter of collective security.[9]

The United States was offered a mandate for the Kurds. But Wilson, weakened by his respiratory illness, did not want the US to become a colonial power in the Middle East and declined Clemenceau's proposal. Turkey's delegation rejected the division of any Ottoman territories. They insisted that the six vilayets were an integral part of the Ottoman Empire and should be included in its successor state.

The US signed the Treaty of Versailles, but Senate approval was required to accept its terms. Wilson collapsed in the White House on 2 October 1919 after an exhausting national tour to raise support for the treaty and the League of Nations. The White House indicated that Wilson was suffering from "nervous exhaustion." Rumors swirled about a debilitating stroke, and Wilson practically disappeared from public view. The Treaty of Versailles was rejected by the US Senate on 9 March 1920.[10] According to the *New York Times*, "The Treaty was now dead to stay dead."[11] Self-determination as a new guiding principle in world affairs was a casualty of Wilson's illness.[12]

The Turkish National Movement

The Mudros Armistice was so severe and punitive that it sowed the seeds for Turkey's War of Independence. The Ottoman army was fully demobilized through the Armistice and the Ottomans surrendered their remaining garrison in Hejaz, Yemen, Syria, Mesopotamia, Tripoli and Cyrenaica. Turkish ports, railways and other strategic points were made available for use by the Allies. The Straits of the Dardanelles, connecting the Sea of Marmara and the Aegean Ocean, and the Bosphorus, linking the Black Sea to the

Mediterranean, were also ceded to the Allies. "In case of disorder," the Allies reserved the right to occupy six Armenian provinces in Anatolia. The Allies reserved the right to take control of "any strategic points" should their security be threatened.[13]

Neither representatives of the Sultanate in Constantinople nor members of the National Movement were invited to the Paris Peace Conference. Excluded from diplomacy, the National Movement adopted a bellicose approach. Mustafa Kemal Atatürk launched the War of Independence (19 May 1919 to 29 October 1923). He fought Greece on the Western Front, France on the Southern Front and Armenia on the Eastern Front. Atatürk rallied his National Movement, disparaging Europe and opposing Kurdish national aspirations.

The Amasya Protocol (22 October 1919) was a memorandum of understanding between the National Movement and the Ottoman Imperial Government in Istanbul. It declared that the unity of the motherland and national independence were in danger. It sent a message to occupying powers and pro-independence Kurdish groups, asserting the primary importance of Turkish independence and national unity. It called for the creation of a national committee to unify Turks. Delegates to Amasya agreed to hold a National Congress in Sivas. The Kurdish issue would be considered at a preparatory conference in the eastern city of Erzurum.

The Erzurum Conference (23 July 1919 to 7 August 1919) sent a strongly worded telegram to Wilson in Paris. The Erzurum delegates adamantly opposed the division of Ottoman territories. They also repudiated Wilson's Fourteen Points. The telegram was a declaration of Turkish nationalism, adamantly rejecting the intention of the Great Powers to create an independent state of Kurdistan.

All 14 leaders of the National Movement were present at the Sivas Congress (16–29 October 1919). In his opening remarks to the Sivas Congress, Atatürk heralded "independence and integrity" as core principles inspiring the National Movement. The Sivas Declaration demanded that the sultan surrender his authority. It called for a new government and parliament to be established in Ankara. It reaffirmed the Erzurum Declaration and called for the creation of the Society to Defend the Rights and Interests of the Provinces of Anatolia and Rumeli, as a vehicle to prevent the rise of Kurdish nationalism.

The Erzurum Declaration set the stage for the National Oath, which was approved by the Ottoman Parliament on 28 January 1920. It declared, "In response to the world of hostility and great evil opposing us [...] We will defend our nation's will and independence, even if we are on the last piece of rock of our country."[14] Atatürk announced the creation of the Turkish Grand National Assembly (TGNA) on 20 March 1920. The TGNA included members of the Ottoman parliament who escaped from Constantinople and deputies from around the country representing the National Movement. Atatürk was elected the Assembly's first president on 23 April 1920. The Assembly rejected the conclusions of the Paris Peace Conference as well as the disposal of Ottoman territories reached at the San Remo Conference on 26 April 1920.[15]

Furthermore, the Sivas Declaration challenged Kurdish self-determination. Not only did Atatürk reject the creation of Kurdistan as an independent state, he also rejected Kurdish autonomy. He went further, endorsing measures to limit Kurdish cultural and political identity; proposing restrictions on the right of Kurds to organize politically; and restricting Kurdish cultural events, even the traditional Newroz celebration.

Kurdish Disunity

Atatürk's National Movement was launched while the Paris Peace Conference was under way. The Kurds sent a delegation to Versailles, headed by Serif Pasha of the Istanbul-based Society for the Ascension of Kurdistan (KTJ). Serif Pasha proposed boundaries for North Kurdistan:

> The frontiers of Turkish Kurdistan, from an ethnographical point of view, begin in the north at Ziven, on the Caucasion frontier, and continue west to Erzurum, Erzican, Kemah, Arapgir, Besni, and Divick. In the south they follow the line from Harran, the Sinjar Hills, Tel Afsar, Erbil, Suleimani, Akk-el-man, Sinne. And in the East Ravandiz, Baskale, Vezirkale, that is to say the frontier of Persia as far as Mount Ararat.[16]

In exchange for Britain's support, Serif Pasha proposed that British officials administer the Kurdish region and control its finances.

The Kurdish delegation did not have a unified negotiation strategy. Serif Pasha and Amin Ali Bedirhan, another KTJ member, publicly argued about the demarcation of political and administrative boundaries. Kurds were also divided on their overall approach to self-rule. Serif Pasha endorsed an administrative entity in Turkey with local control over government, economy,

natural resources and cultural affairs. The Bedirhan faction rejected autonomy and demanded outright independence. It sent a map to the Paris Peace
Conference that included almost all lands in greater Kurdistan. Bedirhan
took an even more maximalist position, seeking sea access as well.

Bedirhan condemned Serif Pasha's concessions and demanded that he
and Seyyid Abdulkadir, another backer of autonomy, resign from the KTJ
and leave Versailles. After stormy internal discussions, Serif Pasha and
Abdulkadir did indeed resign and left the Paris Peace Conference. Serif
Pasha's departure undermined the confidence of Europeans in the Kurdish
delegation. From his headquarters in Eastern Anatolia, Abdulkadir sent a
cable that was non-specific on policy matters. In his message Abdulkadir
insisted on the right to reopen any decision that he believed contravened
Kurdish interests, which alienated European mediators. Adding to the
confusion, Kurdish tribal groups showed up in Versailles to raise local issues
of grazing and water rights.

Britain adopted a pro-Kurdish policy, supporting the establishment of
an autonomous Kurdish region across greater Kurdistan. In March 1918, the
Foreign Office assigned two British officials with long experience of Kurdish
affairs, E.B. Sloane and E.W.C. Noel, to engage local Kurdish leaders in
discussions about self-rule. Sloane and Noel believed that law and order
could best be achieved by delegating authority to a Kurdish Council, but
the success of their plan to administer Kurdish territories required Kurdish
unity. They hoped Kurdish leaders would set aside their differences and unite
in common purpose to realize the greater goal of independence.

On 30 October 1918, Sloane and Noel proposed the establishment of
a British-sponsored Kurdish Tribal Council, envisioned as the first step
towards self-rule. Sir Percy Cox, the British Civil Commissioner in Baghdad,
recommended the setting-up of a Kurdish state extending as far north as Van
in Eastern Anatolia, east to Suleimani, and south to Kirkuk. With support
from Colonial Secretary Winston Churchill, the Kurds believed they were
on the verge of realizing their dream of independence.

But disunity was an impediment to Cox's plan. Kurds are a fragmented
people, organized along tribal lines where kinship ideology is dominant. The
diversity of dialects spoken by Kurds exacerbates this disunity: Kurmanji
is spoken in north and west Kurdistan, Sorani in south and east Kurdistan.
There are also many local dialects such as Zaza and Gorani. South Kurmanji
and Gorani use a Persian alphabet, whereas north Kurmanji uses a Latin
alphabet.

Kurds are also divided by religion and culture. Although about 75 percent are Sunni Muslim, Kurds are not a pious people by Arab Wahhabi standards. A group of Islamist Kurds live above Halabja on the Iran–Iraq border, while other Kurds are Shi'ite, Alawite, Yazidis, Christians and Sifyis, which is linked to Zoroastrianism. An ancient Jewish community also lives in Kurdistan. Kurdish divisions are further exacerbated by Kurdistan's rugged geography. There are nine major mountains in Kurdistan, which is crisscrossed by great rivers, supplied by winter's melting snow. Lake Dukan in Iraqi Kurdistan is nestled beneath snow-capped peaks. The Great Zab, Little Zab and Adhaim rivers flow into the Euphrates, which joins with the Tigris downstream to create the Shatt-al-Arab in the Persian Gulf.

Sir Rupert Hay, a British political officer stationed in Kurdistan between 1918 and 1920, wrote a memoir that provides a window into the views of the Foreign Office, which emphasized self-reliance by the Kurdish tribes.[17] Hay writes, "After the Armistice, especially in Kurdistan, every effort was made to teach the people to rule themselves." The British sought to govern through salaried tribal chiefs. But British officers struggled to establish security and collect taxes. According to Hay, Kurds are "the wildest of brigands." They are "a collection of tribes without any cohesion, and showing little desire for cohesion." But Hay also described Kurds as a noble people with great potential. "The day that the Kurds awake to a national consciousness, the Turkish, Persian, and Arab states will crumble to dust before them."

Tribal society was a mosaic of peoples with conflicting loyalties: "Some tribes have no recognised chief; some have many." Tribes have layers of leadership: "aghas" function as landlords while mullahs represent another layer of local leadership; almost every village has a mullah or local religious leader to advise on community relations.

Kurds and Arabs dislike each other, Hay writes, and Kurds and Turkic peoples also had an uneasy co-existence, as Hay described in his account of Kirkuk.

Kirkuk is the main centre of this Turkish population, and before the war possessed 30,000 inhabitants. Several villages in its vicinity are also Turkish speaking, whereas the other towns are isolated communities surrounded by Kurds and Arabs. The origin of this population, which sometimes refers to itself as Turcoman, descends from a line of colonies settled by the Seljuks, a Turkish race who, starting from their home in Central Asia, in the eleventh and twelfth centuries, overran Asia Minor and Mesopotamia. They eventually fell under the sway of the great descendants of Osman, the founder of the Osmanli or Ottoman Empire.

Kurdish tribes disliked the Ottoman administrators, and Hay describes how the Turks, who had an obsession with Pan-Turanism, made efforts to suppress the Kurdish tongue, and that few or no grammars or educational books existed in the language.

In October 1918, British troops reached Altun Kupri on the Lesser Zab. Hay describes how the Mosul column had come to within a few miles of its objective when the news arrived that the Allies had concluded an armistice with the Turks. The general idea of the policy was to govern through the tribal chief, and wherever possible to dismiss corrupt Turkish officials. But after the armistice, the anarchy and chaos only increased."

Kurds initially welcomed British administration, as an alternative to the corrupt and abusive Ottoman bureaucracy. Kurdish mullahs prophesized that an enlightened British rule would bring a peaceful and prosperous Golden Age to Kurdistan. In a bid to consolidate Kurdish control, Britain appointed Sheikh Mahmud Barzinji as King of Kurdistan in November 1918. However, Mahmud failed to foster national unity and the British removed him.

Anti-British propaganda increased, spurring violence. "Notorious malcontents preached open sedition in the coffee shops. Anonymous notices appeared in the town calling upon all good Muhammadans to revolt against the infidel Government."[18] The security situation continued to deteriorate. Between July 1921 and December 1922 eight British officers were killed on the northern frontier; some were ambushed, and others killed on active military service.[19] British administrators pushed for Kurdish self-rule, which they believed was critical to Britain's exit strategy.

Turkey's defeat produced a short-lived unity among the Kurds, a solidarity based on fears that the Allies would hold them accountable for the genocide of Armenians and attacks against Assyrians during the collapse of the Ottoman Empire. But the Kurds resumed their rivalries when it became apparent that no court would judge their crimes.

Kurdish leaders took seriously the assurances they had received from Cox, Sloane and Noel. After helping to vanquish the Ottoman armies, the Kurds expected British protection for their security as well as support for their political project. But Britain increasingly shied away from confrontation with Atatürk. World War I had taken a heavy toll and Britain was unwilling to engage in a new conflict with Turkey. It focused instead on retaining territories in Mesopotamia, present-day Iraq. Thus the Kurds faced two bad options: partition, dividing the Kurds in Mesopotamia from their brethren in Anatolia, or a unified Kurdistan under Turkish rule.

Treaties of Sèvres and Lausanne

The Great Powers met at Sèvres to formalize agreements from Versailles, and the Treaty of Sèvres was signed on 10 August 1920. It officially abolished the Ottoman Empire and required that Turkey renounce all claims in Arab Asia and north Africa. Greece was given control of Eastern Thrace, the Aegean Islands and the west coast of Anatolia. The Treaty recognized the region of Kars and most of Western Armenia as part of Armenia. The rump of Anatolia, about 25 percent of the Ottoman Empire's territory, was all that remained of Turkey.

The Allies discussed the disposition of Kurdish territories in Anatolia and Mesopotamia. They deferred final agreement on Kurdistan as well as the Mosul vilayet, proposing a commission comprised of officials from the British, French and Italian governments to develop "a scheme of local autonomy for the predominantly Kurdish areas, east of the Euphrates, south of the boundary of Armenia, and north of the northern frontier of Syria and Mesopotamia." The Allies agreed that the Kurds would have the right to appeal for independence to the League of Nations within one year. Mosul would adhere to Kurdistan in the event of independence.[20]

Article 62 of the Sèvres Treaty indicated:

> A Commission sitting at Constantinople and composed of three members appointed by the British, French, and Italian governments respectively shall draft a scheme within six months of the present Treaty's coming into force of local autonomy for the predominantly Kurdish areas lying east of the Euphrates, south of Armenia as it may be determined hereafter, and north of the frontier of Turkey with Syria and Mesopotamia.[21]

Kharput, Dersim, Hakkari and Siirt would be a part of Kurdistan with Diyarbakir its capital. Kurdish territories west of the Euphrates were assigned as France's zone of interest.

According to Article 63: "The Turkish government hereby agrees to accept and execute the decisions of both Commissions mentioned in Article 62 within three months of their communication."[22] Article 63 also pledged the protection of racial and religious minorities, with specific reference to Chaldo-Assyrians.

Article 64 stated:

> If within one year of the coming into force of the present Treaty the Kurdish peoples within the area defined in Article 62 shall address themselves to the Council of the League of Nations in such a manner as to show that the majority of the population of these areas desire independence from Turkey, and if the Council then consider that these people are capable of such independence and recommends that it should be granted to them, Turkey hereby agrees to execute such a recommendation, and to renounce all rights and title over these areas […] If and when such a renunciation takes place, no objection will be raised by the Principal Allied Powers to the voluntary adhesion to such an independent Kurdish State of the Kurds inhabiting that part of Kurdistan which has hitherto been included in the Mosul vilayet.[23]

By then, the War of Independence was in full swing. Atatürk was indignant at the terms imposed by the Allies: Sèvres directly contradicted his National Oath, and principles of sovereignty and independence, and was presented to him as a done deal, without consultation. Atatürk rallied support within the National Movement by opposing Sèvres. Across Anatolia and North Kurdistan, the "Defense of Rights Committees" offered armed resistance to foreign occupation, advancing the political agenda of the National Movement.

Turks still suffer from the "Sèvres syndrome." They believe that Great Powers are conspiring to diminish and dismember Turkey. The Sèvres syndrome comes from insecurity and weakness, although it is often masked by aggressive assertiveness. Turkey is neither European nor Middle Eastern. Turks are outliers and do not feel welcome in either world.

Fighting on three fronts intensified as Atatürk's Republican forces battled to liberate Turkish lands from foreign control. Foreign troops ceded Anatolia and Western Thrace, giving control to Turkey. Atatürk also took steps to undermine Sèvres through diplomatic initiatives. Sèvres provided that Armenia would be recognized as a free and independent country, with its final borders determined by Woodrow Wilson. The Treaty of Moscow (16 March 1921) and the Treaty of Kars (13 October 1921) pre-empted Wilson's role, defining Turkey's border with Armenia. Through the Treaty of Moscow, Turkey received the region of Kars, the southern portion of Batum and the Armenian province of Surmalu. The Treaty of Kars confirmed the Treaty of Moscow, sanctioning Turkey's annexation of Mount Ararat, the Ani ruins and the cities of Artvin and Igdir. However, the validity of these treaties was contested: Turkish signatories lacked authority to sign international agreements until the Republic of Turkey was formally recognized in 1923.[24]

Kurds believed that the Treaty of Sèvres was an ironclad guarantee of their right to self-determination. They grew increasingly concerned as Atatürk's War of Independence gained momentum, reversing territorial gains by the Allies and undermining the Mudros Armistice. The Chanak incident of September 1922 marked a turning point in Britain's policy towards Turkey.

Turkey had succeeded in pushing Greek troops out of Istanbul. Turkish troops captured Izmir, then called Smyrna, immolating Greek civilians in a church where they sought sanctuary. Turkish troops mobilized to attack the Dardanelles, which was treated as a neutral zone by Sèvres. With his army poised to attack, Atatürk demanded that the Allies cede all territories in Asia Minor. He also demanded Constantinople and Thrace up to the Maritsa River.

Lloyd George and Churchill were incensed by Atatürk's violation of Sèvres and threatened a declaration of war. However, they lacked support from fellow Conservatives in the British Government, while the Commonwealth and the public were skeptical of the wisdom of going to war with Turkey. Lloyd George failed to consult the Dominions, and Canada refused to join the fight. Italy and France were also opposed, and France conducted secret negotiations with Ankara, culminating in the Franklin–Bouillion Agreement (20 October 1921). The Accord bestowed legitimacy to Atatürk, as well as territories. France abandoned its claim to Ottoman lands, with the exception of Syria. Turkey gained Cilicia and parts of northern Syria such as Nusaybin.

France's Prime Minister Raymond Poincaré ordered French troops to withdraw from Chanak, leaving Britain on its own. With British troops readying to fight in Chanak, French diplomats brokered the Armistice of Mudanya (11 October 1922), Britain ceded control of Eastern Thrace, which the Greek army abandoned without a shot, and the Dardanelles remained a neutral zone under control of the Allies. However, its neutral status was reversed the following year by the Treaty of Lausanne. Lloyd George was disgraced and removed as prime minister for his bungling of the Chanak affair, which marked a turning point in relations between Turkey and the Allies. It emboldened Atatürk to demand a new treaty, enshrining the terms of the Mudanya Armistice.

The Lausanne Conference opened in November 1922 and lasted 11 weeks. By then, Atatürk had marginalized the sultanate in Istanbul and was the sole representative of Turkey. Turkey's Foreign Minister Bekir Sami Kunduh mocked Kurdish national aspirations:

> The populations of Kurdistan possessed complete representation in the Grand National Assembly. The Kurds always proclaimed that they constituted an indivisible whole with Turkey. The two races [Kurds and Turks] were united by a common feeling, a common culture, and a common religion.

Only a "small committee" of Kurds sought sovereignty and this minority "in no way represented the populations for whom they claimed to speak."[25] Percy Cox proposed reversing British policy towards Kurdistan.

> It might considerably ease frontier negotiations if we could give a preliminary official pledge to Turkey that in the changed circumstances we have abandoned the idea of autonomy included in the Treaty of Sèvres, and that our aim is to incorporate in Iraq as far as may be feasible under normal Iraqi administration all the Kurdish areas which may fall on the Mosul side of the frontier as the result of negotiations.[26]

The Treaty of Lausanne was finalized on 24 July 1923. Unlike Sèvres, which had been imposed on Turkey, Lausanne was the product of negotiations. According to Atatürk,

> This treaty is a document declaring that all efforts, prepared over centuries, and thought to have been achieved through the Sèvres Treaty to crush the Turkish nation have been in vain. It is a diplomatic victory unheard of in Ottoman history.[27]

Turkey signed on one side; Britain, France, Italy, Japan, Greece, Romania and the Kingdom of Serbs, Croats and Slovenes signed on the other. The national aspirations of Kurds were dashed as Lausanne superseded Sèvres and ignored the Kurdish question. Lausanne initiated a process of reform, spearheaded by Atatürk, which aimed to make Turkey truly modern and secular, on a par with European states.

Lausanne marked the formal end of the Ottoman Empire. The Ottoman Caliphate was officially abolished and the last caliph was exiled. Lausanne recognized Turkey within its current boundaries and abandoned the idea of an independent Armenian state. In exchange, Turkey surrendered claims to former Arab regions including Libya, Sudan and Egypt. Cyprus was awarded to Britain. The Dodecanese Islands went to Greece. The Dardanelles were opened to commercial maritime activities.[28]

With the Kurds and Chaldo-Assyrians in mind, Lausanne included provisions to promote and protect the rights of ethnic, religious and racial minorities. It assured minorities local administration and local police (Article 13); freedom of religion (Article 38); use of minority languages (Article 39); local control of education (Article 40); employment rights in the civil service (Article 41); and customary law (Article 42). However, Lausanne lacked a monitoring mechanism. It did not establish the capacity to monitor and report to the international community, and so the commitment to minority rights was more a statement of intent than an enforceable policy.

Mosul

In 1918, the Kurds had been in a position of strength and rejected the partition of Kurdistan into British and French zones of influence. By 1923, however, they had no good options. The only viable Kurdish entity was the Mosul vilayet, east of Turkish-controlled Anatolian territories.

George Curzon focused on Mosul during his opening remarks in Lausanne. Britain lacked the fortitude to enforce Sèvres, establishing Kurdistan as a single territory under its control. Faced with a protracted conflict with Turkey and without support from its Dominions or Allies, Britain abandoned its greater Kurdistan project, ceding Anatolia to Turkey.

Atatürk succeeded in his War of Independence. Freed from the fight with France in Cilicia, Russia on the Black Sea coast, and with Armenians in the Caucasus, Atatürk deployed his forces along the border with Mesopotamia in a show of force. Britain was diplomatically isolated and at a military disadvantage after Chanak. To stabilize its claims in Mesopotamia, Britain turned to Hashemite King Faisal I who had organized the Arab revolt of 1916 that swung the War in Britain's favor. Faisal incited the Kurds to launch a series of rebellions along the so-called Brussels line, demarcating Turkey from the Mosul vilayet.

Kurdish nationalists sought separate status for the Mosul vilayet. Turkey's defeat and the occupation of Mosul by Britain presented an opportunity to press their claim. Britain focused on decentralization and self-rule. Cox concluded:

> To my mind it seems that it would be a reasonable course to work for the inclusion of Kurdish districts and their participation in National Assembly on conditions of local assent and special supervision by British Officers and if necessary by the High Commissioner.[29]

Churchill replied, "Appreciate force of arguments subject to proviso that Kurds are not to be put under Arabs if they do not wish to be."[30] Noel reported,

> We have abandoned the idea of Kurdish autonomy included in the Treaty of Sèvres. Our aim is to incorporate in Iraq as far as may be feasible under normal Iraqi administration all the Kurdish areas which may fall on the Mosul side of the frontier as the result of the negotiations.[31]

Faisal pursued his own interests, while appearing to serve Britain. He had a vision to build a state in Iraq, governed by Arab tribes with himself as the head. In March 1921, Britain sponsored Faisal as king of Iraq and promised a treaty offering eventual independence. Faisal returned from Britain to Iraq and was crowned in August 1921. He was, however, concerned by Britain's decision to abandon the Kurds in Anatolia. He feared the Mesopotamian Kurds would join their Kurdish brethren in Turkey or Iran to marginalize Iraq and undermine his rule. Faisal rejected Kurdistan's independence, wanting the Kurds to be a part of Iraq. Most Kurds are Sunni Muslims and he needed their support in the Iraqi Assembly as a counterweight to Iraq's Shi'ite majority.

British troops adopted a "forward policy," using military force to stabilize the situation until a frontier delimitation commission could formalize the border. The Turks wanted to drive the British out of Mosul. Britain fostered a revolt by the Kurdish tribes along the border between Kurdish and Turkish forces. The Kurds also fought the British, chafing under a foreign power. According to E.B. Sloane, "Generally the mass of people desire no change at all. Above all they do not want a council for Kurdistan, they rejoice at being saved from Sheikh Mahmud…We could not do anything if they chose to rise against us."[32] Britain sought circumstances to rule out the possibility of an independent Kurdistan. It also took steps to dissuade the Kurds from thinking independence could be achieved.

With violent conflict escalating and discussions over Mosul at an impasse, Britain proposed arbitration by the League of Nations. Britain was confident that the League would rule in its favor, as Turkey was not a member of the League of Nations and Sir Eric Drummond, a British diplomat, was the organization's secretary general. Turkey initially rejected a role for the League of Nations, proposing a plebiscite instead. Eventually it relented and Mosul's status was referred to the League in June 1924.

A fact-finding commission from the League of Nations visited the region to assess local attitudes. It interviewed directly affected populations to determine if they wanted to be a part of Iraq or to join Turkey. The Kurds were hardly homogeneous. Kurds living north of the Zab are culturally and linguistically similar to their brethren in Turkey, while those south of the Zab are similar to Kurds in Iran. Kurds were given a choice between joining Iraq or Turkey. Most Kurds rejected Baghdad's rule, but independence was not an option.

The League of Nations awarded the Mosul vilayet to Britain on 18 December 1925. In an attempt to mollify Kurdish opposition, its report proposed safeguards preserving the character of the Kurdish areas. The commission called for extensive self-rule by Kurds. "Officials of the Kurdish race must be appointed for the administration of their country, the dispensation of justice, teaching in the schools, and that Kurdish should be the official language of all these services."[33] Turkey appealed the decision to the Permanent Court of International Justice in The Hague. On 18 July 1926, the Court upheld the League's finding as binding on Britain and Turkey.

Britain was required to promulgate a new Treaty with Iraq, ensuring their alliance for 25 years. Britain's treaty obligations would end if Iraq was admitted as a member of the League of Nations. The Anglo-Iraqi Treaty of January 1926 enshrined the League's recommendations.[34] Faisal negotiated a series of treaties culminating in Iraq's independence and membership of the League of Nations by 1932.[35]

Kurdistan was remote and relatively insignificant when the League of Nations conducted its assessment in 1925. Kirkuk assumed greater importance with the discovery of oil. The Baba Gurgur oil field in north Kirkuk gushed in October 1927; with huge estimated reserves, the field was 100 kilometers long and 12 kilometers wide, stretching all the way to Mosul. Baba Gurgur means "Father of the Flames" in Kurdish, but it was an asset of Iraq, with little benefit flowing to Kirkuk's residents.

Today

The Islamic State and the Kurds share similar views about Sykes–Picot. When ISIS swept across Iraq and Syria in 2014, its self-declared caliph, Abu Bakr al-Baghdadi, declared: "This blessed advance will not stop until we hit the last nail in the coffin of the Sykes–Picot conspiracy."[36]

Kurdish political parties also condemned Sykes–Picot for creating nation states where Kurds were captive. According to Masoud Barzani, head of the KDP and former President of the KRG: "Sykes–Picot has failed, it's over. There has to be a new formula for the region. I'm very optimistic that within this new formula, the Kurds will achieve their historic demand and right [to independence]". Barham Salih, ex-KRG Prime Minister, said: "The system in place for the past one hundred years has collapsed. It's not clear what new system will take its place."[37]

The United States and other countries emphasize the territorial integrity of Iraq and Syria. Washington wants to stabilize Iraq and Syria within their current borders; US policy is a de facto endorsement of Sykes–Picot. Conflict in Iraq and Syria occurred because the central governments had too much power. Decentralizing Iraq and Syria is the best way to promote democracy and prevent their violent break-up. Regions want control over local government, economic affairs, natural resources and cultural rights.

Britain abandoned its Kurdistan project, in exchange for assurances from Iraq and Turkey that they would uphold the rights of Kurds as an ethnic minority. Kurds warily accepted Britain's assurances. However, both Iraq and Turkey failed to devolve power. Instead of protecting and promoting minority rights, Iraq and Turkey abused them. Failure to fulfill commitments made in Sèvres was the Kurds' first betrayal in the twentieth century. It was not the last time Kurds would be betrayed.

2 VICTIMS OF THE COLD WAR

"Covert action should not be confused with missionary work."

HENRY KISSINGER[1]

The Mahabad Republic

The Kurds continued their struggle for sovereignty after Lausanne, led by the legendary nationalist and freedom fighter, Mulla Mustafa Barzani, who was born in the village of Barzan in Iraqi Kurdistan. Central governments in Iraq, Iran, Turkey and Syria imposed draconian security measures to control the Kurds. Their villages were burned and many Kurds were killed. In 1931, Mulla Mustafa Barzani led a rebellion against Baghdad's attempt to limit power of the Kurdish tribes and became a Kurdish national hero for unifying Kurds in opposition to ruthless central authority. Mulla Mustafa Bazani's rebellion was a source of pride for Kurds, who felt dignified by his armed struggle in defense of their rights. His struggle for autonomy and self-determination became a defining principle for Kurds everywhere.

Qazi Muhammad and Mulla Mustafa Barzani established the Republic of Mahabad in northwestern Iran on 22 January 1946 with the aim of autonomy for the Kurds and democracy for Iran. However, it collapsed in less than a year on 15 December 1946. The Republic of Mahabad arose at the same time as the Azerbaijan People's Government in northern Iran. Both were supported by the Soviet Union, and both were casualties of the Cold War. Indeed, the first salvo of the Cold War occurred in Iran over Mahabad.

The joint Anglo-Soviet Invasion had been launched five years earlier in August 1941, at the height of World War II and several years prior to the period of superpower competition. Britain and the Soviet Union sought to secure Iranian oil fields, as well as supply lines for the Soviet Union's ongoing war with Axis powers. The Allies accused Reza Shah Pahlevi of disloyalty and removed him from power on 16 September 1941. With Reza

Shah out of the way, Britain and the Soviet Union divided up the Iranian territory between them. Northern Iran went to the Soviet Union and the southern provinces to Britain.

Winston Churchill, Franklin D. Roosevelt and Joseph Stalin met at the Soviet Embassy in Tehran to finalize the Tehran Declaration on 1 December 1943. The Declaration affirmed support for democracy, tolerance and human rights in Iran.

> With our diplomatic advisers we have surveyed the problems of the future. We shall seek the cooperation and active participation of all nations, large and small, whose peoples in heart and mind are dedicated, as are our own peoples, to the elimination of tyranny and slavery, oppression and intolerance. We will welcome them, as they may choose to come, into a world family of democratic nations.[2]

Kurds interpreted the Tehran Declaration as support for their national cause. The Society for the Revival of Kurdistan (SRK) harnessed Kurdish nationalism and launched an independence movement for Mahabad. The SRK was a nationalist left-wing ideological party organized under the banner of "Islam, Kurdishness, and modernization."[3] The SRK became the Kurdistan Democratic Party of Iran (KDPI) on 16 August 1945, under the leadership of Qazi Muhammad, a well-educated Kurd who was inspired by egalitarian and leftist ideologies prevalent at the time. The KDPI's military wing, known as the Mahabad army, was headed by Mulla Mustafa Barzani.

Qazi Muhammed and Mula Mustafa Barzani launched a pan-Kurdish movement aimed at uniting all Kurdish territories beyond Mahabad. They did not deny that the Mahabad Republic was funded and supplied by the Soviets; the KDPI had no backers other than the Soviet Union. However, Qazi Muhammad insisted that the KDPI was not a communist party. Turkey and Iraq opposed the Kurdish national movement; Turkey did not want its restive Kurds to seek a state of their own. Demands for self-determination by the Kurds in Iraq were also a potential source of instability for Baghdad.[4]

After the war, the United States put enormous pressure on Moscow to drop Qazi Muhammad, cease supporting the Azerbaijan People's Government and withdraw entirely from the Persian Gulf. President Harry Truman threatened a nuclear strike when the Soviet Union refused to withdraw from the territories in Iran it had seized during the war. Despite Washington's objection, Iran gave the Soviet Union an oil concession in exchange for its withdrawal. The US rejected Russian oil interests in the Persian Gulf, seeking sole control of the region's vast energy resources. When the Soviet Union withdrew from Iran in early 1947, Kurds were left without a patron.

Qazi Muhammad turned for assistance to the United States, but to no avail, as Washington believed that the KDPI was comprised of inveterate leftists. Qazi Muhammad's Kurdish national movement was crushed by the Iranian authorities and he was sentenced to death by an Iranian military court and hanged in the central square of Mahabad on 30 March 1947. Mulla Mustafa Barzani escaped to fight another day.

The Baghdad Pact

Communist influence spread through anti-Western and anti-colonial movements. Egypt was a case in point. In 1952, Gamal Abdel Nasser led a military coup that overthrew Egypt's King Farouk. Nasser implemented sweeping land reforms as part of his program to counter imperialism. He confronted the capitalist system in a bid to transform Egypt into a modern and economically developed country where assets were distributed in a more egalitarian way. Nasser tried to rally other countries to his ideological cause.

The US was concerned about Egypt's drift into Moscow's sphere of influence. Measures were adopted to prevent other countries from following its course. The Baghdad Pact was established by Turkey, Iran, Iraq, Great Britain and Pakistan in 1955. It was ostensibly a vehicle for advancing shared political, military and economic goals, as well as peace in the Middle East.[5] However, the Baghdad Pact was really established to counter the spread of Communism.

The Suez Crisis of 1956 highlighted serious rifts in the region. The US and Britain withdrew financing for Egypt's Aswan Dam project because of Egypt's increasingly pro-Soviet position. Nasser responded in July 1956 by nationalizing the Suez Canal, a vital international shipping lane connecting the Mediterranean to the Red Sea. The Israeli Defense Forces (IDF) invaded Sinai on 29 October 1956, joined by French and British forces, exacerbating the crisis. This involvement of Western powers nearly brought the Soviet Union into the conflict.

The US played a critical role behind the scenes to prevent the Suez Crisis from spiraling into all-out regional war. Washington signed bilateral agreements with members of the Baghdad Pact, but was not itself a member.

Washington wanted a light footprint, lest involvement in the Baghdad Pact make the US a lightning rod and adversely affect Israel's position in the region. Israel was a polarizing force during the Cold War, but Kurdish issues were also divisive. Arab countries were wary of Kurdistan becoming a "second Israel."[6]

The Soviet Union was friendly towards Israel when Nasser came to power in 1952, and Israel's socialist ideals resonated with Soviet policy planners. However, Moscow reversed its position in response to Israel's increasingly pro-Western orientation and the Soviet Union branded Zionism as a tool of "racist imperialism." According to the Communist Party of the Soviet Union, "The main posits of modern Zionism are militant chauvinism, racism, anti-Communism and anti-Sovietism […] overt and covert fight against freedom movements and the USSR."[7]

Israel's foreign policy emphasized peripheral alliances to balance the larger Arab bloc. It focused on non-Arab states, such as Iran and Turkey, as well as minorities, such as the Kurds. Israelis and Kurds are strikingly similar: both are relatively small nations surrounded by hostile Arab neighbors. Both Israelis and Kurds have been traumatized by persecution and violent conflict. Both have struggled to gain a state of their own. Kurds in Israel are also a factor in domestic politics: Kurdish Jews emigrated to Israel in the 1940s and 50s, with as many as 400,000 living in Israel today. Israel's support for Kurdistan made the Kurds a factor in the Cold War.

Members of the Baghdad Pact were uncomfortable entering into an alliance that served US and Israeli interests, and Iraq pulled out of the Baghdad Pact in 1959. With Iraq's withdrawal, the secretariat was moved from Baghdad to Ankara and the Baghdad Pact evolved into the Central Treaty Organization (CENTO). The US focused on the "Northern Tier," a band of countries forming a security belt between the Soviet Union and Middle East countries: CENTO linked Turkey, the southernmost member of the North Atlantic Treaty Organization (NATO), with Pakistan, the westernmost member of the Southeast Asia Treaty Organization (SEATO). Through CENTO, the US sought to build a web of alliances to prevent Soviet expansionism. It facilitated a security agreement between Turkey and Pakistan in 1954 and Iraq and Turkey signed a "pact of mutual cooperation" in February 1955. While individual states in CENTO had formidable militaries, CENTO had no joint command or military capabilities of its own. Unable to provide collective security for its members, CENTO was a better conduit for economic and technical cooperation than a military alliance, and it was formally disbanded in 1979 in the wake of the Algiers Accord, which normalized relations between Iraq and Iran at the expense of the Kurds.

The Kurdish Rebellion

Mulla Mustafa Barzani took temporary refuge in Soviet Azerbaijan after the collapse of the Mahabad Republic. In 1958, he returned to a hero's welcome in Iraqi Kurdistan after an 11-year exile in the Soviet Union. Abd Al-Karim Qasim was a nationalist Iraqi army brigadier who led the 14 July Revolution, which eliminated the British-backed Hashemite dynasty. Qasim established the precedent of military officers leading Iraq's government, serving as prime minister until 1963. He exercised arbitrary power, putting Iraq on a path of socialism and Arab nationalism, was intolerant of ethnic minorities in Iraq and rejected Kurdish identity politics. In response, Mulla Mustafa Barzani launched an insurgency from remote encampments in the mountains on the Iran–Iraq border. Barzani felt he had Iran's backing and US support; America's commitment was extended on the personal orders of Nixon and Kissinger.[8] The US backing allowed Mulla Mustafa Barzani to hedge his bets, as he believed that Iran would never cut him off, so long as the US was committed to the Kurds.

When Barzani issued a platform of political demands, setting the stage for rebellion, the Iraqi Air Force indiscriminately bombed Kurdish villages. Instead of suppressing Kurdish aspirations, the Iraqi military offensive rallied popular support behind Barzani. Qasim's failure to win a decisive victory against the Kurdish insurgency went down badly with members of the Iraqi armed forces and created conditions for a coup by young disaffected officers, in February 1963. They launched a military offensive, which ended in May 1966 with the Iraqi army's defeat at the Battle of Mount Handrin in which Peshmerga eliminated an entire Iraqi brigade. Barzani's Peshmerga were a resilient force, defending their homeland and using guerilla tactics against Iraq's potent conventional army.

Cooperation between Israel and the Kurds initially focused on humanitarian issues, involving the delivery of food and medicine. For example, Israel donated a field hospital in 1966 and trained Kurdish medics. Israeli experts in dry-land farming worked in Kurdistan and Israel financed support for the publication of school books in Kurdish.

Israel and the Peshmerga also cooperated discreetly but decisively on security issues. Barzani visited Israel in 1968 and 1973 to coordinate the provision of non-lethal assistance. After the 1973 visit, Israel supplied small arms and ammunition, as well as anti-tank and anti-aircraft weapons. Kurds were sent to Israel for military training and Israeli paratroopers trained Peshmerga in Kurdistan.[9] Israel did not admit to working with Kurdistan until 29 September 1980 when Prime Minister Menachem Begin gave official acknowledgment on Radio Israel.

Cooperating with the Kurds was in Israel's national interest. Iraq was one of the most hostile and aggressive Arab countries towards the Jewish State, refusing to sign the ceasefire agreement with Israel after the 1948 Arab invasion, joining Arab armies in the 1967 and 1973 Arab–Israeli wars and supporting Jordan in border skirmishes with Israel. Israel supported the Peshmerga because they served as a distraction that helped keep the Iraqi armed forces away from Israel's borders.[10]

The First Iraqi–Kurdish War erupted on 11 September 1961 and lasted until 1970. More than 100,000 people died in nine years of fighting. The US gave Mulla Mustafa Barzani just enough support to sustain the fight, but not enough to prevail. According to the House Select Intelligence Committee,

> The recipients of US arms and cash were an insurgent ethnic group fighting for autonomy in a country bordering our ally [...] Documents in the Committee's possession clearly show that the President [Richard M. Nixon], Dr. Kissinger and the foreign head of state hoped that our clients would not prevail. They preferred instead that the insurgents simply continue a level of hostilities sufficient to sap the resources of our ally's neighboring country [...] Even in the context of covert action, ours was a cynical enterprise.[11]

Iraqi Kurds used violent conflict to bring Baghdad to the negotiating table. Mulla Mustafa Barzani negotiated an Autonomy Agreement, finalized on 11 March 1970, which ended the Kurdish rebellion. It included 15 points:

1. Kurdish language shall be, alongside the Arabic language, the official language in areas with a Kurdish majority; and will be the language of instruction in those areas and taught throughout Iraq as a second language.
2. Kurds will participate fully in government, including senior and sensitive posts in the cabinet and army.
3. Kurdish education and culture will be reinforced.

4. All officials in Kurdish majority areas shall be Kurds or at least Kurdish-speaking.
5. Kurds shall be free to establish student, youth, women's and teachers' organizations of their own.
6. Funds will be set aside for the development of Kurdistan.
7. Pensions and assistance will be provided for the families of martyrs and others stricken by poverty, unemployment or homelessness.
8. Kurds and Arabs will be restored to their former place of habitation.
9. The Agrarian Reform will be implemented.
10. The Constitution will be amended to read "The Iraqi people is made up of two nationalities, the Arab nationality and the Kurdish nationality."
11. The broadcasting station and heavy weapons will be returned to the Government.
12. A Kurd shall be one of the vice presidents.
13. The Governorates (Provincial) Law shall be amended in a manner conforming with the substance of this declaration.
14. Unification of areas with a Kurdish majority as a self-governing unit.
15. The Kurdish people shall share in the legislative power in a manner proportionate to its population in Iraq.

The Peshmerga were a symbol of Kurdish self-reliance, and the Autonomy Agreement preserved the honored role of Peshmerga in Kurdish society. It envisioned autonomy in three Kurdish governorates and other adjacent districts with a Kurdish majority.

According to Iraq's Vice Premier Sidan Hussein Taarit, the Autonomy Agreement represented "the total and final settlement of the Kurdish question." Foreign Minister Tariq Aziz stated, "We were sincere when we announced the March 11th Manifesto. It wasn't propaganda."[12] The Autonomy Agreement was broadly supported by Kurdish parties. It was endorsed by Mulla Mustafa Barzani and the politburo of the Kurdistan Democratic Party (KDP), as well as Jalal Talabani, who headed the Patriotic Union of Kurdistan (PUK). On paper, the deal was a model for power-sharing. However, implementation languished, while the Government of Iraq also took steps to undermine the Agreement.

Iraq adopted a policy of "Arabization." Hundreds of thousands of Kurds, Turkmen and Assyrians were displaced from their farms and properties to make room for landless Arab settlers from central and southern Iraq.[13]

Arabization in Kirkuk and Khanaqin was driven by a political agenda. It was an effort to change the region's demography, diluting the presence of Kurds in advance of the census which would determine Kurdish lands for inclusion in the Autonomy Agreement.[14] Infuriating Mulla Mustafa Barzani, the census was postponed twice. Iraq ultimately demarcated the Kurdish area to exclude oil-rich Kirkuk.

Peshmerga received support from the United States via Iran. In parallel, Iraq drew closer to the Soviet Union. Iraq and the Soviet Union signed a treaty of friendship in April 1972, establishing cooperation in political, economic and military affairs. The treaty also facilitated the transfer of sophisticated Soviet-made weapons to Iraq.

By 1973, Mulla Mustafa Barzani had concluded that the Baath Party had turned against the Kurds and was planning a military campaign to gain control of Iraqi Kurdistan. He believed that Iraq's Baathist leadership lacked any sincere intention to implement the Autonomy Agreement, and was playing for time. When fighting resumed between Peshmerga and Iraqi armed forces the Autonomy Agreement collapsed and the second Iraqi–Kurdish war commenced.[15]

Algiers Accord

Mulla Mustafa Barzani made Iran his base of operations when Iraqi armed forces invaded Iraqi Kurdistan in 1974. Assistance from Iran was indispensable with the Shah, Mohammad Reza Pahlavi, supporting the Peshmerga to weaken Iraq. Iran, a Persian country, and Arab Iraq had long-standing disputes over territory, culture and regional hegemony. In the Cold War context, the US sponsored the Peshmerga because of Iraq's tilt towards the Soviet Union. Other important factors were Israel and oil.

Iraq was Israel's chief antagonist. As we have seen, Iraq had participated in the Arab–Israeli wars of 1948, 1967 and 1973. Iraq and Syria were strategic allies and neighbors, both ruled by a Baath Party, and both seeking Israel's destruction. In the 1973 Arab–Israeli War, Israel recaptured lost land in the Golan Heights and pushed back Syrian forces, advancing along the Tiberias–Damascus highway to within 35 miles of the Syrian capital. Iraq came to the rescue of fellow Baathists in Syria, deploying up to 30,000 troops, 100 Russian-made MiG aircraft, an armored division and other supporting units to prevent the Israeli Defense Forces from marching on Damascus.[16]

An embargo of the Organization of Arab Petroleum Exporting Countries (OAPEC) led to the 1973 oil crisis. In response to America's support for Israel during the Arab–Israeli War of 1973, OAPEC reduced production by 5 percent from regular levels. It pledged to further reduce production by 5 percent each month until oil-consuming countries agreed to discontinue support for Israel, and recommended that its members "subject the United States to the most severe cut in proportion to the amounts of crude oil and products it imports from every exporting country."[17] After the October 1973 Arab–Israeli War, world oil prices increased ten times from their level of the 1960s. Oil prices quadrupled between October 1973 and March 1974, causing serious financial disruption in oil-dependent Western economies.

Iraq took a harder line than other OAPEC members. It called for a complete halt in production and the imposition of embargoes on countries that supported Israel. Iraq also called on OAPEC members to nationalize the assets of Western oil companies, break off diplomatic relations with these countries, and withdraw Arab funds deposited in countries targeted by the embargo. When OAPEC refused to go along with this, Iraq withdrew from OAPEC and announced it would nationalize the assets of Dutch and US oil companies.

Oil flows were put at further risk by the maritime border dispute between Iraq and Iran in the Shatt al-Arab, a 200-kilometer river in southeastern Iraq formed by the confluence of the Tigris and Euphrates. The Shatt al-Arab passes the Iraqi port of Basra and the Iranian port of Abadan before emptying into the Persian Gulf. Iraq's Vice President Saddam Hussein inflamed relations by claiming the entire waterway up to the Iranian shore as Iraq's territory. In April 1969, Iran abrogated the pre-existing maritime boundary between Iraq and Iran and Iranian oil tankers, escorted by Iranian warships, refused to pay tolls to Iraq when they passed through the Shatt al-Arab. In April 1969 both armies deployed along the banks and Iran seized four islands in the Persian Gulf. In response, Saddam Hussein expelled all Iranians from Iraq and called on the Arabs of Khuzestan, a region in Iran, to rebel. The United States supported Iran.

The Shah of Iran was indebted to the United States for organizing the coup that had deposed the left-leaning Prime Minister Mohammed Mossadegh in 1953. Through a policy that was known as the "blank check," Iran became the largest purchaser of US military equipment worldwide. Within the space of a few short months in 1972, Iran purchased over $3 billion worth of arms from the US, a twentyfold increase from the previous year. Iran's arms purchases dwarfed those of other US allies such as Israel and NATO nations.[18]

At the 1974 Arab League Summit, Iraq and Iran launched a committee chaired by Jordan's King Hussein to address the Shatt al-Arab boundary dispute. When Iraq insisted on its territorial demands, Iran expanded its assistance to the Iraqi Kurds in order to put more pressure on Baghdad. Saddam Hussein and Mohammad Reza Pahlavi met at the Organization of Petroleum Exporting Countries (OPEC) Summit in Algiers, hosted by Algeria's President Houari Boumédiène in March 1975. Behind the scenes, Kissinger worked with Boumédiène to broker a deal between Iraq and Iran.

The Algiers Accord resolved the maritime border dispute between Iraq and Iran, thereby guaranteeing safe passage of oil tankers and commercial ships through the Shatt al-Arab. It also addressed disputed territories such as Khuzestan and served as the basis for other bilateral agreements between Iraq and Iran. The Algiers Accord was finalized on 5 March 1975 and formally signed on 13 June. Saddam Hussein relinquished Iraq's claim to disputed territories in exchange for Iran abandoning support of the Kurds. Upon returning from Algiers, Mohammad Reza Pahlavi immediately ordered that all Iranian military support and financial assistance to the Kurds should cease immediately. He ordered the border between Iran and Iraq to be sealed on 30 April, thirty days later. He also requested that the CIA and the Mossad, Israel's intelligence agency, stop assisting the Peshmerga.

Just two weeks before the Algiers Agreement, Kissinger wrote to Barzani: "I want you to know of our admiration for you and your people and for the valiant effort you are making."[19] Kissinger was irritated that Mohammad Reza Pahlavi was rushing to normalize relations with Iraq. He hoped to sustain Iraq's conflict with the Kurds in order to tie down the Iraqis and prevent Iraq from acting more aggressively towards Israel. But Kissinger was disingenuous, manipulating the Kurds as well as Iraq to advance US interests in the Cold War. Loyalty was expedient and alliances were trans-actional. When I asked Kissinger about the Kurds, he replied, perhaps in a bid to obscure his own deceit, that they were "the most treacherous people I ever met."[20]

Settlement of the border dispute diffused the threat of an all-out war between Iraq and Iran. The Peshmerga were outgunned and outmanned, and without foreign support. More than 100,000 Peshmerga fled to Iran and Turkey. Under Iran's control, Mulla Mustafa Barzani became a "guest" in Tehran, staying at a villa of the Savak, Iran's secret police agency. Defeated, demoralized and betrayed, Barzani came to the United States in June 1976. He was suffering from lung cancer and underwent treatment at the Mayo Clinic in Minnesota. Haunted by an overwhelming sense of failure, Barzani died in McLean, Virginia on 1 March 1979.

Mulla Mustafa Barzani lived a life of legend. Kurds loved him for asserting their interests against states hostile towards them. When his remains were returned to Iraqi Kurdistan on 6 October 1993, Kurds lined the road to welcome him back to the land he had fought for decades to liberate. Barzani epitomized the struggle of Kurds for dignity and statehood. Used and discarded, he was also a symbol of their betrayal by the West. He and the Kurds were victims of cynical Western policy during the Cold War. The Algiers Accord was the second time in the twentieth century when the Kurds were betrayed by the United States.

3 CRACKDOWN

*"There is another way for the bloodshed to stop and that is for the
Iraqi military and Iraqi people to take matters into their own hands."*

FORMER US PRESIDENT GEORGE H.W. BUSH[1]

Desert Storm

Iraq invaded Kuwait in 1990, claiming it was Iraq's 19th province. After
taking Kuwait, Saddam Hussein threatened to continue his territorial grab
and attack Saudi Arabia. By seizing Kuwait, Iraq controlled 20 percent of
the world's oil supply. If Saddam seized Saudi Arabia, he would cripple
world oil supplies and hold the West hostage.

The US response was swift and sure. President George H.W. Bush
affirmed, "This will not stand, this aggression against Kuwait." He immediately took steps to organize "collective action" against Iraq. The US
led a debate in the United Nations Security Council (UNSC), which
unanimously condemned Iraq's military action. The UNSC demanded an
immediate withdrawal from Kuwait and imposed a worldwide ban on
trade with Iraq. The stage was set for a showdown between the international community, led by the United States, and Iraq's dictator, Saddam
Hussein.

Vice President Dick Cheney went to Riyadh, Saudi Arabia to coordinate a response with the Saudi leadership, including use of Saudi territory
for military operations. Bush insisted on an Arab solution that restored
Kuwait's territorial integrity, but Arab leaders were prone to appeasement
and reluctant to counter aggression by an Arab "brother." Collective action
would require solidarity among members of the Arab League, of which Iraq
was an influential member. Bush, however, demanded the complete and
unconditional withdrawal of Iraqi forces. He was adamant that, "Nobody
is willing to accept anything less than total withdrawal of the Iraqi forces
and no puppet regime."[2]

The US reinforced bases in Saudi Arabia, as a tangible measure of its resolve to staunch Iraq's further aggression. Preventing Saddam from occupying Saudi Arabia was a strategic imperative, for not only was Saudi Arabia the world's largest oil producer, it was also a critical US ally in the Persian Gulf and a counterbalance to Iranian influence in the region. The Bush administration organized an international coalition aimed at compelling Iraq's withdrawal from Kuwait. Saddam was belligerent, deploying up to 300,000 Iraqi troops and vowing a stiff resistance. He promised "the mother of all battles."

The "Powell Doctrine," articulated by Chairman of the US Joint Chiefs of Staff Colin Powell, called for the overwhelming use of force against an adversary. With Saddam amassing forces in Kuwait, the US deployed its assets to reverse Iraq's occupation. Operation Desert Storm was launched on 16 January 1991. It involved up to 900,000 ground forces from 32 nations, including Britain, Egypt, France, Saudi Arabia and Kuwait. The United States was the primary contributor of troops and took the lead in war planning. The coalition launched an intensive five-week bombing assault from air and sea to soften the Iraqi lines and degrade Iraqi command and control. Saddam offered little resistance except for firing Scud missiles against Israel. He hoped to provoke a response from Israel that would undermine the international coalition and drive a wedge between Western and Arab countries; the Arab countries did not agree on much, except their antipathy to the Jewish State. Under pressure from the US, Israel was dissuaded from responding to Iraq's missile attacks. Coalition forces swiftly drove into Iraq from Kuwait. They overwhelmed the Iraqi army, which asked for a ceasefire after just 100 hours. Kuwait was liberated on 28 February 1991.[3]

Resolutions passed by the UNSC authorized "all necessary measures" to restore Kuwait's sovereignty. But it did not sanction an attack on Iraq or authorize regime change. Officials from the Bush administration debated whether to remove Saddam from power. Most opposed marching on Baghdad and occupying Iraq. They warned that it would unleash a civil war between Iraq's ethnic and sectarian groups, and the ensuing bloodbath would destabilize the region. Secretary of Defense Dick Cheney was strongly opposed to invading Iraq and toppling Saddam. He warned of a "quagmire" with regional consequences. Powell invoked the Pottery Barn rule: "Break it, you own it."

United States policy in the Middle East was driven by two linked objectives: first, supporting Israel; and second, countering Iran. The overthrow of Shah Reza Pahlevi and the 1979 Islamic revolution brought Ayatollah Khomeini to power. The Iran hostage crisis, where 52 US diplomats and citizens were held captive for 444 days, scarred US–Iran relations. Washington supported Saddam Hussein in the Iran–Iraq war, which lasted from 1980 to 1988, as a counterweight to Iran. To this day, the Sunni–Shi'ite divide and competition for influence in the Persian Gulf between Iran and Sunni Arab states shape US policy in the region.

The US abandoned its support for Iraq after Saddam invaded Kuwait, but hedged its response to avoid disrupting the balance of power in the region. Powell explained, "Our practical intention was to leave Baghdad enough power to survive as a threat to Iran that remained bitterly hostile to the United States."[4] Concern about Iran was shared by Arab leaders. Egyptian President Hosni Mubarak advised the US not to invade Iraq for fear it would strengthen Iran. According to Mubarak, "Iraq needs a strong leader—and toppling Saddam Hussein would open the gate for Iran."[5]

Despite Saddam's rhetoric, the outcome of Operation Desert Storm was never in doubt. At least half of Iraq's tank battalions were disabled. Tanks and armored vehicles lined the road from Basra to Baghdad, destroyed in flight as Iraqi troops retreated across the desert. Saddam's much-vaunted Republican Guard forces turned out to be a paper tiger. The Iraqi military was adept at bullying, but it was unable to withstand the multifaceted attack coordinated by Desert Storm Commander General Norman Schwarzkopf. The UNSC's Resolution 687 demanded Iraq's unconditional surrender.[6]

Uprisings

As we have seen, some members of Bush's national security team wanted to invade Baghdad and remove Saddam from power. Bush's National Security Advisor, Brent Scowcroft, even proposed that the US organize a coup. For a coup to occur, however, Iraqis would have to take matters into their own hands and undertake an armed rebellion. Arabists in the State Department argued that this would unleash a "Pandora's box" of consequences, as Iraq's simmering ethnic and sectarian tensions boiled over and reprisals spiraled out of control.

Washington could not predict Iran's response, perhaps intervening on behalf of Iraq's Shi'ite majority and protecting holy shrines in Najaf, Karbala and other Iraqi cities. Rather than take matters into its own hands, the Bush administration decided to foment rebellion by Iraqis with the goal of removing Saddam Hussein and establishing a democracy in the heart of the Middle East. The CIA-funded Radio Free Iraq broadcast an appeal from Salah Omar al-Ali, an exiled member of Saddam's Revolutionary Command Council, calling on Iraqis to take up arms against their president.

> Rise to save the homeland from the clutches of dictatorship so that you can devote yourself to avoiding the dangers of the continuation of the war and destruction. Honorable Sons of the Tigris and Euphrates, at these decisive moments of your life, and while facing the danger of death at the hands of foreign forces, you have no option in order to survive and defend the homeland but put an end to the dictator and his criminal gang.[7]

Bush endorsed regime change in a direct address to the Iraqi people on Voice of America. On 15 February 1991, Bush said:

> There is another way for the bloodshed to stop: and that is, for the Iraqi military and the Iraqi people to take matters into their own hands and force Saddam Hussein, the dictator, to step aside and then comply with the United Nations' resolutions and rejoin the family of peace-loving nations.[8]

On 1 March, right after the liberation of Kuwait, Bush reiterated his message of rebellion:

> In my own view […] the Iraqi people should put [Saddam] aside, and that would facilitate the resolution of all these problems that exist and certainly would facilitate the acceptance of Iraq back into the family of peace-loving nations.[9]

Iraqis believed that Saddam was vulnerable and, with the expectation of US support, rose up in rebellion. Between March and April 1991, Arab Shi'ites in the south launched the Sha'aban Intifada and Kurds in the north launched the National Uprising. Military mutineers, including many Shi'ite and Kurdish recruits, joined the rebellion. Violence spread across the country as Saddam's forces lost control. It was a heady time. Convinced that the United States had their back, Iraqis believed it was their moment to overthrow Saddam's "Republic of Fear" and take retribution against Saddam and their Baathist oppressors.

The rebellion started in Shi'ite cities south of Basra. The first salvo came from a T-72 tank, which fired on a huge portrait of Saddam Hussein in Basra's main square. Violence spread quickly with cities across southern Iraq—Hilla, Karbala, Nasariyah and others—swept up in the uprising. Members of the Badr Brigades, based in Iran, crossed the border and occupied sacred Shi'ite shrines in Najaf and Karbala. They called on the Shi'ite faithful to join them. A gun battle erupted between mutineers and Iraqi forces near the Imam Ali Mosque in Najaf, which fell to the rebels.

Unlike the spontaneous and chaotic uprising in southern Iraq, the Kurdish uprising was relatively well organized. The KDP and the PUK called their Peshmerga to attack Iraqi forces and symbols of the regime. Jaish, government-sponsored Kurdish militias, turned on their patrons and joined the Peshmerga. The Kurdish rebellion started in Rania on 5 March. Kurdish cities in the north fell in rapid succession when the 24th Division of the vaunted Republican Guard surrendered. Peshmerga celebrated the liberation of Kirkuk on 20 March 1991.

Peshmerga seized the headquarters of Saddam's secret police in Suleimani, taking 14 tons of files maintained by the Directorate of General Security. The files chronicled in excruciating detail crimes committed by the regime against the Kurds during the Anfal Genocide. In addition to the use of chemical weapons to terrorize the Kurds, the file described "liquidations," "expulsions" and "transfers" of Kurdish victims, who were referred to as "saboteurs," "criminals," "traitors" and "human cargo."[10] The files were transported to the United States and preserved in a warehouse at the US Library of Congress.

As the Kurds rolled up territory during the Kurdish rebellion of 1991, they giddily chanted for "biji, azadi and democrasi" (human rights, freedom, and democracy). The PUK Secretary General, Jalal Talabani, called on his forces to march on Baghdad and arrest Saddam Hussein. By the spring, 14 of 18 provinces were in rebel hands.

The Aftermath

General Norman Schwarzkopf, commander of Operation Desert Storm, negotiated the Gulf War ceasefire agreement. The terms of the ceasefire

prohibited fixed-wing aircraft from flying in Iraqi airspace but, because of
Iraq's destroyed transport infrastructure, Schwarzkopf allowed the Iraqi
military to use helicopters for logistics and to transport government officials.
Iraqi helicopter gunships, equipped with automatic weapons and bombs, had
a devastating effect strafing and bombing the rebels. Helicopters were also
used to disburse chemical weapons, such as sarin and CS gas, while mustard
gas was used to attack Shi'ite civilians near Najaf and Karbala. Kurds lacked
the heavy weapons and surface-to-air missiles to counter the gunships. When
regime loyalists saw that Saddam was mounting a counter-offensive, they
regrouped and launched attacks against the rebels in major cities. About
half of the Republican Guard's tanks were able to escape Kuwait and were
mobilized for the counter-offensive.

Saddam was brutal in suppressing the rebellion, and the US was concerned about the spiral of violence it helped unleash. Cheney cautioned,
"It would be very difficult for us to hold the coalition together for any
particular course of action dealing with internal Iraqi politics, and I don't
think, at this point, our writ extends to trying to move inside Iraq."
Richard Boucher, the State Department spokesman, outlined a policy of
non-interference in Iraq's internal affairs. "We don't think that outside
powers should be interfering in the internal affairs of Iraq." According
to Spokeswoman Margaret Tutwiler, "We never, ever, stated as either
a military or a political goal of the coalition or the international community the removal of Saddam Hussein." Tens of thousands of people
died and nearly two million people were displaced in the immediate
aftermath of the Gulf War. As events spiraled out of control, Washington
feared it would be drawn into the fighting. It also feared a repeat of
Lebanon's civil war as factional violence caused the "Lebanonization" of
Iraq, symptomized by deadly violence and reprisals between ethnic and
sectarian groups.[11]

According to Human Rights Watch,

In their attempts to retake cities, and after consolidating control, loyalist
forces killed thousands of unarmed civilians by firing indiscriminately
into residential areas; executing young people on the streets, in homes
and in hospitals; rounding up suspects, especially young men, during
house-to-house searches, and arresting them with or without charge
or shooting them *en masse*; and using helicopters to attack unarmed
civilians as they fled the cities.[12]

The Peshmerga suffered a series of crushing defeats. They were driven from Kirkuk on 29 March and the following day T-72 tanks were used in operations against Kurds in Erbil and Dohuk. Mosul was lost on 31 March. Saddam exercised vicious victor's justice, killing Kurds randomly as a form of collective punishment. In addition to executing Peshmerga, civilians were targeted indiscriminately. Many thousands simply disappeared, their bodies buried in hundreds of mass graves. The crackdown in Kirkuk was intense. According to Human Rights Watch,

> After the establishment of the curfew government security forces began going door to door, rounding up men who could possibly threaten the regime. These men were taken to compounds outside of Kirkuk, where they endured brutal conditions including torture. Most of the men detained were Kurdish, and ranged in age from early teens to their fifties. In total more than 5,000 were detained.[13]

Rumors spread that mustard gas was used in Erbil and Dohuk. Mass hysteria spread among the Kurds causing approximately 1.5 million to take frantic flight to the mountains along Kurdistan's borders with Turkey and Iran. Turkey sealed its border, concerned that an influx of Kurds from Iraq would rile its own restive Kurdish population. Desperate for safety, about 300,000 Kurds gathered on the rugged cliffs along the Iraq–Turkey border. According to the US Department of State and international relief organizations, between 500 and 1,000 Kurds died each day along the border.[14] Additionally, at least 6,700 Kurds perished in Turkish refugee camps nearby.[15] Secretary of State James A. Baker flew to Turkey and inspected conditions in the camps and the plight of Kurds on the Iraqi side for whom entry into Turkey was barred. In accordance with international humanitarian law, he demanded that Turkey's President Turgut Ozal give them entry. Ozal had Kurdish ancestry and was favorably disposed to helping the Kurds.

Many Kurds also headed to Iran. Landmines left over from the Iran–Iraq war maimed thousands of Kurds who were fleeing Saddam's forces. Princeton N. Lyman, Director of the State Department's Bureau for Refugee Programs, called the displacement "a human tragedy of tremendous proportions."[16] On 5 April, the Iraqi government gloated over its victory, announcing "the complete crushing of acts of sedition, sabotage and rioting in all towns of Iraq."[17]

Bush tried to disassociate the US from the unfolding tragedy, stating that "I made clear from the very beginning that it was not an objective of the coalition or the United States to overthrow Saddam Hussein." He added,

> I don't think the Shi'ites in the south, those who are unhappy with Saddam in Baghdad, or the Kurds in the north ever felt that the United States would come to their assistance to overthrow this man. I have not misled anybody about the intentions of the United States of America, or has any other coalition partner, all of whom to my knowledge agree with me in this position.[18]

Officials in the US acknowledged their role in the tragedy. Powell belatedly admitted that Bush's rhetoric "may have given encouragement to the rebels." Partly out of guilt for egging on the Kurds and then allowing their slaughter, and partly because US interests were ill-served by a resurgent Saddam, the US led a diplomatic initiative calling attention to the plight of the Kurds, recommending measures to prevent further reprisals by Saddam; UNSC Resolution 688 was adopted on 5 April 1991. Not only did the resolution condemn Iraq's human rights abuses, it sanctioned the establishment of a no-fly zone, barring Iraqi war planes from flying north of the 36th parallel. The no-fly zone created conditions of security that allowed nearly all of the Kurds to return to their homes, and it also helped establish a no-drive zone, preventing operations by Iraqi ground forces. Without air power, a level playing field was created between the Peshmerga and the Iraqi army. The Peshmerga knew the terrain and were defending their homes. They were highly motivated to prevent another genocide. The resulting safe haven enabled the emergence of a de facto autonomous Kurdish area.

The physical presence of US troops in Iraqi Kurdistan also deterred Iraqi forces. On 17 April, US forces took control of territories north of the 36th parallel. The safe zone penetrated 60 miles into Iraq. The US also launched a massive humanitarian operation, which included the construction of temporary camps for Kurds displaced by the conflict. Operation Provide Comfort defined the initial humanitarian phase. Beyond emergency assistance, Kurds needed protection, so Operation Provide Comfort was complemented by Operation Northern Watch, which institutionalized the no-fly zone. Incirlik Air Force Base near Adana in southeast Turkey became the major staging ground for relief operations, as well as a base for US and British warplanes that patrolled the skies of Iraq. According to Assistant

Secretary of State David Mack, "We informed the Iraqi government that we were establishing the no-fly zone, and that we would shoot down any of their aircraft that entered the airspace."[19] Iraqi officials protested, asserting that the no-fly zone was a violation of the ceasefire agreement. They were technically correct, but their complaints fell on deaf ears given the regime's crimes against civilians and Iraq's pariah status.

Saddam wanted to punish the Kurds for their rebellion and for collaborating with the United States. He therefore imposed an embargo on Iraqi Kurdistan. The Kurds enjoyed a modicum of security, but their relative peace could be shattered at any moment. Also, hardships remained. The Iraqi army set up checkpoints on the roads to Kurdistan, preventing the transport of food, fuel and other supplies from Iraqi-controlled territory. At the same time, Kurds struggled with an embargo imposed by the UN on Iraq as a whole. Not only did the UN embargo prevent the import of materials to Iraqi Kurdistan, it also denied the Kurds a major source of revenue by blocking the export of oil from Kurdistan. To circumvent the embargo, Kurds filled canisters with crude oil and strapped them to the bottom of trucks crossing into Turkey at the Habur border gate. For miles on either side of the border, the road was covered with the slick surface of crude oil that spilled from makeshift Kurdish oil tankers.

While conditions stabilized in Iraqi Kurdistan, the plight of Shi'ites south of the 32nd parallel steadily worsened. The Iraqi government systematically drained the Mesopotamian marshes in the Tigris–Euphrates estuary. Forty percent of the southern marshlands were drained, forcing the relocation of Marsh Arabs. Other marshlands were flooded in order to deprive rebels of their hideouts. Facing an environmental catastrophe, tens of thousands of Shi'ites fled to Iran. US officials now faced a quandary: should they defend the Iraqi Shi'ites that Bush had incited to rebel, or abide by the terms of the ceasefire and stand aside to let them be slaughtered? On 22 August 1992, Bush announced that the US and its allies had established a second no-fly-zone barring Iraqi aircraft south of the 32nd parallel.

Opportunity

Stabilizing Iraq represented the first test of the international community in the post-Soviet period. On 25 December 1991, the Soviet flag was lowered from the Kremlin and Mikhail Gorbachev resigned as President of the Soviet Union, giving way to the newly independent Russian state. The

Soviet Union's demise signaled the beginning of a unipolar period when US power was ascendant and its leadership consequently essential. Scowcroft heralded the possibilities presented by the new era. "Aggression—simple, naked aggression ought not to be allowed as part of this new world order."[20]

The Gulf War was a moment of both peril and opportunity for the Kurds. The Peshmerga were observers as the US mounted Operation Desert Storm. However, they were hardly neutral. Kurds cheered as the coalition pummeled the Iraqi army and Kurdish leaders developed a close working relationship with US officials during and after the Gulf War. They believed the Kurdish uprising was in their own interests as well as in service of America's agenda. A conference on "Iraq after Saddam Hussein" was held in the Dirksen Senate Office Building on the day the Gulf War ended. Jalal Talabani represented the PUK and Hoshyar Zebari represented Barzani and the KDP. Kurdish political parties came together to affirm their gratitude to the United States, and their endorsement of America's pro-democracy agenda. Senator Claiborne Pell, Chairman of the Senate Foreign Relations Committee, and Senator Edward M. Kennedy assured the Kurds of America's protection.

Though the Kurds were incited by Bush, the Kurdish uprising was a natural response to Saddam's defeat in Operation Desert Storm. The Kurds rose up to finish the job that the coalition had started in the deserts of Kuwait and southern Iraq. With the US military mobilized, it was unfathomable to the Kurds that the US would stand down and allow the survival of Saddam's regime. While the Kurds had trusted America, they learned the hard way that Iraq's stability was more important to Bush than their goal of self-determination. Washington's fear of Iran was greater than its commitment to democracy in the region. A foreshadowing of future events, Bush's call to arms and cynical abandonment of the Kurds was the third betrayal of the Kurds by the United States.

Part II

Struggle

4 SELF-RULE

"Without unity, the road ahead will remain very difficult. With unity there is every reason for Iraqi Kurds to look forward with hope."

FORMER PRESIDENT OF IRAQ, JALAL TALABANI[1]

Personalities

Masoud Barzani and Jalal Talabani dominated Kurdish politics for decades. Masoud, the eldest son of Mulla Mustafa Barzani, headed the Kurdistan Democratic Party (KDP) and served as president of the Kurdistan Regional Government (KRG) from 2005 until 2017.

Masoud was born under the flag of Kurdistan in Mahabad on 16 August 1946. "I was born in the shadow of that flag [...] All of my life has been for the independence of Kurdistan."[2] At the age of 16, he became a Peshmerga. As a fighter and politician, Barzani lived through Kurdistan's tragedies. "Under the regime of Saddam Hussein, the Kurds suffered through wars, genocide, and persecution. The Anfal campaign, chemical bombardment, the destruction of our villages, the mass graves, genocide—that was the lot of the Kurds." Though slight in physical stature, Masoud exudes authority born from his lineage to Mulla Mustafa Barzani. Recognized for his pursuit of independence and leadership fighting the Islamic State, Masoud was shortlisted by *Time* magazine for Person of the Year in 2014.[3]

Jalal Talabani's political life began as a teenager when, after the Algiers Accord, he joined a group of radical students opposing Iraq's King Faisal II. While both were members of the KDP, Masoud had his father's backing whereas Talabani used his charm, intellect and political instincts to advance. Jalal broke from the KDP and established the PUK in 1975.

Jalal was progressive and left-leaning, an avowed Marxist and Maoist. He visited China in 1955, was inspired by his meeting with Premier Zhou Enlai, and translated Mao Zedong's "little red book" of quotations into

Kurdish. Jalal regularly attended conferences of the Socialist International, a worldwide association of political parties supporting democratic socialism. Gregarious by nature, Jalal schmoozed conference delegates from his perch in the coffee shop at the London Conference of Iraqi Opposition in 2002. After Saddam Hussein was deposed, Jalal became a member of the Iraqi Governing Council and played a pivotal role negotiating Iraq's 2005 constitution. Rather than take a confrontational approach to constitutional negotiations, he used guile and pragmatism to extract concessions that were in the interest of Kurdistan. Jalal served as president of Iraq from 2006 to 2014. He regularly visited New York for the UN General Assembly. In his suite on the 38th floor of the Waldorf Astoria, he had a revolving door of visitors whom he entertained with dates and sweets from the Middle East.

The PUK was founded by scholars and intellectuals who defected from the KDP. Cadres of the PUK had a more left-leaning, democratic and socialist political philosophy, while KDP members were more traditional, conservative and tribal in their political philosophy and constituency. Despite stylistic and substantive differences, Masoud and Jalal were both Kurdish nationalists who aspired to independence for Iraqi Kurdistan. Both ran their parties like a family business with political leadership and commercial opportunities apportioned to relatives, embedded throughout the KDP and PUK hierarchies.

Masrour Barzani, Masoud's son, is chancellor of the powerful Kurdistan Region Security Council (KRSC) and heads the KDP's Intelligence Agency, the Parastin. His other son, Mansour, is a Peshmerga commander though not involved in politics. Masoud's nephew, Nechirvan Barzani, is a capable technocrat and shrewd politician who has served as KRG prime minister from March 2006 to August 2009, and from March 2012 to the present.

Jalal has two sons. Bafel, the oldest, received military training from British Special Forces and France's Foreign Legion before establishing the PUK's Counter-Terrorism Group in 2004. Qubad, the second son, is the KRG deputy prime minister and former KRG representative to the United States. Jalal has a half-brother, Sheikh Jengy, who has more than a dozen children (that we know of). Lahur, the most prominent, is director of Zanyari, the PUK's intelligence agency and counterpart to the KDP's Parastin. Araz, the older son of Sheikh Jengy, and Lahur's brother, is a "businessman." For aspiring politicians in Iraqi Kurdistan, opportunities are limited without the pedigree of being a Barzani or a Talabani. Kosrat

Rasul Ali is a respected veteran Peshmerga who became Vice President of the KRG and deputy prime minister. He might have become prime minister, but his path was blocked by Jalal. His influence today is diminished by Parkinson's disease. Najmaldin Karim was governor of Kirkuk from 2011. He has political clout based on his personal relationship with Mulla Mustafa Barzani and his friendly relations with both Masoud and Jalal. He is also competent and principled. However, Karim has no blood ties to either the Barzani or Talabani families. Therefore, his KRG prospects are limited. Barham Salih is another player, who served as deputy prime minister of the Iraqi federal government and KRG prime minister from 2009 to 2012. He assumed the office as part of a power-sharing deal with the KDP whereby the parties agreed to rotate control of the premiership. Barham's term ended a year early in 2012. Since Barham spent many years abroad in the United Kingdom and the US, he could not develop a strong domestic political base. Iraqi Kurdistan experienced a "Kurdish Spring" in 2011, along with Arab countries that demanded reform. The Movement for Change Party, Gorran, which means "change" in Kurdish, won the PUK stronghold of Suleimani that year. Led by Nawshirwan Mustafa, a former member of the PUK Politburo, Gorran emerged in response to alleged corruption and nepotism of the KDP and PUK.

The PUK's constituency comes from Suleimani and Kirkuk. Gorran's victory in a PUK stronghold represented a seismic shift in Kurdish politics, reducing the PUK's power. Unlike any other place in Iraq, Suleimani is known for its intellectual and social life, where both men and women are active in society. Suleimani is situated near the Iranian border, a diverse crossroads where Kurdish, Arab and Persian cultures come together. The climate in the Suleimani governorate is refreshing compared to the oppressive heat elsewhere in Iraq. Not far from Lake Dukan, it is a vacation destination for Iraqis and people from across the region. Jalal is a product of Suleimani. His outsized personality was shaped by and helped shape the city's dynamic cosmopolitanism.

Dohuk, a mountain town near the Turkish border, was Masoud's stronghold. Erbil, a larger city contiguous with the Nineveh Plains leading to Mosul, is also a KDP base. Erbil is more conservative than Suleimani. Many women wear the hijab or abaya as a sign of modesty and purity. Erbil is a traditional place with a history of 5,000 years. Its famous citadel, used to defend against invaders, is unique in the region. Erbil, until the opening of its airport in 2005, has been more isolated from Iraq's neighbors than

Suleimani. The Barzanis have close security and commercial cooperation with Turkey, whereas the PUK is more closely associated with Iran.

Kurds have a bond forged through struggle and shared suffering. They faced a fork in the road after the Gulf War. They could aggregate their interests, work more closely together across party lines and forge a national identity as the basis for their nascent statehood. Or they could revert to tribal and identity politics, emphasizing regional loyalties and pursuing narrow self-interest.

The Civil War

The Gulf War and the West's security guarantee created an opportunity for the political and economic development of Iraqi Kurdistan. On 19 May 1992 Kurds voted for the first time to elect delegates to the Kurdistan National Assembly, the newly formed parliament of Iraqi Kurdistan. Elections were held in all areas of Kurdistan, with the exception of the disputed territories under Iraqi control. Kurds celebrated their ability to vote and make choices about their future. They welcomed the opportunity to exercise their democratic rights and vote for elected representatives. International monitors observed conditions at 178 polling stations, where they found that the vote was free and fair. Initial results gave KDP candidates 50.8 percent and PUK candidates 49.2 percent.[4]

As a result, the KDP emerged with a two-seat advantage in the Assembly—51 to 49. The PUK objected to the final tally, alleging electoral fraud. As a conciliatory gesture, the KDP agreed to a power-sharing formula with each party having 50 seats. The KDP Secretary General Jawhar Namiq Salim was elected Assembly Speaker on 4 June 1992 and Fuad Masum, a prominent PUK member, became prime minister of the KRG. The number of ministers was equally distributed. In instances when a KDP representative was the minister, the deputy minister was from the PUK, and vice versa.[5] The negotiated 50/50 split helped overcome conflict arising directly from the election. Power-sharing averted an immediate crisis, but disputing the returns set the tone for confrontation rather than cooperation. The Kurdistan Front was established to arbitrate differences. However, both the KDP and PUK took steps to consolidate their gains by establishing separate administrations in Erbil and Suleimani.

The KDP and PUK administrations were primarily responsible for collecting customs and tariffs, the principal source of revenue. The PUK collected fees at Iraqi Kurdistan's border with Iran, while the KDP controlled the border crossing with Turkey. Despite the apparent symmetry, revenues were not equal. More trade occurred across the Ibrahim Khalil border crossing with Turkey, generating far more revenue for the KDP, which led to further conflict between the KDP and PUK.

The Kurdistan National Assembly met in an emergency session on 30 June 1993, at which Masoud and Jalal presented their grievances. While the forum temporarily mitigated the chance of violent conflict between Kurdish factions, tensions remained high. In May 1994, fighting broke out between KDP and PUK Peshmerga in Raniya, northwest of Suleimani. The PUK proved more powerful. It launched successful attacks against the KDP, seizing Erbil. Only Dohuk and Zakho on the border with Turkey remained under KDP control. The Kurdish civil war marked the end of Kurdistan's short-lived unity government. It was a deep disappointment to Kurdistan's supporters in the international community.

In January 1995, CIA case officer Robert Baer traveled to northern Iraq with a five-man team to set up a CIA station. Baer was looking to organize a rebellion and overthrow Saddam Hussein. It was a ripe moment for revolt. The Iraqi economy was depressed; Saddam's security services were demoralized. Soldiers were deserting to safe areas in the Shi'ite south and Iraqi Kurdistan. "We had a window then—it was an absolutely crucial window—to get rid of Saddam Hussein," Baer said.[6] However, his plan had uneven support in Washington, and US officials concluded that Baer's plan had little chance of success with the Kurds divided. Internal Kurdish tensions were exacerbated by third parties who sought to take advantage of the crisis to advance their goals. Iran launched cross-border operations, targeting the Kurdistan Democratic Party of Iran (KDPI), a dissident group with offices in Iraqi Kurdistan that opposed Tehran's clerical regime. Iran flouted territorial sovereignty, while Kurdish militia engaged in a long-running armed struggle against Tehran. Talabani had a villa in Tehran prior to the Gulf War, and developed good relations with Iranian officials. Iran used the PUK to facilitate its ambitions in Iraq, and its growing influence within the PUK was of great concern to Baer. His concerns were borne out when Iran launched military operations from Haibat Sultan near Koya against the KDP on 28 July 1996. The presence of Iranian Revolutionary Guard Corps in Iraqi Kurdistan further complicated the battlefield.

Saddam Hussein also tried to exploit Kurdish rivalries to undermine Iraqi Kurdistan and restore Iraqi control. There was no love lost between Masoud and Saddam. But Masoud was a pragmatist and a willing partner to Saddam as PUK forces seized Safin and Shaklawa and marched on Sari Rash northeast of Erbil. With the KDP reeling from a series of defeats, Masoud sent a message to Saddam Hussein requesting assistance.

Erbil was the headquarters of the Iraqi National Congress (INC), an umbrella organization of Iraqi dissident organizations led by Ahmed Chalabi, who was backed by the CIA. The INC office in Erbil was a bunker stocked with state-of-the-art communications equipment. Chalabi warned Jalal of Masoud's collusion with Saddam, but Jalal did not believe that the US would allow Erbil to be overrun and dismissed Chalabi's warnings.

In the early morning of 31 August 1996, KDP Peshmerga along with 30,000 Iraqi infantry and 500 tanks looped around Mosul and advanced on Erbil from the north, where the KDP Peshmerga and Iraqi army forces crushed the PUK's resistance, seizing the city. The INC office was ransacked and its personnel were arrested, while PUK members were also taken prisoner. Approximately 1,500 dissidents were arrested by the Mukhabarat, Iraq's intelligence agency. Some were hung from lampposts near the citadel as a demonstration of what would happen to Saddam's opponents. Baer recognized the severity of the crisis and helped organize an emergency evacuation of INC personnel and NGO staff to Guam. A frantic scene occurred at the airfield with 2,500 dissidents desperately trying to board C-130 transport planes. From Guam, thousands of asylum seekers were relocated to cities across the United States.[7]

The PUK Peshmerga launched a counter-offensive in October 1996. They took control of Suleimani and fought to liberate Erbil from KDP and Iraqi control. The battle was joined by the Kurdistan Workers' Party (PKK), a leftist political movement, and armed groups of Turkish Kurds who were seeking a greater Kurdistan comprising all territories where Kurds reside. The PKK attacked KDP positions in Barzan, Zakho, Bamerne and Mergasure. Triangulating the battlefield, Turkish war planes targeted the PKK. Airstrikes also assisted the KDP, preventing PUK forces from advancing.

The Washington Agreement

The civil war underscored the importance of Kurdish unity in preventing Saddam Hussein's aggressions. Turkey and Great Britain played an important mediation role between the KDP and PUK, culminating in the 1996 Ankara Accord, which set the stage for more robust US-led mediation. According to US Secretary of State Madeleine Albright, the KDP and PUK "recognize the irreplaceable role of our separate consultations in Ankara and London in making these talks a success."[8] But reconciliation was shallow and short-lived. In January 1997, the PUK announced a new government based in Suleimani. The KDP ignored the announcement. Both the PUK and KDP claimed jurisdiction over the whole of Kurdistan. Masoud and Jalal established an uneasy peace, signing a ceasefire agreement in November 1997. The need for a comprehensive and sustainable agreement was critical for the region, as well as for the United States. The KDP and PUK negotiating teams came together under Albright to hammer out the terms of a deal. Four committees were established to come up with the details. Their work culminated in the Washington Agreement, which established terms for normalizing relations between the Kurdish factions, issued on 9 September 1998.

The Washington Agreement was a declaration of principles, enshrining confidence-building measures. It committed the Iraqi Kurds to avoid factional fighting and to prevent incursions by Iraq's Army. The KDP agreed to share more money from tariffs and customs with the PUK. The "Oil for Food Program," established through UNSC Resolutions 986 and 1153, stipulated that 13 percent of all revenue from Iraq's oil sales should be distributed to Iraqi Kurdistan. It established a steady flow of funds to the KRG, easing tensions from the unequal distribution of customs and tariffs. The KRG received $4.6 billion via the Oil for Food Program between 1997 and 2001.[9] The Washington Agreement included a formula for power-sharing, and a pledge to conduct new elections for the Kurdistan National Assembly. It also included security arrangements, affirming the essential role of Peshmerga. KDP and PUK Peshmerga would remain separate, as would their respective intelligence agencies.

Albright publicly reiterated US support for UN Security Council Resolution 688, which condemned the repression of civilians and demanded that Iraq end repression and respect human rights in order to preserve international peace and security. Albright had zero tolerance for the use of chemical weapons by Saddam and pledged action in the event of an Iraqi incursion. In her private discussions with Masoud and Jalal, Albright offered an ironclad guarantee. She pledged that the US would "protect you as we protect Kuwait."[10] Her guarantee was conditioned on Kurdish compliance with the Agreement. She warned the Kurds not to provoke Saddam for the purpose of causing the US to retaliate. Albright's pledge was a departure from US policy. In his 1996 Congressional testimony, Assistant Secretary Robert Pelletreau stated that protecting Kurdistan is "not the policy of this administration."[11]

The Washington Agreement included an ambitious schedule of milestones. Masoud and Jalal agreed to reconvene the Kurdistan National Assembly to authorize the deal. Chairman Roj Shawess of the KDP called a special session to order. After Masoud and Jalal, Mme. Danielle Mitterrand, the wife of France's former president and a great friend of the Kurds, spoke in support of the Agreement.

With the Assembly committed to implementation, KDP and PUK representatives planned to meet alternately in Erbil and Suleimani to define the details of "normalization." Kurdish parties started work on a new constitution, based on "the general principles of federalism." They agreed on "Iraq as a federal state with a republican, democratic, parliamentarian and multi-party system." Drafters agreed that Iraq would consist of two regions: 1) The Arab region, which includes the middle and southern parts of Iraq along with province of Mosul, Nineveh, in the north, excluding [Kurdish] districts; and 2) The Iraqi Kurdistan region, that includes the provinces of Kirkuk, Suleimania, and Erbil within the administrative boundaries in place prior to 1968 and the province of Dohuk and the districts of Akkra, Sinjar and Sheikhan and the sub-district of Zimar in the province of Nineveh, the districts of Khanaqin and Mandili in the province of Diyala, and the district of Badra in the province of Al-Wasit. According to Article 5 of the draft constitution, "The city of Kirkuk shall be the capital of the Kurdistan region."[12]

The draft constitution envisioned that Iraq would have a president; a council of ministers, with a prime minister; a judicial authority; and a legislative authority made up of two chambers: a national federal assembly, elected on proportional representation of the population in each of the regions, and an assembly of the regions, made up in equal numbers of members from the two regional assemblies. Each region of the Federal Republic, such as Iraqi Kurdistan, would have its regional president, its regional council of ministers and regional prime minister, its legislative authority and its regional judiciary.

Iraq's incursion into Iraqi Kurdistan was a reminder of the fragile peace that existed after the Gulf War. Despite the no-fly zone, Iraqi forces were dominant on the ground and could attack Iraqi Kurdistan at a moment's notice. Saddam remained defiant, threatening the Kurds, obstructing efforts by the international community, and rejecting UN demands for periodic weapons inspections. Washington's approach towards Saddam evolved from containment to regime change. President Bill Clinton signed the Iraqi Liberation Act on 31 October 1998, pledging US military assistance to the KDP, PUK and other Iraqi opposition groups.

The Kurds were acutely aware of Turkey's concerns. Ankara strongly objected to Kirkuk as the capital of Iraqi Kurdistan. Giving the Kurds control over Kirkuk's oil would give Kurdistan the financial means to become a viable state. Ankara feared that Kurdistan's control of Kirkuk's oil would encourage Kurdish independence, inspiring Kurds in Turkey to seek the same. Turkey was also concerned about the fate of ethnic Turkmen living in Kirkuk governorate. Turkmen are Iraqi citizens of Turkic origin whom Turks call their ethnic brethren, and many of them live in the Nineveh Plains between Kirkuk and Mosul. Turkmen are the third largest ethnic group in Iraq, after Arabs and Kurds, representing about 10 percent of Iraq's population. Ankara feared the Turkmen would become a persecuted minority in Kurdistan. However, Turkey's concern for the Turkmen was insincere. The Turkmen were manipulated by Turkey as a way of curtailing Kurdistan's ambitions. Including a reference to the PKK in the Washington Agreement was an attempt to assuage Turkey's concerns. Since the mid-1980s, Turkey and the PKK had fought a vicious civil war that killed tens of thousands and displaced millions. Turkey was also concerned about the Agreement's endorsement of federalism for Iraq. Ankara feared that a federal Iraqi state would motivate Kurds in Turkey to demand decentralization and power-sharing. The Kurdistan National Assembly was supposed to set up a committee to draft the federal constitution, in which KDP experts, including Sami Abdul Rahman, would take the lead. A joint KDP–PUK committee would review and modify the draft. The KRG deferred action drafting the federal constitution because it did not want to antagonize Turkey.

Ankara also opposed UN sanctions on Iraq after the Gulf War. According to Turkish officials, the embargo cost Turkey $100 billion in energy transport fees and missed commercial opportunities. To balance nascent nationalism in Iraqi Kurdistan, Ankara engineered a rapprochement with Baghdad, upgrading diplomatic relations with Iraq to the ambassadorial level. Iran and Syria also objected to the Washington Agreement, and tried to undermine it.[13] In addition to concerns about the substance of the Agreement, they objected to America's role and its close ties to the Kurds.

The Washington Agreement tolerated the division of Kurdistan into two zones, one controlled by the KDP and the other by the PUK. It did not restore the level of co-existence that had existed before May 1994, but it created conditions for the Kurds to upgrade their administration and improve mutual relations. The Agreement created a network of shared interests at the political, financial and security levels which would become the KRG.

Masoud and Jalal announced the Washington Agreement during a joint statement at the US Department of State on 17 September 1998. Albright spoke first, heralding the Washington Agreement as a breakthrough in Kurdish relations and an important measure in containing Saddam Hussein. According to Albright, "The two important Kurdish parties of northern Iraq have agreed to a specific timetable to reconcile their decades-old differences with the goal of power-sharing, revenue sharing, and elections next summer." She explained,

> Our sessions here follow six months of working-level talks between the two parties in northern Iraq and recent consultations by each in Ankara and London. The renewed spirit of reconciliation between Mr Barzani and Mr Talabani, exemplified in their joint meeting and joint statement today, will make it easier for the United States and others to help their people. They have set a timetable for resolving their differences fully consistent with the principles laid down in the 1996 Ankara Accords. We encourage them and will help where we can to see that this agenda is met. Without unity, the road ahead will remain very difficult. With unity, there is every reason for the Iraqi Kurds to look forward with hope.[14]

Jalal responded,

> It is a historic day. We closed a sad chapter of the history of the Kurdish people, who suffered too much in their history. It is a new day, and I hope that it will be a day that we both, Mr Barzani and myself, and our two parties, the PUK and KDP, will do their best to implement this historic accord which we have achieved with the support of our American friends, especially Secretary Albright, whom we are very much grateful to—to her personal contribution, to her personal encouragement and advice to us, and to our friends. Our people are looking forward to having a

united, democratic, federative Iraq. It is an opportunity for us to assure that we are not a separatist force; we are for strengthening the national unity of Iraq.

He noted that the two parties have been "convinced, under popular pressure and international pressure, that they need each other". The Agreement would help "disperse many clouds." Masoud was less ebullient. "We have accomplished something important in the last few days. With God's help, we must implement what we have agreed to."[15]

While the Washington Agreement ended the civil war between the KDP and PUK, it did not decisively advance reconciliation between Kurdish factions. Reconciliation is a process, not an event. It would take time for Kurds to overcome their distrust. Speaker Roj Shawess indicated: "For the time being, the two regions will keep their separate governments. We need to work together for a longer period, inside the parliament and with the opposition, to set up a transition government and to prepare for elections."[16] The Washington Agreement left Kurdistan divided into two zones, with the KDP in the northwest and PUK in the southeast. The boundary was controlled by several heavily armed checkpoints. Driving between the two parts of Kurdistan felt like crossing the border between two distinct countries.

5 DYSFUNCTIONAL IRAQ

> *"The consequences of what we set in motion were beyond imagination. But inaction also has consequences."*
>
> AMBASSADOR RYAN C. CROCKER[1]

US–Kurdish Partnership

The Kurds played an active role in the US State Department's Future of Iraq Project, which made plans for governing Iraq after Saddam Hussein was deposed. Kurds such as Najmaldin Karim and Qubad Talabani played an important part in postwar planning, focusing on long-term challenges to nation-building. Kurds still dreamed of independence but did not want to pursue an unattainable goal. In lieu of independence, the Kurds sought to create a federal and democratic republic of Iraq, which would guarantee their interests.

Kurds enthusiastically supported Operation Iraqi Freedom, which was launched on 19 March 2003. After the toppling of Saddam's statue in Firdos Square on 9 April US troops had no instructions for Phase IV stability operations so they stepped aside, allowing looting by Iraqis. Iraqi Shi'ites, who represent about 55 percent of Iraq's population, and Kurds welcomed the US invasion and occupation of Iraq. However, Iraq's Sunnis mourned Saddam's removal from power and the loss of their power and privileges. The spasm of violence that ensued after the regime's removal was an expression of pent-up frustration and rage after decades of dictatorship.

The Bush administration needed an interim arrangement to govern Iraq until Iraqis could draft a constitution and hold elections. It established the Coalition Provisional Authority (CPA), which was headed by Ambassador L. Paul Bremer III. At the behest of neoconservatives in the Bush administration, Bremer took steps to remake Iraq. "Neocons" believed in the unbridled exercise of US power to promote democracy and free markets around the world. They believed that regime change in Iraq would catalyze an irreversible movement towards democracy in the Middle East, assuring US interests in the region's oil sector and enhancing Israel's security.

Iraq's Sunnis were infuriated by Bremer's decrees targeting Baathist and security structures, such as the one issued to "dis-establish" the Baath Party on 16 May 2003. The decree dismissed 120,000 Iraqis from their jobs. But not every Baathist was a war criminal; many Iraqis joined the Baath Party because they had no choice. Party membership was the ticket to education and employment opportunities. On 23 May, Bremer issued a companion decree that disbanded Iraq's military and intelligence agencies. His decree banned salaries and pensions for members of the Iraqi armed forces and security services. By banning the Iraqi army, four hundred thousand Iraqis employed in the security services and their family members were effectively turned into antagonists. Bremer is often criticized for eliminating institutions that could have played a stabilizing role during the transitional period after Saddam.

The Kurds, however, cheered Bremer's decrees. Karim and other prominent Kurds refused to join the chorus of criticism leveled at Bremer for dismantling institutions that included the perpetrators of Saddam's Arabization policy and the Anfal Genocide. For Kurds, the Baath Party and armed forces committed horrible crimes committed against them. Kurds would never feel secure as long as Saddam's institutions remained intact.

Secretary of Defense Donald H. Rumsfeld described the transition to stabilize Iraq as "messy." Bremer urged the Kurds to work with Iraqis to draft a constitution and then hold elections, especially as they had a head start on constitution-making. Sami Abdul Rahman, the KDP head in Dohuk, had been working on a draft constitution for Kurdistan, which defined federal and local powers. The draft included a bill of rights for Iraq and a power-sharing formula between the central government and the governorates. Other Iraqis criticized Rahman's draft for devolving too many powers to local authorities. They saw it as a Trojan Horse advancing the Kurdish goal of independence.

Iraq's Shi'ite majority, inspired by Grand Ayatollah Ali al-Sistani, the leading Shi'ite cleric in Iraq, insisted that elections should come first, then duly elected representatives could draft the charter defining Iraq's future governance. They maintained that focusing on elections would give the constitution greater credibility. Conditions grew increasingly volatile as Iraqis debated the sequence of events. Reprisals and sectarian violence intensified.

To show progress with Iraq's transition to democracy, Bremer endorsed a Transitional Administrative Law (TAL), which was adopted on 8 March 2004. With considerable input from the Kurds, the TAL established basic principles and rules for governing Iraq during its transition.

According to the TAL,

> The people of Iraq, striving to reclaim their freedom, which was usurped by the previous tyrannical regime, rejecting violence and coercion in all their forms, and particularly when used as instruments of governance, have determined that they shall hereafter remain a free people governed under the rule of law.

The law affirmed that "The federal system shall be based upon geographic and historical realities and the separation of powers, and not upon origin, race, ethnicity, nationality or confession."[2]

The TAL addressed core Kurdish concerns. It recognized the KRG as the legitimate government of the Kurds, enshrining the existence of the KRG within the new federal state. The Peshmerga were recognized as the lawful army of Kurdistan, to receive financial support from Baghdad. The TAL established both Arabic and Kurdish as official languages of Iraq. It affirmed that mineral wealth was an asset belonging to the people of Iraq with revenue-sharing based on the region's proportion of the population. Article 58 of the TAL addressed the issue of disputed internal boundaries, "remedying unjust changes […] to the demographic character of certain regions, including Kirkuk." Resolution of disputed territories "shall be consistent with the principle of justice, taking into account the will of the people of those territories."[3] Article 58 outlined a process for resolving disputed territories, starting with a fair and transparent census, followed by ratification of a permanent constitution, and a popular referendum to approve the constitution. In Article 61, the TAL affirmed that a "no" vote by two-thirds of the people in three provinces would veto the constitution. Kurds feared a tyranny led by Iraq's Shi'ite majority. Article 61 gave Kurds control of the final constitution, since Kurds represented a super-majority in the governorates of Dohuk, Erbil and Suleimani.

Shi'ites resented the influence of Kurds over US officials during the process of drafting the TAL. Sistani and other Shi'ite clerics wanted to establish a theocratic Shi'ite state, modeled on Iran. He was wary of the secular and pro-western tendencies of the Kurds. The TAL addressed the role of religion in Iraq's governance, describing Islam as a "source" of legislation. It did not, however, require Islam as the basis for all laws. Shi'ites also objected to the two-thirds provision in Article 61. Not only would it give Kurds a veto, but it also empowered Sunnis who are a majority in the governorates of Nineveh, Anbar and Salahuddin.

Drawing on the TAL, Iraqis established a Constitutional Drafting Committee made up of Iraq's ethnic and confessional groups to prepare a permanent constitution. The draft constitution reflected many of the principles and provisions in the TAL. However, the drafters could not agree on some fundamental issues. They disagreed on the role of religion and especially of Islam as the basis of law. An impasse arose over the ownership and distribution of Iraq's vast energy wealth. Drafters hotly debated a process for demarcating internal boundaries, addressing the thorny issue of disputed territories such as Kirkuk. Rather than get stuck on the details, the Constitutional Drafting Committee punted by either deferring final decisions or including ambiguous language that allowed different sides to claim victory.

The US pushed the Iraqis to finalize the constitution. Delaying its adoption could spark violence and undermine Bush's claim of "mission accomplished." The constitution guaranteed religious freedom. It recognized Islam as the official religion, mandating that Islam be considered a source of legislation and that no law should contradict the provisions of Islam. Regarding the energy sector, the 2005 constitution limited the federal government's functions to shared management over oil fields already in production with revenues from existing fields to be distributed on a per capita basis. The federal government was excluded from the ownership of oil fields discovered after 2005. Development of new fields was the responsibility of relevant regions and governorates.

The Constitutional Drafting Committee could not resolve the issue of Kirkuk so it deferred a decision through Article 140, which placed obligations on the federal government to engage in a process addressing the status of Kirkuk and disputed territories. Normalization would involve the return of people forcibly displaced by Saddam's regime and the correction of border changes that had been arbitrarily imposed to augment the Arab population of Kirkuk governorate. A census would follow the return of displaced people to Kirkuk. Finally, a referendum would determine if Kirkuk should become part of the Kurdish Autonomous Region. Article 58 of the TAL would:

extend and continue to the executive authority elected in accordance with this constitution, provided that it accomplishes completely (normalization, census, and referendums in Kirkuk and other disputed territories to determine the will of the citizens) by a date not to exceed December 31, 2007.[4]

The US brokered a further compromise over the process of finalizing the constitution. Agreement was reached allowing Iraqis to review and amend the constitution after it was adopted. In such event, the first parliament after the constitution was adopted would establish a committee to consider amendments. Another referendum would be held to authorize amendments.

Iraqis voted to authorize the constitution in a referendum on 15 October 2007. Though some Sunni groups called for a boycott, 9.8 million Iraqis, 63 percent of eligible voters, cast ballots, in which 78 percent voted to adopt the constitution while 21 percent opposed it. Voters in the Kurdistan Region of Iraq voted overwhelmingly in favor of the charter. More than two-thirds of the voters in Anbar and Salahuddin, Sunni-majority provinces, rejected it. Only 55 percent of voters in Nineveh province rejected it. Since this number did not meet the two-thirds threshold in a third province, the constitution was approved.

The Kurds made a strategic decision to forego their dream of independence in favor of a federal, democratic republic that devolved political, economic and cultural rights from the central government to Iraq's regions. The constitution addressed the core concerns of Kurds. It enshrined democratic government through a federal system. It included a robust system of checks and balances to guard against majoritarian rule. The constitution's bill of rights included significant protection and affirmative duties to promote linguistic, religious and ethnic minority rights. It enshrined Kurdish cultural symbols such as a flag, anthem, and cultural and national holidays.[5] It assigned responsibility for security in Iraqi Kurdistan to the Peshmerga, while restricting their deployment outside of Kurdistan without authorization by the Kurdistan parliament.[6]

Kurds welcomed the outcome. They had bargained hard in order to achieve their goals. But other Iraqis complained. They felt the process of drafting the constitution lacked transparency. They believed that the outcome was skewed in favor of the Kurds. President George W. Bush commended Iraqis for resolving their differences through negotiations rather than violence. However, Iraqis—already distrustful towards the United States—questioned America's role as an honest broker. Iraqis believed that a federal, democratic republic was an interim arrangement for the Kurds. An overwhelming number of Kurds wanted independence, as confirmed by the Kurdistan Referendum Movement (KRM) of 2005.

Polarization

A group of Kurdish intellectuals in Suleimani launched the KRM in July 2003 as an expression of their desire for self-determination. The KRM quickly spread beyond Suleimani, a progressive stronghold, across Kurdistan to other Kurdish communities in Kirkuk and Mosul.

The KRM organized a petition demanding the right to an official referendum on Kurdistan's political status. The petition garnered 1,732,535 signatures, which KRM representatives presented to the UN Office of Electoral Assistance on 22 December 2004. As a next step, an unofficial referendum on independence was conducted on 30 January 2005.[7] Voters could either choose to stay a part of Iraq or opt for independence. The referendum was held across Kurdistan including disputed territories such as Kirkuk, Khanaqin and Kurdish communities in Nineveh province between Erbil and Mosul. Kurds in predominantly Arab areas, such as Baghdad, were not able to participate. Voters overcame logistical and security challenges to cast their ballots. Of the 1,998,061 people who voted, 1,973,412 voted for independence. This represented 98.8 percent of the total. Only 19,560 voted to stay a part of Iraq.[8]

Legislative elections for Iraqi Kurdistan and governorate council elections were held in parallel with the referendum on 30 January 2005. The KDP and PUK established a unified list of candidates in order to resolve differences between them. The KDP, PUK and a few smaller parties formed the Democratic Patriotic Alliance of Kurdistan. The unified list swept the vote with more than 90 percent, winning 104 of 111 seats in the Kurdistan National Assembly.

Kurdistan's elections were held at the same time as Iraq's national elections, the first ballot since Saddam was overthrown. Sunni parties were disorganized; some boycotted the vote. As a result, the Kurdish Alliance came in second, seating 77 deputies in Iraq's 275-member parliament. Kurds showed they were a force to be reckoned with nationally. To the Kurds, however, all politics is local. Their focus was on Kurdistan.

After the 2005 landslide of the Democratic Patriotic Alliance of Kurdistan, Kurds committed to genuine power-sharing between Kurdish parties, dividing key positions in government. The Kurdistan Regional

Assembly elected Masoud Barzani as President of Iraqi Kurdistan, with a four-year term limit. Masoud established a government of national unity, creating the Kurdistan Presidency Council. The PUK's Kosrat Rasul Ali became Deputy President. The Speaker of the Kurdistan Regional Assembly was from the KDP and the deputy speaker was PUK. Other leadership positions included the posts of prime minister, deputy prime minister and chief of staff of the presidency.

When Masoud's term expired in 2009, the KRG decided that the president should be directly elected by popular vote rather than by the parliament. Direct elections were held on 25 July 2009. Masoud was elected to a second four-year term with 69.6 percent.[9] Masoud was presidential, but lacked the skills of a retail politician. Despite the popular mandate, Masoud could be distant and remote from the average Kurd. This remoteness was dramatized by the setting of his office compound, Sar-e-Rash, outside of Erbil in Sallahudin. Sar-e-Rash was a vacation resort before Saddam appropriated the property as a presidential palace. Masoud took it over from Saddam and used it for work meetings, as well as his residence. The presidential palace was like a heavily guarded fortress with multiple checkpoints. At the end of the long driveway, a set of white marble stairs covered with a red rug led to the front door. The palatial facility burnished Masoud's aura of leadership.

The Gorran Movement morphed into a political party. The joint KDP–PUK list won 59 seats and Gorran gained 25 seats in elections for the Kurdistan National Assembly on 25 July. The other seats were assigned: five reserved for Turkmen; five for Assyrians; and one for an Armenian; small parties won the rest of the seats. Gorran capitalized on popular discontent. Its message of anti-corruption and accountability resonated with voters, who were tired of the nepotism and corruption of the major parties. Particularly in Suleimani, voters were angered by the government's inability to provide basic services such as garbage collection and a reliable supply of electricity. Gorran's gain came at the expense of the PUK, which served to strengthen the KDP.

Both the KDP and PUK accused Gorran of opportunism and Nawshirwan Mustafa of populism. Nawshirwan had been an establishment figure for years. The PUK believed that he was disingenuous to criticize the political order that he helped establish. Nawshirwan was a former PUK politburo member and Jalal's deputy since 1976. He was familiar with the PUK's inner workings—and its dirty laundry.

Nouri al-Maliki

A US intelligence report characterized Iraq as a "civil war" in February 2006. With official Iraqi security services unable to provide security, Iraqis increasingly relied on sectarian militias for protection. Most Iraqis wanted the US to withdraw from Iraq. Bush instead announced "The Surge," deploying 20,000 additional troops and adopting a new counter-insurgency strategy (COIN). Bush hoped the deployment would create space for reconstruction, economic development and greater political participation. The US supported Arab Sunni tribal leaders in the "Anbar Awakening" to counter al-Qaeda and Sunni extremists. Radicalized Sunnis posed the gravest threat to peace and stability in Iraq.

Nouri al-Maliki of the Dawa Party was a populist, who gained support by railing against the US occupation of Iraq. Maliki became prime minister in 2006 with the backing of the US Government and assistance from Qasem Soleimani, a leader of the Iranian Revolutionary Guard Corps (IRGC) and commander of the Quds Force. Maliki catered to his Shi'ite base, accusing Sunnis of terrorism and Kurds of separatism.

Maliki was a weak prime minister, who initially proved his bona fides by confronting Shi'ite radical groups such as Muqtada al-Sadr's Madhi Army in Basra and Baghdad. Confronting Sunni extremists in Anbar, he took credit for the killing of Abu Musab al-Zarqawi, head of al-Qaeda in Iraq, in Baqubah on 8 June 2006. After US warplanes dropped two 500-pound bombs on Zarqawi's safe house, Maliki addressed the Iraqi people: "Today, Zarqawi has been terminated. Every time a Zarqawi appears we will kill him. We will continue confronting whoever follows his path." Maliki further burnished his credentials as a champion of Shi'ite interests by presiding over the execution of Saddam Hussein on the sacred Muslim holiday of Eid al-Adha. From an enhanced position of strength, Maliki brokered a ceasefire with Sadr and consolidated his power over rival Shi'ite factions. He ended the year-long boycott of parliament by Sunni legislators. Maliki also took on the Kurds.

Maliki ignored the deadline for determining Kirkuk's status, 31 December 2007, and set an alternative date for the referendum. He contested Kurdish claims in disputed territories, rejecting claims to Khanaqin, Kifri and Baldrooz in Diyala province; Sinjar, Tall Afar, Akra, Shekhan and Tell Kaif in Nineveh province; Tooz in Sallahudin province; and Badra in Wasit province. He threatened the Kurds, naming himself as commander in chief and creating the Baghdad Brigade, which reported directly to him. Maliki refused to share weapons with the Peshmerga, which the United States provided to the Iraqi army through the train-and-equip program, including armored Humvees and M1A Abrams tanks, as well as other sophisticated weaponry. The Kurds feared that Iraq would use US weapons against Pehsmerga in the event of violent conflict with Baghdad.

Iraq's national elections in 2010 were postponed when hundreds of candidates with alleged links to the Baath Party were prevented from standing. Waves of violence further undermined the vote. Elections were finally held on 7 March 2010. Al-Iraqiya, a multi-ethnic party led by Ayad Allawi, received 91 seats. Maliki's State of Law Coalition came in a close second with 89 seats. A coalition of Shi'ite parties, the Iraqi National Alliance, which included the Supreme Council for Islamic Revolution in Iraq, gained 70 seats. The Kurdistan Alliance ended up with 43 seats.[10]

Maliki's State of Law Coalition and the Shi'ite Iraqi National Alliance were natural partners to form a coalition government. However, their combined total of 159 seats was four short of a majority. After months of political gridlock, Masoud stepped in to help mediate differences between Iraqi parties in what was called the "Barzani process." The Erbil Agreement of 11 November 2010 established 19 power-sharing principles, including the allocation of government posts to different ethnic and sectarian groups. The Agreement stipulated that a Kurd would be Iraq's president, a Shi'ite would be prime minister and a Sunni would be speaker of the parliament. Maliki was awarded a second mandate on 21 December 2010. Resolving political differences was key to stability, as Washington and Baghdad negotiated a Status of Forces Agreement (SOFA) that would be the legal basis for a continuing US military presence.

Talks collapsed after half-hearted negotiations on the SOFA. President Obama was more focused on fulfilling his pledge to withdraw from Iraq than extending the deployment of US troops, and US forces left Iraq on 18 December 2011. The US always protected Kurdistan's interests. Absent the US presence in Iraq, relations worsened between Maliki and Masoud at the same time as tensions spiked between Shi'ites and Sunnis. Maliki was furious when the KRG granted asylum to the Sunni vice president Tariq al-Hashemi in December 2011, after he was found guilty in absentia by an Iraqi Court for his role in Iraq's civil war. The Kurdistan Alliance joined Allawi's Iraqiya and Sadr's political bloc in a vote of no confidence. In June 2012, Maliki gave an interview to a private Kurdistani television station denouncing the

Barzani family for corruption and nepotism.[11] Maliki deployed the Dijla Operations Command, which squared off with Peshmerga in the disputed territories of Kirkuk, Diyala and Sallahudin governorates. A month later, Peshmerga blocked the Iraqi national army from reaching the Fish Khabur crossing into Syria at a time when Syria's civil war was escalating. Maliki and Iran supported Bashar al-Assad, whereas the Kurds and Turkey were sympathetic to Sunni rebel groups.

As President of Iraq, Jalal mollified Masoud's confrontational approach to relations with Iraq. A natural conciliator, Jalal also subdued Maliki's most contentious tendencies. However, Jalal had a stroke and slipped into a coma on 18 December 2012, his illness creating a leadership vacuum in the PUK. Many PUK stalwarts, including members of the Talabani family, felt it would be an act of disloyalty to replace Talabani while he was still living. Hero, Jalal's wife, now played a critical role. She controlled the party's finances and no new PUK leader could emerge without her endorsement.

The First Deputy of the PUK, Kosrat Rasul Ali, and Second Deputy, Barham Salih, criticized "unethical" actions by Hero's faction.[12] They announced the establishment of a new front called the "Decision-Making Body," asserting that any action taken outside of this body would not be recognized. Their initiative was backed by prominent members of the PUK's political bureau and members of parliament. Kosrat had strong credentials as a Peshmerga, but was diagnosed with Parkinson's disease, and his condition steadily worsened. Like Jalal, Barham is a strong retail politician with an uncanny ability to connect. However, he lacked a strong base in the electorate. Barham had been away from Kurdistan for many years as the PUK representative in Washington and later as deputy prime minister of Iraq, based in Baghdad. Barham was hampered by the fact that he was never a Peshmerga, which would have given him enhanced status in Kurdish society. Gorran tried to take advantage of Jalal's illness to expand its support among Kurds who had been turned off by corrupt, clan-led dynasties.[13]

Kurdistan's parliamentary elections were held on 21 September 2013. Extraordinary security measures were put into place on election day. All roads leading to Erbil were closed. Guards at polling stations were heavily armed, searching voters before they could enter voting facilities. Rather than offering a unified list, the KDP and PUK ran as individual parties. Gorran also fielded a slate of candidates, challenging the two-party rule. The KDP and PUK defended their record of keeping the region safe; Kurdistan's relative security allowed for greater economic development than other parts of Iraq riven with violent conflict. However, Gorran's charges of graft and nepotism struck a chord. The KDP won 38 seats, Gorran won 24 and the PUK won just 18. Seventeen seats were won by Islamic parties, such as the Kurdistan Islamic Union and the Kurdistan Islamic Society, and three were won by left-wing parties. Other seats were obligated to minority groups. Demonstrating the growing emancipation of women in Kurdish society, 34 women were elected, about one-third of the Assembly seats. In an unprecedented and surprising development, the PUK had become the third party in Iraqi Kurdistan, behind the KDP and Gorran.

There were a total of 111 seats in the Kurdistan National Assembly, meaning that 56 seats were needed to form a government. Overcoming deadlock and dysfunction, the three major parties came together to form a coalition. Nechirvan Barzani, Masoud's nephew and a highly competent technocrat, became prime minister. Qubad Talabani, Jalal's telegenic youngest son, well schooled in western ways, became deputy prime minister. Yousif Muhammed from Gorran was elected speaker of parliament.[14] Other important positions were allocated to Gorran, including the Finance Ministry and the Ministry for Peshmerga Affairs.

Despite the veneer of compromise and power-sharing, lack of unity was still a liability for the Kurds. Rather than establish a thriving democracy, Kurdish political parties proved more interested in consolidating their power and wealth. They gave lip service to the rule of law and democratic institutions. Easy money created the appearance of prosperity, but Kurdistan's economic development was based almost entirely on oil revenues. Kurdish leaders failed to diversify their economy and fell victim to the so-called oil curse, which gave rise to kleptocracy and a political culture where personal rivalries trumped national consensus.

Political polarization and popular discontent increased. In 2014, the Peshmerga were unable to resist the invasion of ISIS. The security crisis accompanied a financial crisis, as world oil prices collapsed. Kurdistan was also beset by a political crisis as relations with Baghdad worsened, and the Government of Iraq (GOI) suspended payment of Kurdistan's share of the national budget. A perfect storm of problems undermined peace and progress in Iraqi Kurdistan, impeding its path to independence.[15]

6 A PERFECT STORM

"Sunnis are afraid of the future; Shi'a are afraid of the past; Kurds fear the past, present, and future."

PRIME MINISTER NECHIRVAN BARZANI[1]

ISIS Crisis

In May 2014, the KDP's intelligence agency learned that ISIS fighters were massing on the Syria–Iraq border. Masoud Barzani warned Iraq's Prime Minister Nuri al-Maliki, who was blind to the imminent threat. Fighters with ISIS crossed the border, seizing Mosul, Iraq's second largest city, on 10 June 2014. "The city fell like a plane without an engine," said a Mosul businessman.[2]

Al-Qaeda in Iraq (AQI) morphed into ISIS as the insurgencies in Iraq and Syria converged in 2014. Abu Bakr al-Baghdadi announced a caliphate, with himself as caliph. ISIS also includes several former Baath Party members, as well as military and security officials who joined forces with AQI. It drew upon the myriad resentments of Sunni Arabs in Iraq, a formerly dominant minority, and Sunni Arabs in Syria, a majority long excluded from power. The ISIS leadership was battle-hardened by the insurgency against US forces in Iraq, as well as fighting in Iraq's sectarian civil war. ISIS foot soldiers came from across the Arab world, as well as from Europe, South Asia and Southeast Asia.

The Mosul garrison, which included 30,000 members of the Iraqi Security Forces (ISF), was overrun by a few hundred ISIS fighters. The ISF showed no will to fight and completely collapsed. Commanders simply disappeared from the frontline and fled to Erbil, 50 miles to the east. The US spent $25 billion on security assistance to the ISF between 2005 and 2013. When the ISF fled, ISIS seized state-of-the-art military equipment, including 2,300 Humvees as well as tanks, artillery, howitzers, other weapons and ammunition. With its success in Mosul, ISIS grew from fewer than 10,000 fighters to over 30,000 in a matter of months, its ranks augmented by jihadis freed from local jails, local fighters and opponents of the Shi'ite-dominated federal government. Additionally, volunteers from around the world joined ISIS, inspired by its social media campaign and military successes. Rather than oppose ISIS, Sunni sheikhs in Nineveh, Anbar and Diyala provinces welcomed them. They preferred a Sunni Salafist caliphate to Iraq's Shi'ite-led government.

In addition, ISIS was well financed. It seized $425 million from the Mosul branch of Iraq's Central Bank and received other revenues from the sale of oil, historic artifacts, ransoming prisoners, racketeering and extortion. Christians in Mosul were told to convert to Islam, pay a high tax or face death. Local women were assigned to ISIS fighters as jihadi brides; ISIS conducted mass executions of Yazidi men and boys while many Yazidi women and girls were raped and sold into sexual slavery. It assumed an aura of invincibility as Tikrit, Tal Afar and the Baiji power plant fell in rapid succession.

As ISIS rolled up territory, advancing down the Tigris river valley, it seized Sadiyah and Jalawla near the Iranian border and threatened Baqubah and Samarra, 80 miles north of Baghdad and home of the al-Askari Mosque, one of the holiest sites in Shi'ite Islam. The Gold Dome Mosque was built in AD 944 and two revered Shi'ite imams who died in the ninth century were buried at al-Askari. According to Shi'ite legend, the mosque is also the site of a tunnel into which Muhammad al-Mahdi, the 12th Imam, descended in 878. Shi'ites believe that al-Mahdi is the revered "Hidden Imam" who will reappear as the Messiah and bring salvation to Shi'ite believers. The Gold Dome Mosque had previously been a flashpoint in Iraq's sectarian civil war. On 22 February 2006, AQI infiltrated the mosque and blew up its gilded dome and minarets. Abu Musab al-Zarqawi, AQI's leader at the time, targeted Samarra because of its spiritual significance to Shi'ite faithful.

In June 2014, ISIS attacked Samarra from the west, taking control of five neighborhoods. They seized the towns of Dhuluiyah, Sadiyah and Jalawla in the southwest, and overran the Dhuluiyah air base. Further south, ISIS battled Iraqi forces in the town of Baiji in an attempt to interdict the Iraqi military and the Shi'ite militias before they could reinforce Samarra and other cities along the road north of Baghdad. They used eastern Anbar province to stage attacks on the city of Karma, just 15 miles west of Baiji. Controlling Highway One and other critical supply routes to Samarra, ISIS was poised to enter the city.[3] Meanwhile ISIS also threatened Baghdad, despite the city's size and majority Shi'ite population.

Grand Ayatollah Ali al-Sistani, who has millions of followers in Iraq and worldwide, issued a call to arms. Casting the fight against ISIS as a patriotic and religious duty, Sistani said it was "the legal and national responsibility of whoever can hold a weapon to defend the country, the citizens, and the holy sites."[4] At Friday prayers in Karbala, Sheikh Abdulmehdi al-Karbalai said: "Citizens who are able to bear arms and fight terrorists, defending their country and their people and their holy places, should volunteer and join the security forces to achieve this holy purpose."[5] He called on volunteers to "fill the gaps within the security forces."[6]

Thousands of Shi'ites responded to Sistani's plea. At first they were a disorganized group. General Qasem Soleimani, of the IRGC, rushed to Iraq to help organize them into disciplined militias. Soleimani was commander of the Quds Force, a branch of the IRGC responsible for extraterritorial military and clandestine operations, and had played an important role in Iraq's sectarian civil war between Shi'ites and Sunnis. He supplied Shi'ite extremists with advanced improvised explosive devices (IEDs), rocket-propelled explosives and other munitions, which killed more than 500 US service members.[7] Soleimani was the architect of Iran's military intervention in Syria, which saved Damascus from Sunni radicals. He gave coherence to Iraq's Shi'ite militias, ready to defend Shi'ite holy sites and become martyrs. Hassan Nasrallah, the spiritual leader of Hezbollah, declared: "We are ready to sacrifice martyrs in Iraq five times more than what we sacrificed in Syria, in order to protect shrines, because they are much more important than [the holy sites in Syria]."[8] In a televised address, Iran's President Hassan Rouhani pledged to fight "violence and terrorism" in Iraq. Foreign Minister Mohammad Javad Zarif called his Iraqi counterpart to offer Iran's support for the "fight against terrorism."[9]

A complex mosaic of Shi'ite militias rushed to defend Samarra. Iraqi Shi'ite militias, called the Popular Mobilization Units (PMU), integrated IRGC personnel and organizational capacity. Asaib al-Haq is one of the most effective Iranian-backed militias. Its flag depicts a white background with a green sketch of Iraq and a Kalashnikov framed between two swords. Its battle-hardened members fought for President Bashar al-Assad's forces in Syria. The radical cleric, Muqtada al-Sadr, formed the Imam al-Sadr Brigade, a militia under a flag with his likeness and the image of a dove. The Badr Brigade, which defended Shi'ites in Basra during the crackdown in 1991, also rushed to Samarra. Other militias included the Khataib Hezbollah and Jaysh al-Mahdi. Each militia fielded a brigade of 2,500 to 3,000 fighters, fervent to defend Baghdad and Shi'ite sacred sites."[10] The involvement of Shi'ite militias was decisive.

Its advance on Samarra thwarted, ISIS pivoted to attack Iraqi Kurdistan. Its fighters seized Sinjar, Makhmur, the Mosul Dam on the Tigris River and Gwer, just 15 miles from Erbil. The Peshmerga had previously earned a reputation as fierce warriors defending their homeland from the Iraqi army. However, they had not engaged in any meaningful combat since 1991 and had failed to maintain a fighting edge through rigorous training. They were used to manning checkpoints rather than fighting a real opponent. Prior to ISIS, their greatest adversary had been boredom. Serving as a Peshmerga became an employment opportunity. Masoud Barzani allegedly had an informal agreement with ISIS commanders that the KRG would not intervene in their fight with Iraqis, if ISIS did not approach. The Peshmerga were taken by surprise when ISIS attacked them.

Highly motivated ISIS fighters used heavy weapons and armored vehicles they had seized from the ISF, and the Peshmerga were simply outgunned. They did not have armor, artillery or anti-tank weapons but were a light infantry with vintage machine guns captured from the Iraqi military or supplied by Iran in the 1970s and 1980s. Some lacked ammunition, engaging ISIS with only 60 bullets for each rifle. In contrast, the Iraqi army had state of-the-art equipment—M-16s, night-vision goggles, and Humvees. Masrour Barzani, the Kurdish intelligence chief, said, "We never got any of that. We've got Kalashnikov rifles from the nineteen-seventies. The Americans never gave us anything, and they've blocked us from acquiring new weapons on our own."[11]

In the 2008 US presidential election, Barack Obama ran on a platform to disengage from Iraq, and in 2011 US forces folded their tents and left Iraq when Baghdad and Washington failed to agree on the terms of a SOFA. The last thing Obama wanted was to send US forces back to Iraq. The Obama administration initially refused to help the Peshmerga against ISIS; US officials insisted that Iraqis resolve their political differences and form a consensus government before the US would rescue the Kurds. However, Washington's position was overtaken by events as ISIS stormed towards Erbil.

United States war planes attacked ISIS columns just in time to prevent Erbil from being overrun. Air power was decisive in stopping its advance. The Obama administration adopted a "light footprint" strategy, which involved air support and intelligence to aid the fight against ISIS while refusing to put boots on the ground in combat operations or as spotters.[12]

Most US sorties returned to base with their munitions, unable to identify and attack high-value targets. Despite these challenges, the multinational coalition launched 5,600 sorties in June and July 2015, 60 percent of which targeted ISIS in Iraq.[13]

The Peshmerga were desperate for weapons and ammunition as they tried to defend their homeland with one hand tied behind their back. Masoud embraced the fight against ISIS, affirming: "It is the collective responsibility of the whole world to defeat Daesh."[14] Iran filled a vacuum resulting from the West's slow support. According to Masoud, "We asked for weapons and Iran was the first country to provide us with weapons and ammunition."[15] Two Iranian jumbo transport planes landed at Erbil Airport within a week of the attack on Mosul. Iran delivered a diverse arsenal, including BM-14 and BM-21 truck-mounted rocket launchers, which were critical to countering ISIS armor. Iranian officials said that Iran's support was limited to providing weapons. However, Iran's 81st Armored Division was spotted on the battlefield in Khanaqin on Iran's border with Iraq's Diyala province. Despite denials about IRGC field participation, Iranian television showed Qasem Soleimani with Peshmerga on the battlefield in October 2014.

Kurds often visit Iran. As we have seen, members of the Iraqi opposition to Saddam Hussein, including Barzani and Talabani, received support from Iran in the aftermath of the Iran–Iraq War (1980–88). Talabani had a villa in Tehran, which he frequented in the 1980s and 1990s. After Saddam was deposed, Kurds and Iranians interacted extensively. Iranian-language television programming was broadcast to viewers in Iraqi Kurdistan. In addition to people-to-people contact, KRG and Iranian officials maintained close communication. Iran's Foreign Minister Mohammad Javad Zarif was a frequent visitor to Erbil. Emblematic of close ties, KRG Prime Minister Nechirvan Barzani went to Tehran for President Hassan Rouhani's inauguration in 2013.

Iran also had security concerns: cross-border incursions by the Free Life for Kurdistan Movement (PJAK), a Kurdish militia fighting the mullahs, were a constant threat. Iranian Kurds, numbering between 10 and 12 million, are a restive minority who chafe under the mullahs' autocratic rule. Protests erupted across Iraqi Kurdistan when Iran hanged two Iranian Kurdish activists in 2013. In response, PJAK attacked Iranian security posts, killing ten members of the IRGC. In 2014, Iran emphasized an even-handed approach towards the KDP and PUK. It tried to repair relations with the KDP, which had suffered when Iran supported the PUK in the Kurdish civil war. Supporting the KRG was part of a broader strategy to enhance

Iranian influence via proxies. Tehran pursued a surrogate strategy in Iraqi Kurdistan, Arab Iraq, Syria, Lebanon and Yemen.

Iran has complex and multifaceted interests in Iraq. It has a 400-mile border with Iraqi Kurdistan, and extensive commercial contact exists between Iraqi Kurds and Iranians. Bilateral trade was worth $100 million in 2000, and in 2014, just prior to the ISIS attack, it reached $4 billion annually.[16] Iran wants to expand the export of oil from Iraqi Kurdistan via tanker trucks and pipelines through Iran to international markets. Energy cooperation also limits Turkey's leverage over the Kurds, as most Kurdish oil was transported via pipelines from Kirkuk and Suleimani to the Turkish port of Ceyhan on the eastern Mediterranean.

Iran's support was not an endorsement of Kurdistan's political project for independence. Its engagement was purely transactional. Moreover, supporting the KRG was a way to challenge US influence in Iraqi Kurdistan. With worsening relations between the US and Turkey, Iran was worried that Iraqi Kurdistan might emerge as the de facto eastern flank of NATO, and its Southern Frontier.

The US did not send arms to the Peshmerga until 8 August 2014. It provided just enough firepower to deter the ISIS advance, but not enough for the Peshmerga to achieve a decisive victory on the battlefield. Washington refused to provide heavy and offensive weapons. It feared that the KRG and Baghdad could come to blows and US weapons would be used by the Kurds to fight for independence. The KRG's wish list included Javelin and TOW anti-tank missiles, Man-Portable Air-Defense systems (MANPAD), M1A Abrams tanks, armored personnel carriers, drones and night-vision equipment. Washington insisted on supplying weapons "by, with, and through" Baghdad.[17] This "Baghdad first" policy was intended to bolster the central government and dissuade the Kurds from misunderstanding Washington's support as an endorsement of Kurdistan's independence.

Masoud and Obama met in the Oval Office on 6 May 2015, when Masoud asked for the same military equipment that the US provided for Iraq, including F-16 jet fighters and Apache attack helicopters. He also requested drones for intelligence, surveillance and reconnaissance.[18] Masoud maintained that the Peshmerga would need heavy offensive weapons to deter future advances by ISIS, and to participate in the fight to retake Mosul. Although the Kurds would join the Battle for Mosul, they would not fight in Arab-majority neighborhoods—Masoud assured Obama that the KRG did not covet territory.

United States officials urged the KDP and PUK to unify their command and control of Peshmerga, as well as to combine intelligence operations. After the 1998 Washington Agreement, KDP and PUK Peshmerga never unified and US officials had questions about where weapons would go, who would get them, and whether the distribution would be fair to both parties. Peshmerga were traditionally voluntary militias acting as armed wings of political parties. Party loyalty was paramount and the parties still influenced decisions over recruitment, appointments and promotions. Such politicization limited their military effectiveness.

Some in the US Congress pushed the administration to arm the Kurds directly. On 16 June 2014, a bipartisan majority of the US Senate voted "To provide for a temporary, emergency authorization of defense articles, defense services, and related training directly to the Kurdistan Regional Government." The measure, supported by a 54 to 45 margin, reflected a broad level of popular support for directly arming the KRG. However, it failed to gain the 60-vote requirement. The House Armed Services Committee released its annual Defense Bill on 27 April 2015, which included $715 million to the ISF. It designated 25 percent of that amount for the Peshmerga, Sunni tribal militias and the Sunni National Guard. The bill "would require that the Kurdish Peshmerga, the Sunni tribal security forces, and the Iraqi Sunni National Guard be deemed a country" so they could "directly receive assistance from the United States." A bipartisan group of US lawmakers, including House Foreign Affairs Committee Chairman Ed Royce and Ranking Member Eliot Engel, also introduced legislation authorizing direct weapons transfers to the Peshmerga.[19]

The Obama administration strongly argued against directly arming Peshmerga, citing the Arms Control Export Act. Secretary of Defense Ashton Carter wrote to Senator John McCain on 10 June 2015:

> I am writing to express concern about legislation that would authorize the President to directly arm forces of the Kurdistan Regional Government or other groups within Iraq, without the specific consent of the Iraqi government in Baghdad. Although I agree that our security partners in Iraq need to be armed expeditiously in order to counter the Islamic State in Iraq and the Levant (ISIL), this type of legislation risks fracturing the Government of Iraq, may have implications for force protection, and is redundant given that Kurdish forces are already receiving defense equipment in an expedited manner.[20]

Obama initially trivialized the threat posed by ISIS, saying: "The analogy we use around here sometimes, and I think is accurate, is if a JV team puts on Lakers uniforms, that doesn't make them Kobe Bryant." As ISIS advanced, Obama looked weak and indecisive. He admitted, "We don't have a strategy yet." The online beheading of US journalist Steven Sotloff drove home the urgency of the ISIS crisis. Obama addressed the UN General Assembly on 24 September 2014: "[The US] will work with a broad coalition to dismantle this network of death." He described strategic objectives, which included rallying global opinion, cutting off flows of cash and the movement of foreign fighters, and preventing online ISIS propaganda, which glorified the organization's heinous crimes. "The only language understood by killers like this is the language of force," Obama said.[21]

The US did ultimately provide unprecedented levels of security assistance to the KRG, setting up an American–Kurdish Joint Military Command Center in Erbil. It embarked on an ambitious train-and-equip program with Kurdish forces. Though the GOI closed Kurdistan's airspace to cargo flights to prevent outsiders from supplying the Peshmerga, the US facilitated the supply of weapons to them from coalition countries.[22] As of July 2015, the US had given the KRG 54 million rounds of ammunition, 4,000 rounds of anti-tank munitions, tens of thousands of rifles, body armor, many vehicles and Humvees, and 25 Mine-Resistant Ambush-Protected (MRAP) vehicles. The US Department of Defense delivered some 70 planeloads of weapons. Of the $1.6 billion in weapons earmarked through the Iraq Train and Equip Fund, about $400 million was directed to helping the Kurds.[23] The US established a "Building Partnership Capacity" site in Erbil. As of May 2015, more than 3,000 military advisors were based in Iraqi Kurdistan.

In the absence of Javelin and TOW missiles, Germany filled the gap. German-made Milan missiles were transferred to the Peshmerga. Milan missiles were effective against ISIS armor and improvised vehicle-borne explosive devices. France and other countries also made emergency transfers of weapons to bolster the Peshmerga.

Obama's thinking was evolving. On 7 August, the US dropped food and water to Yazidis besieged on Mount Sinjar. A few days later, US Special Forces landed on Mount Sinjar to assess the humanitarian emergency. Obama explained in a nationally broadcast speech on 10 September 2014,

Unless you degrade [ISIS's] war-fighting capacity—that means its command and control, its leadership, its armored vehicles, its ability to mass and maneuver and conduct war—there is no local force on the ground in this entire swath of territory that can stand up to it right now.[24]

The Peshmerga fled Sinjar, abandoning the Yazidis to ISIS. After their humiliating retreat, they regrouped and focused on disputed territories. The Kurds, taking advantage of the chaos, seized huge tracts of territory claimed by both Kurdistan and Baghdad. Peshmerga entered Kirkuk on 12 June 2014, filling the gap created when the ISF fled. As we have seen, Kirkuk had always been a flash point for conflict between the KRG and Baghdad. Beginning in 2003, Peshmerga and the ISF worked out an arrangement to jointly secure the city, and US soldiers joined a tripartite security arrangement until 2011 when US forces left Iraq. With the ISF in headlong retreat, Fuad Hussein, President Barzani's chief of staff, received a phone call from Hamid al-Musawi, Maliki's personal secretary, conveying a request from Maliki for the Peshmerga to secure Kirkuk before ISIS was able to seize it. Musawi told him: "It would be a good thing if you moved in."[25]

The Peshmerga paid a steep price in the fight against ISIS. As of March 2018, more than 1,300 Peshmerga have been killed and at least 10,000 wounded.[26] In addition, the fight has been very costly. Military expenditures represented as much as 10 percent of the KRG's budget, making its relative expenditure the highest in the world.[27] Iraqi Kurdistan's path to independence was thwarted by a perfect storm of crises. Iraqi Kurds woke up one morning to a border with ISIS of 1,050 kilometers. No part of Iraqi Kurdistan was contiguous with GOI-controlled territory. In addition, Kurdistan was overwhelmed by a humanitarian emergency and an economy that had collapsed.

Humanitarian Emergency

Iraqi Kurdistan was no stranger to mass movements of people. In the first years of the twentieth century, refugees and internally displaced persons (IDPs) came in waves. The first wave came in 2006 and 2007, formed of Christians and Arabs fleeing Iraq's sectarian bloodletting, especially in Baghdad. The second wave fled Syria's civil war between 2011 and 2014. Of the 247,000 Syrian refugees who crossed Iraq's border, 242,000 ended up in Kurdistan.[28] The third wave comprised Iraqis displaced when ISIS invaded in June 2014.

About 500,000 people fled Mosul the day it fell to ISIS on 10 June 2014 and many sought safety in Iraqi Kurdistan, where IDPs arrived in droves on a daily basis, most of them from Sunni Arab areas. As of June 2015, the UN Office for the Coordination of Humanitarian Affairs (OCHA) reported that 8.2 million people in Iraq required immediate humanitarian support. This figure included three million IDPs and more than a quarter of a million refugees. More than half of those displaced sought safety in the Kurdistan Region of Iraq (KRI).

The number of displaced people continued to grow. At the time of writing, more than 3.5 million Iraqis have sought sanctuary in Kurdistan. In 2017, it cost $2 billion to provide for IDPs in Kurdistan. According to Hoshang Mohammed, who heads the KRG's Joint Crisis Coordination Center (JCC), the international community covers approximately 25 percent of the cost through grants to UN agencies and international non-governmental organizations. The KRG pays the balance.

The KRG Interior Minister Karim Sinjari puts the scope of the crisis in perspective.

> The Kurdistan Region, which has roughly the population of Wisconsin at about five million inhabitants, has welcomed nearly two million people, including hundreds of thousands of Syrian refugees, in the past five years. That would be like the United States, with a population of 325 million, absorbing nearly 100 million refugees—or roughly the combined populations of California, Florida, Texas and New York—virtually overnight.[29]

Iraqi Kurdistan went through a dramatic demographic transition, caused by the resettlement of IDPs. Since 2014, Kurdistan's population has increased by 32 percent. Arab Sunnis fleeing the Baghdad belt and other Sunni areas came to the KRI because they did not feel safe in Shi'ite-majority areas where they were subject to insults, threats, harassment and extortion at checkpoints by Shi'ite police. Many Arabs left the KRI to go home but returned to Kurdistan because of security concerns.

Wealthier IDPs bought properties, contributing to a spike in Erbil's real-estate prices. However, the windfall was temporary as their stays were prolonged and they ran out of money. The KRG accepted many unaccompanied children whose parents had joined ISIS. The Kurdish community of Shaklawa was referred to as "Shakluja" because so many Arabs from Falluja resettled there. Shaklawa formerly had a Christian majority but the balance changed as Shaklawa doubled in size.

Displaced persons require a complex combination of services. They need protection, shelter, sustenance, water and sanitation. Children need schooling; families need livelihoods. Traumatized victims require psychosocial counseling. Public health is a significant challenge. The most vulnerable are young children, pregnant women, women and girls who may be susceptible to sexual and gender-based violence (SGBV) and the elderly, especially those from single households. Many of those who arrived were deeply traumatized by their experience under ISIS. Women and girls had been gang-raped, submitted to sexual slavery and forced into marriage. In Sinjar, Yazidi men and boys had been executed, with women often forced to watch beheadings of their family members. Though they felt betrayed when the Peshmerga fled, most displaced Yazidis came to the KRI. Winter conditions exacerbated problems for IDPs, increasing infectious diseases and the risk of death. The weather also worsened the effects of the housing shortages, poor water supply, sanitation and the disruption of routine immunization programs.[30] Sanitation was a particularly worrisome issue, given the limited numbers of latrines and showers.

The large number of Sunni Arabs resettling in Iraqi Kurdistan exacerbated social tensions, which worsened as the number of Sunni Arab IDPs increased and extended their stay. The KRG rigorously prevented ISIS infiltration, through border security and by imposing travel limitations on mainly Arab populations to and within Iraqi Kurdistan. Long queues formed at, for example, the Maktab Khalid checkpoint outside of Kirkuk, where about 84,000 IDP families were resettled.[31]

Funds were short. In 2014, Saudi Arabia made a one-time voluntary contribution of $500 million to the UN Office for the Coordination of Humanitarian Affairs (OCHA). It earmarked funding for minorities and the people of Anbar province. Financing emphasized quick-impact projects, with the money to be spent between September 2014 and March 2015. The UN and the KRG established the JCC in Erbil and international donors coordinated assistance with Baghdad. Funds were provided to the GOI, which was responsible for allocating funds to provincial governments. As relations worsened between the KRG and Baghdad, less money was made available for activities in the KRI. In June 2015, the World Health Organization (WHO) provided more than $17 million of medicines and medical supplies directly to the KRG's Ministry of Health. The WHO also worked with KRI-based health care providers to offer polio vaccinations to displaced persons.[32] The WHO's direct collaboration with the KRG was exceptional, as the response to Iraqi Kurdistan's health emergency was limited by the "Baghdad first" policy.

After the initial spasm of violence, the KRG appealed to donors by developing a National Recovery Plan, which focused on the transition from relief to development. However, the non-stop flow of IDPs made the transition difficult. The KRG succeeded in including a dedicated section on Kurdistan in the UN humanitarian appeal for Iraq. Direct financing to agencies of the KRG, such as the Ministry of Health and the Ministry of Planning, was proposed. Though the World Food Program (WFP) works with the Barzani Foundation on shelter and Sweden supports the Qandil Foundation's camp management via the United Nations High Commissioner for Refugees (UNHCR), Baghdad objected to direct links between donors and the KRG. Its objections limited direct contact between donor countries and the KRG's MOH to procure and store medicines and supplies.

The UN launched a Humanitarian Response Plan in Brussels on 4 June 2015, requesting $197.9 million, but pledges were lower than expected. According to a senior KRG official,

> The UN does prepare a Humanitarian Response Plan for Iraq every year. This year, upon our request and insistence, they have included a section within the plan for Kurdistan and it covers several basic areas such as food, protection, shelter, health, education, water and sanitation. There is no clear and transparent mechanism for fund earmarking for Kurdistan. It has been left for the discretion of Baghdad and UN Agencies. We do not know how much of the funds are being allocated or spent for the displaced in Kurdistan and they are very reluctant to share information with us and they truly lack transparency.[33]

The US did not provide humanitarian assistance directly to the GOI or the KRG. Instead it worked through UN agencies, such as the WFP, and international NGOs like the International Rescue Committee (IRC). The US was the global leader in responding to the humanitarian crises in Iraq and Syria, and as of 2014 it had provided more than $4 billion since the start of the Syria crisis. More than $183 million assisted 250,000 Syrian refugees in Iraq, and more than $416 million was earmarked for Iraqis resettled in Kurdistan.[34]

Though its capacity was seriously overstretched, the KRG accepted its humanitarian role. The humanitarian emergency had an important security dimension, as without humanitarian aid, the victims of ISIS easily could have become radicalized. If the KRG did not resettle them, these people would remain displaced. Sinjari called for international cooperation to help the KRG face the humanitarian emergency, lest it metastasize into a broader security crisis. Addressing the humanitarian emergency took political will and leadership. The KRG extended a helping hand at a time when it could least afford such largesse.

Economy

After the Gulf War, Kurdistan went from a war-torn country to an economically buoyant region. Cranes dotted the horizon, a measure of the rapidly expanding construction industry. Glass and chrome structures suggested modernity and wealth. Five-star hotels such as the Divan, Kempinsky and Rotana opened for business. Jaguar and Mercedes dealerships sold luxury vehicles.

The *Economist Intelligence Review* ranked Iraqi Kurdistan high on its macroeconomic environment, market opportunities and Foreign Direct Investment (FDI) policy. The KRG implemented a friendly tax environment, manifest through low corporate and personal taxes, which encouraged international trade and investment. It also instituted a 15 percent corporate tax rate and tax exemptions for companies with production-sharing agreements in the hydrocarbons sector, as well as a flat five percent income tax rate and no value-added tax. Its 2006 Regional Investment Law was progressive, allowing foreign investors to own land and hold majority positions in joint ventures. It spurred opportunities in construction, transport, storage, communications and wholesale and retail trade, as well as service sectors, manufacturing and agriculture.

The KRG radically improved infrastructure; in 2013 alone, it spent \$2 billion on infrastructure projects.[35] Plans were finalized for a new bridge and five new crossings on Iraqi Kurdistan's border with Turkey to ease the transport bottleneck, where trucks often lined up for miles on both sides. Turkish construction companies built modern international airports in Erbil and Suleimani. There were daily flights to Europe and Turkey as well as other Middle Eastern cities, such as Beirut, Dubai and Amman.[36]

Electricity production increased steadily from 2008, nearly doubling between 2011 and 2012. Businesses had barely two to three hours of electricity each day in 2003. In the first half of 2014, businesses enjoyed nearly uninterrupted power supplies.[37] Most electricity came from plentiful supplies of natural gas.

The information technology (IT) and communications sectors also advanced. In 2014, 21 companies provided internet services. Newroz Telecom and KurdTel were dominant digital network companies. Three mobile operators with GSM licenses emerged: Zain Iraq, a unit of Kuwait's Zain; Qatar Telecom (Qtel)'s subsidiary, Asiacell; and France Telecom, which is affiliated with Korek Telecom. The mobile telephone penetration rate was about 80 percent.[38]

Economic growth was fueled by dynamic trade relations between Iraqi Kurdistan and Turkey, as well as Iran. As of February 2014, 2,830 foreign companies were registered in the KRI. Of these, 45 percent were Turkish. Turkish consumer goods were omni-present in Kurdistan's markets; 80 percent of all goods for sale in the KRG came from Turkey.[39]

Relations between Iran and the KRG were dynamic. In 1988, Iran was the first country to open a consulate in Erbil. The KRG exported 50,000 barrels of oil per day by truck from Suleimani, across Iran to oil terminals in Iran's Bandar Abbas in the Persian Gulf. Numerous border crossings between Iraqi Kurdistan and Iran exist at Haji Omeran, Penjwen, Bashmagh, Garmiyan and Raperin. Border crossings were upgraded to include registries and customs collection for traffic in both directions. Iran was a significant supplier of foodstuffs to Iraqi Kurdistan, including staples such as potatoes and onions. Beyond economic relations, the KRG helped address Iran's security concerns; Kurdish officials helped negotiate a ceasefire between Iran and the PJAK in 2011.

The web of regional economic and political connections contributed to the impression of an integrated and growing economy. But despite the appearance of steady growth, systemic problems existed. Smuggling and illicit economic activities were normal during the period of double sanctions between 1992 and 2003, and smuggling continued to take place. Iraqi Kurdistan's cash-based economy, which expanded dramatically after 2003, fostered a freewheeling approach towards capital accumulation. The concentration of power, nepotism and patronage gave rise to the widespread perception that connections were needed to conduct business, and that the elites sanctioned corruption.

The KRG tried to address corruption and promote transparency, taking steps to create a culture of accountability, establishing the Office of Governance and Integrity in February 2010 and charging a number of high-profile officials with corruption, including the former Mayor of Suleimani. However, the KRG's anti-corruption efforts were mostly symbolic and largely ineffective. Its failure to effectively enforce the rule of law or publish data on oil revenues were indicative of endemic problems.

Kurdistan suffered from a phenomenon known as the "oil curse," under which countries with a paradox of plenty—fossil fuels and minerals—typically have less economic growth, less democracy and more corruption. In a 2012 poll, 88 percent of respondents were critical of government efforts to combat corruption.[40]

Iraqi Kurdistan's economy went into recession in 2014. Economic problems were triggered by a combination of factors: the suspension of oil payments by the Iraqi government in February 2014; depressed energy prices affecting revenue from the sale of Kurdish oil directly to international markets; and the collapse of investor confidence stemming from the ISIS attack. Iraqi Kurdistan was supposed to receive 17 percent of the Iraqi budget, although the actual payout was less. With the cut-off, Iraqi Kurdistan was left to rely mainly on its oil reserves, the revenues from which decreased dramatically as world oil prices collapsed. The KRG's overall budget was $13 billion in 2013, with a budget deficit of $1 billion. The deficit ballooned to $6.5 billion in 2014, and doubled the following year.[41] The KRG was unable to pay the salaries of civil servants, which were slashed or unmet for long periods.

The KRG's economic governance was affected by the absence of a consolidated balance sheet, inadequate financial planning and budgetary excesses. Contributing to the deficit, the KRG spent $4 billion subsidizing fuel in 2014. The budget was bloated by ghost workers, individuals on the payroll who did not show up for work or sometimes did not even exist. Civil servants numbered about 1.2 million; 70 percent of the workforce. With revenues slashed, the KRG was unable to pay salaries. The import-reliant economy came to a standstill. Queues at gas stations stretched for miles. The KRG experienced a 70 percent revenue reduction in 2014. The situation was so dire that Empire Construction, an Erbil-based construction and engineering firm, subsidized meals for Peshmerga on the frontline.

Deputy Prime Minister Qubad Talabani led the KRG's efforts to reform its economic governance. He sought to create a stable and predictable environment for doing business through a legal system that governed commerce and property rights, as well as taxes and tariffs levied in a more consistent and transparent way. He took steps to review and strengthen the investment law. Qubad also sought to improve economic planning by developing a consolidated balance sheet; improving communications between relevant ministries; and harmonizing budgetary practices across the three governorates of Iraqi Kurdistan. He took steps to increase revenues to the KRG through a tariff structure that accurately reflected the real cost of electricity and water. He reduced costs by phasing out fuel subsidies and other allowances. Qubad's public-sector reforms helped curb rampant inefficiency after Iraqi Kurdistan's economy collapsed in 2014. The arrival of ISIS was a wake-up call for the KRG.

Hydrocarbons

Iraqi Kurdistan has oil reserves estimated at up to 45 billion barrels.[42] Estimates vary, but if correct, Iraqi Kurdistan would rank tenth among the world's largest oil-holding countries. One giant field, Shaikan, contains at least 12 billion barrels of heavy crude. Other fields—Taq Taq, Tawke, Akri Bijeel, Barda Rash, Garmiyan and Kurdamir—contain seven billion barrels of oil-in-place.[43] The oil is high-quality low-sulfur crude.

Iraqi Kurdistan also has bountiful supplies of natural gas. Estimated reserves are between 100 and 200 trillion cubic feet (tcf), equivalent to around 2.8 to 5.7 trillion cubic meters (tcm).[44] The gas field at Miran contains at least 6.8 tcf (c. 0.2 billion cubic meters (bcm)); Khor Mor holds at least 1.8 tcf. In November 2013, the KRG signed a gas sales agreement with the Government of Turkey, which envisaged the KRG supplying Turkey with some 4 bcm/y in 2017, 10 bcm/y by 2020 and an option of 20 bcm/y thereafter. Production will come primarily from Genel Enerji's fields at Miran and Bina Bawi, which are not likely to go online until at least 2018.

The KRG works with international partners through production-sharing agreements (PSAs), whereas Iraq structures its deals on a royalty-fee basis. In 2012, the KRG set ambitious targets intended to take oil output to 1.0 million barrels per day (mbd) by 2015 and to 2.0 mbd by 2019.[45] As of June 2015, oil production was around 450,000 barrels per day (bpd) in areas controlled by the KRG.[46] Production came from territories under control of the KRG after 2003, territories seized by Peshmerga during their counterattack against ISIS in 2014, and oil produced by the North Oil Company (NOC), which is exported to the Mediterranean port of Ceyhan via KRG-controlled territory.

Beginning in 2003, the GOI agreed to pay 17 percent of Iraq's total revenues from the sale of hydrocarbons to the KRG each month. The payout was roughly equivalent to $1.2 billion. However, in January 2014, the GOI responded to the KRG's overtures to customers on the global market, suspending the monthly payments because of its own economic crisis in addition to protesting the KRG's export of oil. The KRG insisted that, in accordance with Article 115 of the constitution, it had the rights for exploration and production of new fields. Baghdad disputed Kurdish ownership of new fields, as well as the oil produced by the NOC.

A KRG-built pipeline exported about 400,000 Bpd to Ceyhan, starting in early 2014. The 600-mile long Kirkuk–Ceyhan connection is Iraq's largest crude oil pipeline, but it suffers from poor maintenance and sabotage. The KRG's Khurmala–Fish Khabur pipeline was operational as of 1 January 2014, when it began exporting oil from Kirkuk. However, ISIS posed challenges to monetizing the KRG's oil and gas resources, sabotaging segments of the pipeline and interdicting transport from the Kirkuk oilfield to southern Iraq and the Persian Gulf.

Twenty-nine energy companies, including DNO from Norway, Genel Enerji from Turkey and the US firms Chevron and ExxonMobil, signed PSAs with the KRG. ExxonMobil's CEO, Rex Tillerson, negotiated the deal. Tillerson and other oil executives entered into agreements despite Baghdad's objections. The GOI threatened to boycott companies doing business with the KRG and took legal action to block the sale of Kurdish oil. Iraq's Oil Minister, Hussein Shahristani, disparaged the Kurdish oil project. "These companies have no right to work on Iraqi soil, in violation of Iraqi laws, without the agreement of the Iraqi government."[47] Baghdad threatened to sue any buyer of Kurdish oil, taking a case to the International Court of Arbitration in Paris. The Obama administration feigned neutrality. However, Washington's warnings about buying Kurdish oil had a chilling effect on the sale of Kurdish oil in international markets.

To address competing claims, the KRG and GOI reached the Baghdad Agreement in December 2014. Prime Minister Nechirvan Barzani was the principal architect of the deal, which saw the GOI pledge to resume payments to the KRG. In exchange, the KRG would export 550,000 bpd of Kurdish oil via Iraq's State Oil Marketing Organization (SOMO). The agreement represented a breakthrough at the time. However, it was never implemented. Baghdad did not make its payments and the KRG did not send the full allotment of oil, maintaining that the goal of 550,000 bpd was to be averaged over the year.

The KRG responded by finalizing a 50-year contract to sell oil to Turkey. Revenues from the sale of Kurdish oil would be deposited into a Turkish bank. The deal represented a dramatic about-face for Turkey, which had historically opposed Iraqi Kurdistan. Masoud Barzani was vilified by Turkish officials as enemy number one of the "deep state." Turkish officials could not even bring themselves to use the term "Kurdistan" when referring to the KRI. Largely based on economic interests, Turkey's approach shifted after Recep Tayyip Erdoğan's Justice and Development Party (AKP) won a convincing victory in 2002 and was able to form a single-party government the following year. By 2007, Ankara was fully committed to improving relations with the KRG.

Hydrocarbons were essential to fuel Turkey's fast-growing economy, as it became a dynamic member of the G-20. Energy imports from Russia and Iran were unpredictable, given US sanctions on Iran and Vladimir Putin's volatile relations with the West. If supplies were interrupted, an energy shortage would cause serious price hikes and economic slowdowns, affecting the AKP's electoral prospects. Turkey turned to the KRG to provide energy security. The partnership involved joint pipelines,[48] investment in Iraqi Kurdistan by Turkish oil and gas companies, and a PSA that circumvented Baghdad.[49] In 2009, US Ambassador James Jeffrey reflected on Turkey–KRG energy relations:

> GOT [Government of Turkey] officials recognize what they describe as a special cultural affinity between Turks and Kurds and see Turkey as the most natural outlet to bring the Kurdish region's hydrocarbon resources to world markets as well as the primary source for investment, consumer goods, and technology. In part to help satisfy its own growing energy requirements and in part to make viable plans to bring gas from both Middle East and Caspian Basin sources to European markets, Turkey has begun to sound out possibilities for Turkish companies to help develop oil and gas fields in the KRG-administered region as well as to link those fields to the existing Kirkuk–Yamurtuluk oil pipeline and a proposed northern route gas pipeline into Turkey. The Turks argue that they do not want to undermine efforts to achieve agreement on national hydrocarbons legislation in Iraq, but similarly do not want to be penalized for "doing the right thing" by discovering that contracts signed with the KRG end up being grandfathered under a final deal between Erbil and Baghdad, with Turkish companies sidelined as a result.[50]

Jeffrey's reference to "undermining efforts to achieve agreement on national hydrocarbons legislation in Iraq" reiterated US policy that Baghdad should control all oil and gas exports from Iraq, including Kurdistan. Washington worried that making energy deals that bypass Baghdad would increase the likelihood of Iraqi Kurdistan emerging as an independent and sovereign state.[51] Market forces were a powerful motivator. According to Ashti Hawrami: "Nowhere in the world does one million barrels a day (of crude oil production capacity) remain stranded forever."

Aydin Selcen, who was then the Turkish Consul General in Erbil but later went to work for Genel Energy, a Turkish company developing oil and gas fields in Iraqi Kurdistan, explained Ankara's perspective at the time:

> There are no legal obstacles for public or private firms to sign deals with the KRG. This includes pipeline projects. We respect the Iraqi constitution. And we reject an artificial choice to be imposed between only cooperating with Erbil or only cooperating with Baghdad. We are hopeful that Erbil and Baghdad will reach a peaceful solution to their differences through sustained policy dialogue.[52]

The KRG bent over backwards to build confidence with Turkey. It gave Turkish companies special concessions to invest and trade with the KRI. Trade between KRG and Turkey was $12 billion in 2014, making the KRG Turkey's second largest market after Germany. Barzani was silent in the face of egregious human rights abuses against Kurds in Turkey. He cooperated with Turkey to increase pressure on the PKK, headquartered in the Qandil Mountains of Iraqi Kurdistan. According to Masrour, "They must leave. This is one of the reasons why we are so eager to see the Kurdish peace process inside Turkey succeed."[53] In a further concession to Turkey, Masoud Barzani criticized the Democratic Union Party (PYD) for trying to establish a Kurdish autonomous area in Syria modeled on the KRG.

Masoud went to Diyarbakir, a Kurdish metropolis in southeast Turkey, for a campaign appearance with Erdoğan in November 2013. They were joined by the iconic Kurdish poet and singer, Sivan Perwer, who serenaded him and Erdoğan before a large crowd of Turkish Kurds.[54] Barzani addressed the audience:

> My request from my Kurdish and Turkish brothers is to support the peace project. I want to tell them that we support the peace process with all our force. The time in the Middle East for living together has come. We can carry our people to happier days if we follow the methods of living together. Wars have been tried. The days when the blood of a young Turkish man was spilled by a Kurdish youth or the blood of a young Kurdish man was spilled by a Turkish youth are over.

Barzani concluded his remarks in Turkish: "Long live Turkish and Kurdish brotherhood. Long live peace. Long live freedom."[55] Many Kurds were shocked and dismayed by Barzani's chumminess with Erdoğan, as well as his endorsement of the AKP.

The KRG believed that economic diplomacy would enhance overall relations with Turkey. Cooperation with Turkey was vital to the KRG, as Iraqi Kurdistan needs a corridor to the outside world. Oil exports to Ceyhan were critical for accessing global markets. But relying on Turkey put Kurds in a precarious position. Turkey could close the pipeline in a fit of pique over Iraqi Kurdistan's political declarations or implement a broader economic embargo if the KRG moved towards independence.

Barzani hoped that goodwill would redefine relations. However, Turkey was non-responsive to the KRG's appeals for help in fighting ISIS. Soon after ISIS attacked Iraqi Kurdistan, a senior KRG official met then Foreign Minister Ahmet Davutoğlu in Istanbul to ask for weapons. Davutoğlu declined, citing upcoming presidential elections on 10 August 2014. The envoy met a representative of Turkey's National Intelligence Agency (MIT) several weeks later. He was told that Turkey could not support the KRG because ISIS was holding Turkish hostages from the Turkish consulate in Mosul.[56]

In a further blow to the KRG, Turkish officials refused to release proceeds from the sale of Kurdish oil that had been deposited in Turkish banks. Ankara indicated that it would require the KRG to distribute oil revenues according to the provisions of the Iraqi constitution. As a result, the KRG would receive only 17 percent of the money from the sale of its own oil.

Governance Issues

Masoud Barzani was elected president by the National Assembly of Kurdistan for a four-year term in 2007. He was re-elected in 2011, this time by a popular vote. Though the Kurdish Presidency Law limits the president to two terms, the Assembly failed to adopt a regional constitution clarifying the procedures for electing its president. Without constitutional guidance, the Kurdistan National Assembly voted to extend Barzani's term for two more years in 2013. After two years, Kurdistan's five major political parties failed to reach an agreement on the presidency and Barzani's term was extended for another two years until November 2017.

Barzani's backers and KDP stalwarts argued that Barzani was the only figure who could confront the security risks from ISIS. A steady hand was needed to meet the economic challenges arising from the KRG's budget shortfall. Barzani had become a fixture in Kurdish politics; he appeared irreplaceable. An opposition media channel, NRT, conducted an online poll in June 2015. Of the 150,000 survey participants, 85 percent favored extending Barzani's term.[57]

Negotiations over the Presidency Law highlighted the need to consolidate Iraqi Kurdistan's democratic institutions and reduce family control of its political parties. The presidency crisis also revealed the depth of rivalry between political parties. Gorran castigated the PUK for its role as a submissive, junior partner in Barzani's administration; it also effectively challenged the PUK's base in Suleimani. Gorran, the Islamic Group and the Kurdistan Islamic Union—the three main Kurdish opposition forces—strongly opposed Barzani's presidency. They maintained that the law ratified by parliament extending Barzani's term for two years, from 20 August 2013 to 19 Aug 2015, was illegal. Gorran was a strong proponent of parliamentary oversight of the executive, opposing direct election of the president as diminishing the parliament and undermining the separation of powers.

On 12 October 2015, Speaker Yousif Mohammed Sadiq—from Gorran—was prevented by Barzani's security from entering Erbil to convene the Assembly to debate a new presidency law. A convoy of military vehicles drove through Erbil as a show of force. It was a veiled threat of what might happen if they tried to remove Barzani from the presidency. Gorran accused Barzani of abusing power and charged the KDP with corruption and nepotism. The Kurdish media reported in November 2016 that Barzani's salary was $400,000 dollars per month.[58] Deputies brawled in the parliament, hurling water bottles at one another and the discord spilled onto the streets as a large anti-Barzani protest was held in Suleimani.

Barzani promised to conduct a referendum on independence, but only after ISIS was vanquished. He knew his time was running out and was determined to hold the referendum before stepping down as president. As the US-led coalition fighting ISIS geared up for an assault on Mosul, Peshmerga were needed for the battle. As long as Peshmerga were indispensable, Barzani had leverage over the US for his independence agenda. However, he decided to wait until the after the Battle for Mosul in the hope the US would support Kurdistan's right to self-determination over Baghdad's opposition.

7 COUNTDOWN

"The time has come to decide our fate, and we should not wait for other people to decide it for us."

KRG PRESIDENT MASOUD BARZANI[1]

At the White House

Iraq's 2005 constitution was a compromise. The Kurds agreed to remain in Iraq if it were truly democratic, federal and decentralized. By failing to fulfill its constitutional commitments, the Iraqi government pushed the Kurds towards independence. No legal requirement existed for the KRG to conduct a referendum on independence, but Masoud Barzani believed a referendum would establish a legal, popular and international legitimacy for the referendum and its result. Knowing full well that a declaration of independence would be meaningless unless countries recognized Iraqi Kurdistan as an independent and sovereign state, Masoud welcomed political dialogue with the Government of Iraq (GOI) on the terms of a friendly divorce. The referendum was envisioned as part of a process, initiating negotiations that would culminate in Iraqi Kurdistan's independence.

Masoud promised to conduct the referendum in a deliberative and transparent way, avoiding precipitous decisions or reckless pronouncements. After the referendum, which he believed would provide a ringing endorsement for independence, Masoud pledged a dialogue with all regional and international stakeholders. The Kurdistan Regional Government (KRG) would keep the US Government and other members of the international community informed. In Washington on 6 May 2015, Masoud declared: "I cannot say if it will be next year, or when, but certainly independent Kurdistan is coming."[2] The message was echoed by Masrour Barzani, his son and the Kurdish intelligence chief. "We need our own laws, our own rules, our own country, and we are going to get them."[3]

The KRG believed it was acting lawfully. Its lawyers concluded that a referendum was consistent with Iraq's 2005 constitution, which allows regions to have their own constitutions. The charter defines relations between the KRI and the federal government. It asserts that Iraqi Kurdistan voluntarily entered into a federal union and, as an equal party, has the right to secede. "The people of Iraqi Kurdistan have the right to self-determination, and under this right they are free to determine their politics and free to achieve their economic, social, and cultural development."[4]

Masoud made his case to President Barack Obama during a White House meeting on 5 May 2015. Obama and his team were agnostic on the independence issue. They did not endorse it; nor did they deny its possibility. Vice President Joseph R. Biden, who played a leading role in determining the Obama administration's Iraq policy, did not rule out independence. The US officials played to Masoud's vanity. After the Gulf War, Barzani and Talabani had not even been allowed on the premises of the State Department but met US officials at a coffee shop in Columbia Square on 23rd Street. When Masoud visited Washington in 2015, the US rolled out the red carpet, offering meetings with the President, Vice President, the Secretary of Defense and other senior officials. They made him feel like a head of state. Treating Masoud as a valued partner was an effort to convince him to abide by their wishes.

Masoud took away two important messages from the White House meeting. First, the Obama administration was focused on degrading and destroying ISIS. Until that was accomplished, Kurdistan's push for independence was a distraction. Second, Washington blamed Iraqi Prime Minister Nuri al-Maliki's polarizing approach for making Iraq's Sunnis susceptible to Abu Bakr al-Baghdadi's sectarian appeal. The US officials welcomed Maliki's removal and the formation of a new government led by Prime Minister Heider al-Abadi, calling it a "promising step forward." They hoped Abadi would govern in a more conciliatory fashion, draining support for ISIS in Iraq's Sunni-majority regions. Additionally, truly implementing federalism would obviate the Kurds' push for independence.

Masoud addressed a prominent Washington audience after meeting Obama, affirming the goal of independence. He maintained, however, that independence would not be necessary if Iraq fulfilled its constitutional power-sharing commitments. He surprised the audience by stating that his first priority was to defeat ISIS. Masoud indicated that once ISIS was destroyed, the KRG would evaluate Abadi's performance. Only then would the KRG consider a referendum on independence. He set no timetable, nor did he rule out other constitutional arrangements.

Brendan O'Leary, the Lauder Professor of Political Science at the University of Pennsylvania, served as an advisor to the KRG. In addition to outright independence, confederation was also seen as an option. Confederation is the union of autonomous political units, which band together because their individual interests are enhanced through common action. In a confederation, each entity retains sovereignty and the right to seek independence. Confederations are often established by treaty between confederation members who enjoy equal status. As a transitional measure, it would create breathing space. Iraqis would have an opportunity to gradually redefine their relations with one another, aggregating interests to achieve greater self-rule through the formation of states: one Kurdish, one Sunni, and one or more Shi'ite regions. Confederation may have been a good option on paper but it was easier said than done. Constitutional changes require a referendum and approval by the majority of Iraqi voters. Any three governorates can defeat a constitutional amendment with a vote of two-thirds. Given the fragmented nature of Iraqi politics, a negotiated settlement was a high bar to meet.

Biden, then the ranking member of the Senate Foreign Relations Committee, and Leslie H. Gelb, president emeritus of the Council on Foreign Relations, published an op-ed in the *New York Times* on 1 May 2006, entitled "Unity through Autonomy in Iraq." Drawing on a report by the Council on Foreign Relations, *Power-Sharing in Iraq*, the article offered a reality-based approach to Iraq's transition.[5]

Biden and Gelb outlined a process "to maintain a united Iraq by decentralizing it, giving each ethno-religious group—Kurd, Sunni Arab and Shi'ite Arab—room to run its own affairs, while leaving the central government in charge of common interests." They envisioned

> three largely autonomous regions with a viable central government in Baghdad. The Kurdish, Sunni and Shi'ite regions would each be responsible for their own domestic laws, administration and internal security. The central government would control border defense, foreign affairs and oil revenues.

They pointed out that their decentralization plan was consistent with Iraq's constitution, which "already provides for a federal structure and a procedure for provinces to combine into regional governments." They considered the perspectives of Iraq's ethnic and sectarian groups, noting:

> Increasingly, each community supports federalism, if only as a last resort. The Sunnis, who until recently believed they would retake power in Iraq, are beginning to recognize that they won't and don't want to live in a Shi'ite-controlled, highly centralized state with laws enforced by sectarian militias. The Shi'ites know they can dominate the government, but they can't defeat a Sunni insurrection. The Kurds will not give up their 15-year-old autonomy.

A strong federal system would prevent sectarian cleansing, and, as an alternative to partition, Sunnis would accept this arrangement because it was better than being dominated "by Kurds and Shi'ites in a central government or being the main victims of a civil war." Biden and Gelb proposed giving Sunnis 20 percent of all revenues. They also addressed the need for security, while recognizing that the US commitment of troops was not open-ended.

> The president must direct the military to design a plan for withdrawing and redeploying our troops from Iraq by 2008 (while providing for a small but effective residual force to combat terrorists and keep the neighbors honest). We must avoid a precipitous withdrawal that would lead to a national meltdown, but we also can't have a substantial long-term American military presence. That would do terrible damage to our armed forces, break American and Iraqi public support for the mission and leave Iraqis without any incentive to shape up.

They also proposed an international contact group of regional countries and major powers to coordinate assistance. The Biden–Gelb plan offered a "plausible path to that core political settlement among Iraqis, with the economic, military and diplomatic levers to make the political solution work."[6]

George W. Bush was depleted by the war in Iraq, which a growing number of Americans opposed. By the end of his second term, he was also undermined by the faltering US economy, which further tainted his presidency. In response to policies of the Bush administration, which favored Iraq's Shi'ites, Sunnis banded together to support Salafist and extremist groups. Zarqawi was killed, but other jihadists took his place. There was no end in sight to America's involvement in Iraq, which deepened with the ISIS invasion in June 2014.

The Battle for Mosul

The Obama–Barzani meeting was a reality check. Masoud accepted that negotiating constitutional alternatives or scheduling the referendum was premature with Iraq under attack and a third of the country occupied by ISIS. He recognized that liberating Mosul was the priority. As horror stories emerged about the draconian rule of ISIS, the US and its coalition partners planned the Battle of Mosul, in which Peshmerga and Iraqi partners would be indispensable.

Mosul is Iraq's second largest city and the capital of the Nineveh governorate. Today, Arabs and Sunnis are the majority. It was not always that way. In 1923, Mosul was 50 percent Kurdish and 13 percent Arab. The balance of the population was a combination of Turkmen, Assyrians, Chaldeans, Shi'ites, Christians, Zoroastrians and Jews. Saddam Hussein's Arabization program changed Nineveh's ethnic balance, leading to social tensions. The Iraqi Revolutionary Command Council issued Decree No. 795 in 1975, authorizing the confiscation of property from Kurds and resettlement by Arabs. The Nineveh and Kirkuk governorates were most affected by Saddam's Arabization policy, which created an Arab belt around the oil fields from Kirkuk to Mosul. A 1997 census found that 58 percent of Mosul's population was Arab. Kurds contest the figure, claiming that the Arab majority was a result of "internal colonialism." Western Mosul was almost entirely Arab, while the population is more mixed east of the Tigris River, which divides the city. Villages on the Nineveh Plain from Mosul to Erbil are diverse, but mostly Kurdish.[7]

Ninety percent of Mosul's Arab population supported ISIS when it invaded in June 2014. However, life under ISIS proved to be a nightmare. Mosul suffered from water shortages and electricity was available for only three hours each day. There was no heat in the winter. Cooking oil and other staples were in short supply. Unemployment rose as Mosul's economy collapsed. The media was used by ISIS as a tool for intimidation; big-screen televisions in public squares publicized beheadings. Shaving was declared illegal and ISIS issued instructions on the proper length of a man's beard. Smoking and cell phones were banned and anyone caught with a cigarette or a mobile phone was executed. Women were not allowed to leave their homes unless accompanied by a male family member and wearing a hijab; women who failed to cover themselves were subject to public lashings. ISIS did not allow girls to attend school. Boys could study, but textbooks were rewritten to reflect the ISIS ideology. One math textbook presented the following problem: "There are 42 bullets and seven unbelievers. How many shots in your sniper rifle do you have for each?"[8] The rules were brutally enforced by Hesba, the ISIS religious police.

The Battle for Mosul was launched in the summer of 2016. It involved about 100,000 Iraqi counter-terrorism forces and Shi'ite militias comprising Popular Mobilization Units (PMUs). Air strikes meant that the US was working in direct support of PMUs, surrogates for the IRGC, but there was no direct contact between the US and PMU commanders. Liaison was done through officers of the Iraqi Security Forces (ISF), who together with Peshmerga commanders coordinated activities on the battlefield.

The parameters of Peshmerga participation were established at the outset. Barzani stipulated that Peshmerga would not fight in Arab sections of Mosul. Nonetheless, they played a decisive role in clearing ISIS fighters from Mosul's suburbs to the north and east. According to Bernard-Henri Lévy, the French philosopher with affinity for the Kurds, "It was the Kurdish Peshmerga that, in October and November 2016, opened Mosul's gates for the Iraqis."[9] Coalition air strikes destroyed bridges across the Tigris, with the aim of limiting the ability of ISIS to resupply or reinforce positions. After fierce fighting, ISIS made a tactical retreat in January 2017, in order to assume more defensible positions in western Mosul.

A wave of counterattacks was launched by ISIS fighters numbering between 5,000 and 6,000, using vehicle-borne IEDs and mortar fire. Sniper attacks were enabled by a labyrinth of tunnels throughout the city. In June 2017, the ancient Great Mosque of al-Nuri, the pulpit from which Abu Bakr al-Baghdadi had declared his caliphate, was blown up, with ISIS claiming it was destroyed by coalition air strikes in the hope of turning the local population against the United States. It was, in fact, destroyed by ISIS themselves in an effort to mobilize Sunni loyalists. Civilians who tried to flee the fighting were shot dead by ISIS while others were used as human shields.

The ISIS fighters made their last stand in West Mosul's old city, a densely packed labyrinth of alleyways and ancient buildings. The small streets were wired with booby traps. House-to-house fighting gave ISIS an advantage.

Bombing from warplanes and Iraqi artillery destroyed whole neighborhoods, burying ISIS fighters under the debris. Small pockets of ISIS fighters held out, fighting for their nihilistic cause until the end.

Surrounded by elite Iraqi counter-terrorism police, Prime Minister Heider al-Abadi entered Mosul and, with the remnants of the al-Nuri mosque as a backdrop, declared victory on 9 July 2017. Abadi was dressed in combat fatigues and Kevlar body gear. US Secretary of State Rex W. Tillerson was more cautious.

> The end of major combat operations does not mean we have achieved the enduring defeat of ISIS. ISIS remains a serious threat to the stability of the region, our homelands, and other parts of the globe. Without continued attention on the part of coalition members, we risk the return of extremist groups like ISIS in liberated areas in Iraq and Syria and their spread to new locations.[10]

The ISIS withdrawal after Mosul triggered a debate over Kurdistan's boundaries. Masoud insisted that Iraqi Kurdistan stretched from Syria in the west to Iran in the east. He pronounced, "These areas were liberated by the blood of 11,500 martyrs and wounded from the Peshmerga. After all these sacrifices, it is not possible to return them to direct federal control." Asserting Iraqi sovereignty, Abadi scoffed at Barzani's claim. Abadi's office issued a terse statement calling for the Peshmerga to pull back. The two sides finalized an agreement with "a specific clause on the withdrawal of the Peshmerga from the liberated areas after the liberation of Mosul." The agreement indicated that Peshmerga would return "to the previous places that they held prior to the launch of liberation operations." In accordance with the de-confliction protocol, the Peshmerga withdrew without a shot.

Iraq's neighbors sought to take advantage of the situation to advance their national interests. Turkey rejected any attempt to change Mosul's Sunni demographic composition by Iraq's Shi'ite-led federal government, maintaining that changing the sectarian demography would be a threat to its security. It also insisted that the Kurds vacate villages in the Nineveh Plains east of Mosul, as well as oil-rich Kirkuk.

Iran celebrated the ISIS defeat in Mosul. Though the PMUs comprised Iraqi Shi'ites, they were under the control of Iran and acted to advance Iran's interests. Ridding the region of ISIS would allow Iran to open a corridor across northern Iraq to Syria and Lebanon. The corridor would be used to send missiles and other weapons to Hezbollah and Hamas. Iran also used the corridor to export its Shiʻite revolution and ideology.

The debate between Abadi and Barzani over disputed territories occurred in the broader context of Kurdistan's push for independence. In September 2016, Fuad Hussein, Barzani's chief of staff, briefed US Secretary of State John Kerry at the Helmsley Hotel during the UN General Assembly. He explained that the KRG and Baghdad had agreed to establish committees to evaluate the question of independence and discuss future relations. Fuad explained that the committees would develop divorce details rather than a modus vivendi for Kurdistan to remain a part of Iraq. To Masoud, independence was already a foregone conclusion. "Independence is the natural right of our people and we will never give up such a right under any condition. We have discussed this matter clearly and openly with Baghdad that gave us positive response."[11]

The Obama administration warned Masoud against a referendum because it would distract from the ongoing fight against ISIS. It would also divide two US allies, Iraq and the KRG. With Mosul liberated, Masoud pushed to achieve his lifelong ambition for independence. However, Masoud did not appreciate the extent to which he had lost leverage after Mosul. By 2017, Iraq was emboldened by Mosul's liberation and armed to the teeth with state-of-the-art US weaponry. Post-Mosul, Abadi was less accommodating of Kurdish aspirations.

Referendum Plans

Abadi sent conciliatory messages. He affirmed that Iraq would not block Kurdish efforts to hold a referendum. Moreover, Abadi indicated that independence was "an undisputed right."[12] At the same time, however, he was under pressure from factions in his Dawa Party and Iran to derail the Kurds.

A joint KDP–PUK delegation met Abadi in Baghdad on 29 August 2016. Fuad Hussein and Prime Minister Nechirvan Barzani held "frank and open discussions" about "self-determination" and "Kurdish independence." Participants focused on areas of agreement rather than intractable differences. A joint statement commended collaborative efforts to liberate Mosul, while both sides recommitted to vanquishing ISIS elsewhere. They also discussed the timing and modalities of the referendum.

Fuad reported on discussions. "Prime Minister Barzani said the situation cannot continue as it is now and that we needed to talk about a fundamental solution which is independence for Kurdistan." He described the process going forward. "We agreed on the formation of two committees: one in Erbil and the other in Baghdad to evaluate all aspects of this question."[13] The two sides agreed on the principle that Kurds and Iraqis should have a sustained dialogue to address differences. The UN could be involved, but only in a technical capacity. Third parties were not welcome; Abadi rejected an offer of mediation by Turkish President Recep Tayyip Erdoğan.

The KRG delegation knew their Iraqi counterparts held different views. "Some of the Iraqi parties said clearly that they were in favor of Kurdistan's right to self-determination," said Fuad. "Others said Kurdish independence could create domestic and regional tensions." Hadi Al-Ameri, head of the Iranian-backed Badr Organization, was a vocal opponent. Representing the views of Iran and the PMUs, Ameri warned that the referendum could cause regional instability and trigger civil war.

Achieving consensus among Kurdish parties and personalities was also a monumental task. The notion of independence had broad appeal to Kurds, as demonstrated by overwhelming support for the informal referendum in January 2005. However, the Kurds were deeply divided over process and timing. Advocates of the referendum worried about voter turnout, since participation was critical to success.

The PUK supported the referendum, albeit unenthusiastically. Less significant rivals opposed the vote. For example, Rebwar Khudar of Jamaa Islamiya, an opposition party, said the referendum was premature. According to Khudar, "Before the referendum, we must put our Kurdish internal affairs in order and hold a real dialogue with our neighbouring countries so they will support us."[14] Rabun Maroof, a member of the Kurdish Parliament and spokesman for the "No for Now" campaign, supported an independent Kurdish state but said that this was not the time. "Everyone knows that without the support of the international community, and especially the United States, it's impossible to establish an independent country here."[15]

In addition, Gorran and the Kurdistan Islamic Group opposed a precipitous referendum. They feared that a bid for Kurdish independence would strengthen Barzani and the KDP. Rather than a popular consultation, they wanted the vote to occur within the Kurdistan National Assembly, where they held greater sway. Gorran refused to join the KDP-led referendum committee, demanding a role for parliament. "The Iraqi Kurds are badly fragmented," said the former US Ambassador to Iraq, Ryan Crocker.[16]

On 7 June, Masoud held a meeting with political figures and parties in Kurdistan. They agreed to hold the independence referendum on 25 September. Masoud announced on Twitter: "I am pleased to announce that the date for the independence referendum has been set for Monday, September 25, 2017."[17]

Kurdistan elections for president and parliament would be held soon after the referendum. They were planned for 6 November 2017. The KDP expected that the referendum would instill nationalist fervor that would carry over to the elections, giving it an advantage. Some Kurds, however, doubted Masoud's sincerity, believing the referendum was a device to help him stay in power four years after his mandate had expired.

Others viewed the referendum as a bargaining chip. They believed that the KDP was using it to gain leverage over contentious issues with Baghdad, such as oil exports, budget payments and control of disputed territories. By scheduling the referendum in advance of Iraq's national elections in April 2018, the referendum would put pressure on Baghdad.

Relations between the KRG and Baghdad had worsened. The KRG wanted Baghdad to resume payments to the KRG, covering its share of the national budget. Baghdad had stopped making payments to the KRG to punish it for moving ahead with international oil sales. Bayan Sami Abdul Rahman, the KRG's representative to the United States, hoped that the referendum would kick-start serious negotiations. According to Bayan, Kurdistan would seek a relationship with Baghdad in which they are "each other's biggest trade partner, [with] agreements on security, banking, finance, currencies, economic trade", and many other issues such as water, boundaries, debt and asset allocation. The most difficult issues involved the sharing of oil revenues, as well as resolution of disputed territories.[18]

Abadi sent mixed signals. On one hand, he indicated respect for the right of Kurds to vote for independence, but on the other he discouraged them from acting because it was not the right time. On other occasions he took a harder line, especially upon returning from visits to Tehran, when Abadi expressed strong opposition to a referendum that he called "illegal." Abadi was Tehran's hand-picked candidate for prime minister and he needed its support to stay in power.

Kirkuk's governor, Najmaldin Karim, was singled out for criticism. Baghdad views Kirkuk governorate, with its diverse population, as an integral part of Iraq, but Kurds view it as "Kurdistan's Jerusalem." Kirkuk not only has emotional significance; it has commercial value too. The Kirkuk oil fields produce at least 435,000 barrels per day, about 10 percent of Iraq's total production. With Kirkuk, Iraqi Kurdistan would have the economic means to support statehood. Karim was an adamant proponent of including Kirkuk and other disputed territories in the referendum.

Abadi criticized Karim and Masoud for their position on independence and sent a motion to Iraq's parliament requesting Karim's removal as governor after the Kirkuk provincial assembly voted to participate in the referendum. Ahmad al-Kinani, a member of parliament from the Maliki's State of Law Coalition, said: "We voted to sack the Governor of Kirkuk because he is violating the constitution and working against the central government to push his constituents towards separation."[19] Karim refused to step down from his post and the tense relations were exacerbated when he raised the Kurdistan flag alongside the Iraqi one above his office in Kirkuk.

The Iraqi parliament rejected the KRG's proposed referendum, authorizing Abadi to take measures against it. The parliament adopted a resolution, calling the referendum a "threat" to the unity of Iraq. It voted to commit "all relevant authorities to take every measure to cancel it." The resolution affirmed, "The Iraqi government will be responsible for preserving the unity of Iraq, taking all measures and decisions that include the protection of the unity of Iraq" and called for "serious negotiations to solve outstanding issues based on the constitution and the laws in place."[20] In response to a request from the Iraqi parliament, the Iraqi Supreme Court ordered the KRG to suspend the referendum until its constitutionality could be assessed.

The KRG enjoyed warm relations with Washington under successive presidents, including Obama. Masoud hoped the US would defend Iraqi Kurdistan in the event of an attack or, at the very least, use its influence to mediate. Iraqi Kurds had been visiting Washington for decades, cultivating support. Karim, who is from Maryland, was an effective advocate for the Kurdish cause. Barham Salih was based in Washington as the PUK representative and he too was an effective advocate. Qubad Talabani cultivated friends for Kurdistan when he served as the KRG's Representative to the United States between 2006 and 2012. He and Iraq's ambassador to the US organized a memorial each year on the anniversary of the Halabja chemical weapons attack. The Kurdish Issues Caucus educated Members of Congress and mobilized action on Capitol Hill. Kurdish hospitality laid the foundation for good relations. Kurds built a relationship with officials from the US Department of Defense and many US officers spent time in Iraqi Kurdistan. Moreover, the KRG learned the ways of Washington, spending $1.5 million on lobbying firms between 2014 and 2017.[21]

United States officials have been debating the future of Iraq since the 1990s. The Kurds believed that their relationship with US officials was based on strategic interests, and that Kurds were a force for democratization in the region. Kurds and Americans have shared values, based on principles of pluralism and human rights. The relationship was also based on common security interests. More than 5,000 US Special Forces and support personnel were based in Iraqi Kurdistan. Oil companies like Chevron and ExxonMobil have a stake in exploration and production of Kurdistan's vast oil reserves.

As the Kurds debated independence, Washington provided lip service to their "legitimate aspirations." However, the US discouraged the Kurds from actually holding a referendum. "If this referendum is conducted, it is highly unlikely that there will be negotiations with Baghdad, and the above international offer of support for negotiations will be foreclosed."[22]

Brett McGurk was the chief architect of US policy in the region. He was appointed by President Obama as Special Presidential Envoy for the Global Coalition to Counter ISIS at the US Department of State in 2015. Previously, McGurk had been nominated by Obama as Ambassador to Iraq in 2012. However, a series of emails surfaced about an affair McGurk was having with a Baghdad-based journalist. It was also alleged that McGurk may have shared sensitive information exclusively with his reporter girl-friend. Though McGurk had to withdraw his name as nominee to become ambassador, he avoided censure and his security clearances remained valid.

McGurk kept his job when Donald J. Trump became president in January 2017. There was nobody else with his qualifications for the position. He had a reputation of supporting the Kurds. As the most senior US official working on security issues in the region, he was a regular visitor to Baghdad and Erbil, and Kurds hoped he would use his influence to sway Washington in support of their cause.

The State Department said it presented an "alternative" to Masoud in an attempt to persuade him to postpone the referendum. However, Masoud said no alternative was actually offered. A growing credibility gap affected US–KRG relations, as well as relations between the KRG and Baghdad. Bayan pointed out that the Iraqi government had violated 55 out of 144 articles in the Iraqi constitution. According to Bayan, "Staying in Iraq offers only a never-ending vista of civil war and uncertainty."[23] Masoud declared an end to the "partnership" with Iraq. Kurds would no longer accept living in a "theocratic, sectarian state." He said, "From now on, Kurdistan will be a neighbor of Iraq, but not part of it."[24]

McGurk viewed Kurdish issues through a security lens in which destroying ISIS was the overarching goal. Coalition spokesperson Colonel Ryan Dillon indicated, "The Combined Joint Task Force priority remains the defeat of ISIS in Syria and Iraq. The current discussions about the Kurdish referendum have been a distraction in the pursuit of a common goal."[25] The KRG decided to go ahead with the referendum, rebuffing McGurk's entreaties.

At the same time, the KRG took other steps to assuage critics of the referendum. They sought assistance from the international community to build the capacity of the Kurdistan Independent High Electoral Commission (KIHEC), so that the design and conduct of the referendum met and indeed surpassed international standards. It invited monitoring by the international community during the pre-election period, on election day and during vote-counting. Masoud offered to count votes in Kirkuk and other disputed territories on district and sub-district levels so that the tally would more accurately reflect the wishes of the local population. If specific sub-districts voted against the referendum, they could opt out when it came to declaring independence.

The day after his Twitter announcement, Masoud instructed the KIHEC to make preparations for the referendum. The KIHEC rushed to finalize procedures for the ballot, on 25 September, as well as presidential and parliamentary elections in November. Though the Kurdistan National Assembly had not met in several years, the KIHEC called for it to be reconvened to reinforce the legality of the referendum and elections. Masoud resisted the mounting pressure, showing no signs of regret; self-doubt was not in his character. Moreover, it would cause him to lose face with the Kurdish electorate and jeopardize the KDP's prospects in elections.

Kurds and friends of Kurdistan rallied around the world. The largest gathering in Europe was held in Cologne on 26 August 2017, where about 20,000 people attended. Kurds rallied across the United States in Michigan, Tennessee and in New York at the Dag Hammarskjold Plaza across from the United Nations. Kurds in traditional clothing joined arms and danced rhythmically in a circle while bystanders waved the Kurdistan flag. Speakers used a bullhorn to address the crowd. Bayan tweeted, "Join the Kurdistan referendum rally in Washington, DC, this Sunday […] Live Kurdish music, flags, and fanfare." Rallies were a celebration of the right to self-determination and imminent independence. The largest rally was at the Washington Monument in DC.

Kurds also rallied across Iraqi Kurdistan. About 20,000 Kurds gathered in Zakho on the Turkish border; Barzani addressed the crowd, vowing that nothing would stand in the way of their right to independence. Other rallies were held in Duhok and Erbil. The "No for Now" movement, led by some PUK and Gorran personalities, called a meeting in Suleimani, which was sparsely attended.

Kurds were joined by old friends who had supported their independence drive from the beginning: former US ambassador Peter Galbraith, former French foreign minister Bernard Kouchner, the French scholar and author Bernard-Henri Lévy and the constitutional expert Brendan O'Leary joined the festivities in Erbil. Their encouragement and counsel had brought Kurdistan to the cusp of independence. As Kurds prepared to vote, the outcome of the referendum was predictable. However, its repercussions were unknown.

Part III

Treachery

8 THE REFERENDUM

"Do you want the Kurdistan Region and Kurdistani areas outside of the [Kurdistan] Region to become an independent country?"

REFERENDUM BALLOT[1]

Intense Pressure

The United States strongly discouraged Masoud Barzani from proceeding with the referendum. US Secretary of Defense James Mattis visited Kurdistan about a month before the vote. According to Qubad Talabani, Mattis admonished the Kurds and encouraged them to postpone. Mattis was not fundamentally opposed to the exercise of self-determination by the Kurds but warned that the timing was not right. He wanted the Kurds to focus on ISIS, to help finish the job of destroying the terror group, then consider Kurdistan's political future.

According to Qubad, "Mattis told us we were in the best position ever. Everybody loves you," Mattis assured the Kurdish leadership. "We'll support you, but the timing has to be right."[2] In the middle of the meeting, Qubad passed a note to Masoud Barzani about establishing a team. The KRG had done almost no planning to follow up the referendum. Planning was a slippery slope. It would identify obstacles, and the referendum's proponents did not want anything to stand in the way.

The KRG was still recovering from the perfect storm of problems it had faced in 2014. It was $28 billion in debt, and unable to meet its payroll and other obligations. The ISF were far superior to the Peshmerga, fortified by sophisticated US weapons. Brett McGurk, the Presidential Special Envoy for the anti-ISIL Coalition, urged patience. By 2020, the KRG could be pumping one million barrels of oil a day, putting it in a stronger position and making it more economically viable.

After the Mattis meeting, Qubad discussed all the issues with McGurk, US Ambassador to Iraq Douglas Silliman and Fuad Hussein,

Presient Barzani's Chief of Staff. They discussed the details of a deal with Baghdad, and America's mediation role. Qubad explained, "We would get certain things up front within a certain time frame—[Article] 140, oil and gas, currency issues, control of the airport." If the KRG agreed to postpone the referendum, the US would mediate the terms and timing of an agreement with Baghdad on the final status of Iraqi Kurdistan.

They went back and forth drafting a letter for Secretary of State Rex W. Tillerson, outlining the US position on Kurdistan in the future. According to Qubad, "It was not a bad deal. I knew the US could not give a rock-solid guarantee for independence. But this was as close as we'd ever get." The PUK leadership agreed that the letter was better than a referendum and they should try to convince Masoud. According to Qubad, "The nearer we got [to the date of the referendum], the more politicized the whole thing became and the more it was about political legacy."

Concessions were not entirely one-sided, as US officials pushed Abadi to let the Kurds control oil exploration and production from the fields in Iraqi Kurdistan. They urged Abadi to resume paying the KRG's 17 percent share of the national budget, as required in the constitution.[3] Iraq would immediately take control of the K1 military base, a former US airfield on the outskirts of Kirkuk. The compromise would be a win–win, diffusing conflict and allowing both sides to claim victory. Abadi went to Ayatollah Ali al-Sistani to explain the deal, in the hope of getting his help in neutralizing opposition from other Shi'ite parties.[4]

The problem was not with Abadi, however. The KRG was unwilling to accommodate the deal. According to a senior US official, "We gave them a golden ticket." The US would mediate negotiations over two years, blessed by the UN Security Council and UN Secretary General Antonio Guterres. An event at the UN on the occasion of Iraqi Kurdistan's independence would be a "big deal."[5] They assured the Kurds that if negotiations failed because of Baghdad's intransigence, the US would support their declaration of independence.

The US had significant information on how other countries were likely to react. The Iranians were warning of ominous consequences, including military action. According to a senior US official, "We knew what Iran would do." Turkey was strongly opposed. President Recep Tayyip Erdoğan was in touch with Baghdad about closing the airspace over Iraqi Kurdistan, blocking commercial flights, and sealing the border. Masoud wanted Washington's support. Some Kurds, including Najmaldin Karim, were convinced that "the US would come around."[6] Masoud was obstinate.

A senior US official believes that "The Kurds were getting bad advice from former officials" and that "They misread the Trump administration."[7] The Kurds set up a Referendum High Committee to manage the planning of the referendum and its aftermath. Nechirvan, Masrour, Hoshyar Zabari, Khaled Saleh and Qubad met with foreign proponents of the referendum. Everyone was very positive about going forward. According to Qubad, "Peter [Galbraith] was practically foaming at the mouth at the idea of it. 'We can't wait for Kurdish unity to happen. The referendum will force Kurdish unity.'" Qubad felt that "There was something wrong in the room. I was the only PUK person. If this becomes an agenda of a political party, it will fail."[8]

Qubad presented the draft letter sent from Tillerson to Masoud at a meeting of the High Refendum Committee in the Presidential Palace offering an analysis of the deal. Qubad explained, "Masoud didn't like it. He practically bristled." Masoud accused the US of making empty promises and started talking about the 1970s when the US had betrayed his grandfather, Mulla Mustafa Barzani. "Most Kurds were begging Masoud not to do the referendum," explained Qubad. "They were asking us to help convince Masoud not to do this." However, Masoud stuck to the plan.

Qubad recalls, "The closer we got, the more people started to panic about the possible repercussions." Special envoys, ministers and ambassadors visited Kurdistan, urging the KRG to delay. Qubad described it as "the most intense pressure I've ever experienced. The world was warning us about consequences and we were basically saying 'fuck you' to everybody. We were all swept up in the momentum, which was irreversible. Logic didn't apply."[9]

Ode to Joy

Referendum day, 25 September 2017, was a day of celebration. Women wore their finest clothes to polling stations, colorful vests over a gown with an underdress or puffy pants gathered by a traditional woven belt at the waist. Headpieces were ornamented with gemstones, bright beads and gold pieces. Men wore a traditional Kurdish suit with wide baggy trousers, a starched shirt, colorful cumberbund and a woven textile hat with geometric designs. Children accompanied their parents to polling stations, also dressed in their best clothes.

The 1920 Treaty of Sèvres had promised Kurds a referendum on independence, but the ballot was never held. A century of betrayal and disappointment had ensued. The 2017 referendum was the long-awaited opportunity for Kurds to democratically determine their future. Billboards across Kurdistan encouraged Kurds to vote, and the Kurds celebrated their right to self-determination. Those who had voted had their index finger marked with purple ink. They raised their stained fingers in proud display. The referendum was more than a political statement: it affirmed Kurdish identity and democratic rights.

Masoud was concerned not about the outcome, but about the turnout. Voter participation of less than 70 percent would undermine the referendum's credibility. Surpassing this threshold would give the referendum a critical mass of participation and enhance its legitimacy. Of 4,581,255 eligible voters, 3,305,925 cast ballots—about 72 percent.[10] The simple act of voting was a resounding statement of Kurdish identity. Fewer than 50 percent voted in Catalonia's independence referendum a week later on 1 October 2017, but unlike the Catalans, Kurdistanis flocked to the polling stations.

Voters were asked a simple question: "Do you want the Kurdistan Region and Kurdistani areas outside of the [Kurdistan] Region to become an independent country?" Ballots were written in Kurdish, Arabic, Turkmen and Assyrian. A total of 92.73 percent voted "Yes."[11]

Kurdistan's Independent High Elections and Referendum Commission (IHERC) performed ably, organizing the tally on a short schedule with scant financial resources. About 2,065 polling stations were open on 25 September. Kurdish political parties sent monitors to polling stations, and international observers also monitored the referendum. Polling stations were set up in cities across the United States and Europe so that the Diaspora could vote, and voting was also held in the disputed territories of Kirkuk, Makhmour, Khanaqin and Sinjar, as the Peshmerga had established control over these cities after the defeat of ISIS. Voting in disputed territories was de facto recognition of their future as part of Kurdistan.

After the result was declared, Masoud was jubilant. He gave a raucous victory speech in Erbil.

You, the people of Kurdistan, you did not allow your will to be broken, and now, after your yes-vote that was a yes for independence and no to Anfal, chemical attacks and another genocide, we have entered a new stage.[12]

Barzani affirmed that an independent Kurdistan would be democratic, with a federal system where the rights of all ethnic and religious groups would be upheld.

Beyond vindicating Barzani's lifelong pursuit of independence, the vote was widely seen as consolidating the KDP's grip on power and giving it an advantage in Iraqi Kurdistan's upcoming parliamentary and presidential elections, scheduled for 1 November. Barzani's future role in Kurdistan's government was uncertain. He had already served as president for 12 years, four years more than allowed by the Presidency Law. With such a resounding victory in the referendum, Barzani would seize the momentum and start negotiations with Baghdad on the terms of Kurdistan's separation. The Kurdish opposition feared that Barzani might try to amend the Presidency Law and run for another four-year term. According to a senior US official, "Barzani made bad decisions."[13]

The referendum marked a bittersweet moment for the PUK and members of the Talabani family. As Kurds went to the polls, Jalal Talabani lay in a hospital bed in Berlin, his life slipping away. The PUK announced that Mam Jalal died a week after the referendum on 3 October 2017. It was a tragic irony that Jalal, who had spent his life struggling for Kurdish rights, was unable to participate. While in a coma he was told about the referendum result, but did not show any reaction to the news.

If Talabani had been well he would have gleefully cast his ballot at a polling station in Suleimani. Kurds imagined him smiling for the cameras, jubilantly inserting his vote and encouraging Kurds to persevere in their freedom struggle. Members of the Talabani family were wobbly in their support for the referendum, however. The issue was not independence itself, but the timing. Hero Talabani, Jalal's wife, and Bafel, their older son, were wary of potential repercussions. The Talabani family had close personal, political and commercial ties with Iran, which strongly opposed independence for Iraqi Kurdistan. Up to 12 million Kurds live in Iran, and independence for Iraqi Kurdistan would inspire them to seek the same thing.

Baghdad's Response

Prime Minister Heider al-Abadi had urged Barzani to postpone the referendum. Iraqi nationalism was strong after the Battle for Mosul, and Abadi was reaping a popular reward for defeating ISIS. As a result, he had no choice but to oppose the referendum; had he condoned it, the Iraqi parliament would have passed a no-confidence motion causing the collapse of the Dawa Party-led coalition government. Iran would also have withdrawn its support, causing the Badr Organization and other Iranian-backed Shi'ite parties to break with Abadi.

Abadi addressed the nation on the eve of the referendum. Warning of dire consequences, he vowed never to accept the break-up of Iraq. "This is an unconstitutional decision against the social fabric of our citizens. We will not recognize the referendum, nor its results." He vowed to take all necessary measures, including the use of force, to prevent a "fight between Iraqi citizens." He warned, "We will impose Iraq's rule in all districts of the region with the force of the constitution."[14]

While intimating the use of force, Abadi pledged to resolve the crisis through negotiations. He vowed that the ISF would never fire on Iraqi citizens of Kurdish origin. Abadi reiterated that he wanted to avoid "fighting among the people of the country."[15] At times confrontational and at other times conciliatory, Abadi was clearly unsure about the right course of action.

In the immediate aftermath of the ballot, Masoud reached out to Abadi and proposed a political dialogue. The KRG offered to send a senior delegation to Baghdad for discussions, but the offer was rebuffed. Abadi could not countenance a discussion about independence. He refused to negotiate unless the Kurds annulled the referendum. In a speech to parliament on 26 September, Abadi insisted that he would "never have a dialogue" about the referendum's outcome. He told parliament, "If [the KRG] wants to start talks, they must cancel the referendum and its outcome."[16] He warned the Kurds of "consequences," sanctions, international isolation and possible military intervention.

Abadi was talking tough but actually wanted a compromise to avoid bloodshed and keep Iraq from falling apart. He focused on Kirkuk and disputed territories, proposing "joint administration." To Abadi, joint administration was not about power-sharing but was a way to assert Baghdad's authority. Iran was pushing him to take a hard line. Parliament Speaker Salim al-Jabouri warned, "We will take follow-up steps to protect the unity of the country and the interests of every citizen living in a unified Iraq."[17] At Jabouri's instigation, parliament voted to approve a 13-point resolution giving Abadi authority to deploy troops. Abadi announced a series of punitive measures against the KRG, which were intended to ratchet up the pressure on Barzani.

First Abadi focused on isolating Iraqi Kurdistan by initiating a ban on international flights to Erbil and Suleimani. Iraq's Civil Aviation Authority notified foreign airlines that it would cancel permits to land and take off from Kurdistan's airports. At least six airlines—three Turkish companies, Lebanon's Middle East Airlines, Egypt Air and Royal Jordanian Airlines—took immediate steps to cancel regularly scheduled flights. Some VIP visitors were almost stranded; Galbraith scrambled to rebook his outbound ticket and got a seat on one of the last flights before the ban took effect. The KRG's Minister for Transportation and Communications, Mawlud Murad, objected to the shutdown, calling it "political and illegal."[18] He argued that functioning airports were not only important for commerce, they were also critical in the fight against ISIS. The GOI ignored Murad's entreaties.

Turkey and Iran aligned themselves with Baghdad, threatening the Kurds over the vote. Both have restive Kurdish populations that were taking inspiration from Iraqi Kurdistan's push for independence. Masoud tried to mollify Kurdistan's neighbors by making clear that the KRG harbored no plan for a greater Kurdistan incorporating the Kurds of Turkey, Syria, Iraq and Iran, and extolled Iraqi Kurdistan as a force for moderation among Kurds in the region.

In a further effort to isolate Iraqi Kurdistan, Baghdad demanded that the KRG relinquish international border posts that had been under its control since 1991. Customs and transit fees collected at border posts represent an important source of revenue, so losing them would further cripple the KRG's finances.

Border crossings at Fish Khabur, Parviz Khan, Tamarchin, Haji Omran and Bashmagh were bustling hubs of intra-regional trade between Iran and Iraqi Kurdistan. Fifty percent of Iran's trade with Iraq went through Parviz Khan. Intra-regional trade between Turkey and Iraqi Kurdistan was also extensive, with Turkish consumer goods sold at retail establishments across the region. Turkish construction and engineering firms profited from building airports, roads, hospitals and other public infrastructure. Ibrahim Khalil was the busiest border crossing between Turkey and Iraqi Kurdistan, with more than $6 billion in goods passing through each year.[19]

Iran and the Popular Mobilization Units (called Hashd al-Shaabi or Hashd) were especially keen to control Fish Khabur, which connected Iran to its allies in Syria. Iran carefully orchestrated its response to the referendum with Baghdad, and President Hassan Rouhani warned about "chaos in the region."[20] Iran's Foreign Minister announced, "At the request of Iraq, we have closed the airspace and ground borders with the Kurdistan Regional Government."[21]

The Kirkuk–Ceyhan pipeline, which is critical for Turkey's energy supplies, also traverses Fish Khabur. Turkey had competing commercial and security interests, and it wanted to keep Fish Khabur open to maintain oil supplies needed for its economic growth; Kurdistan exported 550,000 barrels per day to Ceyhan. Erdoğan threatened to close the pipeline, thereby depriving the KRG of its primary revenue source. According to Erdoğan, "We have the tap. The moment we close the tap, then it's done."[22] Erdoğan threatened to "starve" the KRG. [23]

Turkey was a leading member of the G-20 and an economic powerhouse regionally and worldwide. The bottleneck at border gates, such as Ibrahim Khalil, negatively affected Turkish exports to Iraq and the greater Middle East. Enterprising Turkish truck drivers found alternate routes for delivering goods to Iraq via Tal Afar, where Turkmen were the majority. Despite its threats, Turkey never closed the pipeline. The KRG enjoyed an uninterrupted revenue stream from the sale of Kurdish oil transported via Turkey to international markets. Nor did Turkey seal the Ibrahim Khalil border crossing. Erdoğan proved to be a pragmatist, despite his bluster and duplicity.

Security concerns proved more compelling. Turkey's Foreign Ministry promised to apply "all measures" allowed under international law should the referendum threaten Turkey's national security. Erdoğan warned that Kurdistan would pay "a price" in the event of a yes vote. Turkey already had military bases in Iraqi Kurdistan, at Dubardan and Bashiqa north of Mosul, and now it massed troops on the Turkish side of the border, threatening to invade and establish a buffer inside Kurdistan. The buffer could extend all the way to Kirkuk, capturing the city's oil and protecting Iraqi Turkmen. Erdoğan cautioned, "We may enter at night without warning."[24] To reinforce his warning, Turkey and Iraq conducted joint maneuvers on the Turkish side of its border with Iraq.

Turkey also threatened to close the Fish Khabur border crossing in order to prevent the Syrian Kurds from coordinating with the PKK. Syrian Kurds were establishing a contiguous territory known as Rojava along the Syrian border with Turkey, encompassing the provinces of Jazeera, Kobani and al-Hasakah. The far east of Rojava was contiguous with Iraqi Kurdistan. The PKK maintained its headquarters in the remote and rugged Qandil Mountains of Iraqi Kurdistan. Turkish officials insisted that Syrian Kurds comprising the Democratic Union Party (PYD) and its armed wing, the

People's Protection Units (YPG), were a branch of the PKK. However, Turkey's position did not align with US policy. While Washington considers the PKK a foreign terrorist organization (FTO), neither the PYD nor the YPG is on the US list of FTOs.

The KRG did not overreact to the closing of border crossings but chose to play a long game. Nechirvan Barzani said he had "no problem" with Baghdad's embargo, anticipating that closing the border gates would be temporary. Indeed, as we have seen, some were never closed, while other border crossings reopened in late October 2017. Iran normalized all of its border crossings with the KRI by January 2018.

Baghdad imposed additional punitive measures, slapping sanctions on Kurdish banks and halting foreign currency transfers to the KRI. Iraq's central bank informed the KRG that it would no longer sell dollars to four leading Kurdish banks and would stop all foreign currency transfers to the region. Blocking dollar-denominated transactions, especially for oil sales, could cripple Iraqi Kurdistan's economy. It was impossible to trade internationally using the Iraqi dinar, which was not accepted outside the country.

Jabouri threatened legal action against Kurdish members of the federal parliament who had taken part in the referendum, insisting that the referendum was unconstitutional and those who voted had broken the law. The Iraqi parliament compiled a list of Kurdish deputies who voted in the referendum as a step towards their censure and impeachment.

Abadi demanded that the Peshmerga be brought under federal control. Imposing control over the Peshmerga was part of a broader effort to delegitimize and undermine the KRG's institutions. Peshmerga were a symbol of Kurdistan's national struggle and identity. "The illegal referendum is over, its results invalid and belongs in the past," Abadi wrote on Twitter. "We call for dialogue based on Iraq's national constitution."[25]

The newly elected Trump administration expressed its deep disappointment with Barzani's decision to go ahead with the referendum. Former US Ambassador to Iraq Stuart Jones said,

There is no ambiguity on what the US position was on this issue. The United States has been telling the Kurds and telling [Kurdish President] Masoud [Barzani], and telling Masrour [Barzani] since last spring not to proceed. This would be not good for Kurdistan, not good for Iraq, and would play into the hands of the hard-liners and the hands of the Iranians.[26]

McGurk took Barzani's decision personally. According to Bayan Sami Abdul Rahman, the KRG's representative to the US, McGurk wanted to punish the Kurds for expressing their legitimate democratic aspirations. Bayan said, "We expected opposition. We thought that would be the pattern. Where we were surprised is the hostility to the referendum, the disrespect, the attempt to belittle the referendum."[27] The Trump administration tried to assuage hurt feelings through conciliatory yet hollow statements. A State Department spokeswoman said, "The United States' historic relationship with the people of the Iraqi Kurdistan Region will not change in light of today's nonbinding referendum, but we believe this step will increase instability and hardships for the Kurdistan region and its people."[28]

The US position was echoed by UN Secretary General Antonio Guterres, who expressed concern about the "potentially destabilizing effects" of the referendum. Guterres affirmed the UN's support for "the sovereignty, territorial integrity, and unity of Iraq." At the same time, he called for a "structured dialogue and constructive compromise" between Baghdad and Kurdish leaders and offered the UN's offices to mediate talks.[29]

Some countries were agnostic on the referendum. Putin and Erdoğan spoke by phone on 25 September. They agreed that the vote would strain the territorial integrity of both Iraq and Syria. However, the Kremlin did not issue a public statement directly criticizing the referendum. Putin and Rouhani held a separate call; the Kremlin provided notes about the conversation, which did not mention the referendum.

The KRG and Rosneft, Russia's oil and gas giant, finalized plans for a natural gas pipeline to Turkey just a week before the referendum. The pipeline would have the capacity to transport 30 billion cubic meters of gas per year, more than Kurdistan's current output and over half of Turkey's annual demand. Barzani believed that shared interests in the energy sector would shape the international community's view towards independence. Israel was also a buyer of Kurdistan's oil, and while most countries vocally opposed independence, Israel was the only one to make a public statement supporting the referendum.

Masoud's Demise

Masoud swiftly found that his allies had abandoned him and his enemies were united against him. He had overestimated the KRG's political influence and military capacity, and was accused of a strategic miscalculation for insisting on the referendum. Timing was the primary concern of many Kurds. The optimum moment for the referendum would have been before the Battle for Mosul. The KRG's persuasive power had been greatest when Peshmerga were needed on the front lines, fighting ISIS.

Masoud was blamed for failing to consult and lacking transparency. He knew that Kurdistan could not achieve independence without Washington's backing; US officials had offered to mediate between the KRG and Baghdad if the KRG only postponed the vote. Both the Obama and Trump administrations clearly stated their opposition to the referendum. Masoud naively believed that the US would adjust its policy once the Kurds had clearly committed to independence.

He also failed to bring Baghdad on board. The establishment of two committees to work out the details of separation had been a positive development. However, the committees existed in name only. Their work was overtaken by the announcement of a date for the referendum. The referendum pre-judged the outcome of talks between the KRG and Baghdad, undermining the possibility of compromise.

Turkey and Iran might well have opposed the referendum under any circumstances. But failing to bring them on board was disastrous. Closing the airspace and threatening to restrict the borders isolated the KRI and limited Masoud's room to maneuver. Turkey and Iran opposed independence from the outset, for fear that their own Kurdish populations would seek a similar path. At a minimum, neutrality was needed. Given the extensive economic ties between Turkey and the KRG, a deal could have been made to mollify Turkey's opposition. In retrospect, Masrour believes that

> Turkey has been a critical partner for the KRG. Economically it's been the corridor between Kurdistan and the rest of the world. Throughout the turbulence around the referendum Turkey never sealed its borders, and that helped prevent a humanitarian crisis in Kurdistan. It was a very important gesture. Sure, there are always tensions, ups and downs, in relations, but let's look at the bright future we have together.[30]

The dearth of dialogue between Kurdish factions was another part of the problem. While high-ranking PUK members were part of the High Referendum Council, the PUK and Gorran never assumed ownership of the KDP-led process. They were convinced that the referendum was simply a device for Masoud to enhance his position and gain an upper hand in

Kurdistan's elections. Widespread allegations of corruption against the Barzani family compromised the KRG's integrity while Masoud's autocratic tendencies also compromised his credibility. Opposition parties criticized him for extending his term as president twice. They objected to the KDP's patronage system, as well as efforts to mask Barzani business dealings from public scrutiny. Preventing the Assembly's Speaker, a Gorran member, from entering Erbil was further evidence of autocracy.

Long knives came out for Masoud after the referendum and Gorran was the first to call for him to resign. They insisted that the KRG "must be dissolved" and called for a "national salvation government." Gorran stated, "[The KDP] refused to listen to our demands and those of Baghdad," leaving the Kurdish region "with another terrible crisis." According to Gorran, "What has happened does not demonstrate the failure of our people and the Kurdish nation, rather it is the defeat of the authority and officials."[31] "Our people have lost many of their achievements which they gained shedding their blood. Peshmerga lost their grandeur. We lost many friendly countries. The reason for all of this is due to the failures of the party in power."[32]

Kurdistan's political parties engaged in a heated war of words. Elements within the PUK castigated the KRG for insisting on the referendum and for official corruption. In response, Masoud accused "people from a certain political party" of "high treason" for selling out Kurdistan's national aspirations.[33]

Iraqi politicians also piled on the pressure. Former deputy prime minister of Iraq and energy minister Hussain al-Shahristani said Masoud should accept responsibility for the consequences of the independence referendum and resign. The inclusion of Kirkuk and other disputed areas in the referendum enraged Baghdad, which accused the KRG of a land grab. Baghdad insisted on protecting Arab minorities who lived in ethnically mixed regions. But Baghdad itself was guilty of a land grab. It faced a financial crisis and wanted greater access to Kirkuk's oil.

Many Kurds were bitterly disappointed that their dream of independence had collapsed in such dramatic fashion. Some Kurds grew increasingly convinced that their national interests might be better served if Masoud stepped down. His resignation would facilitate negotiations with Baghdad over a modus vivendi.

Baghdad's rejection of the referendum does not erase the fact that 92.7 percent of voters, more than three million people, voted for independence. The KRG may have bungled the roll-out and failed on public diplomacy,

1 Araz Talabani and Qasem Soleimani at Jalal Talabani's graveside

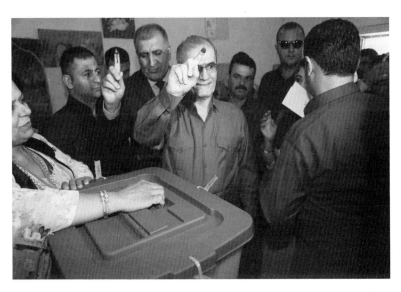

2 Governor Karim on Election Day

3   Brett McGurk and Masoud Barzani meet in Erbil in July 2017

4   Iranian Kurds demonstrate in support of the Kobani people

5 Iranian Kurds march in support of an independence vote in Northern Iraq

6 Children flashing a Turkish nationalist sign and dragging the Kurdish flag

7   Bafel Talabani and Haider al-Abadi

8   Lahur Talabani and Qais al-Khazali in Baghdad at Jalal Talabani's memorial service

9 General Qasem Soleimani at his father's memorial ceremony

10 Presidents Rouhani, Erdoğan and Putin meeting in Ankara

11   Grey Wolf soldiers in front of Governor Karim's office. The Grey Wolves are part of a Turkish ultra-nationalist organization and are frequently described as the MHP's paramilitary or militant wing.

12 Shi'ites and Turkmen display the Iraqi flag, taunting Kurds fleeing Kirkuk after the city was seized by pro-Baghdad forces in October 2017

13   Hadi Ameri and Kata'ib Hezbollah leader Abu Mahdi al-Muhandis (a wanted terrorist) removing the Kurdish flag and raising Iraq flag in front of the Governor's office but the referendum reflected the overwhelming support of Kurds for independence.

Masoud had significant accomplishments, which cannot be obscured by post-referendum problems. Kurdistan's economy was doing well until the collapse of world oil prices, an event beyond Masoud's control. He successfully defended Kurdistan from ISIS, halting its advance and reclaiming territories. He avoided violent conflict with Iraq over disputed territories, at least until 16 October 2017 when the ISF and Iranian-backed militias attacked Kirkuk.

9 KIRKUK CRISIS

"[They] were not coming to oust him or even to arrest him. They were coming to kill him."

PETER W. GALBRAITH[1]

Kurdish Control

The Kurds had taken control of Kirkuk as Saddam's regime collapsed in 2003. The Bush administration asked the Peshmerga to withdraw, promising a referendum to determine Kirkuk's status. The governorate could either join the Kurdistan Region of Iraq (KRI) with special autonomy status, or it could revert to the central government's control. Power-sharing between Iraq and the KRG was also explored. Washington was not wedded to an outcome; its priority was to prevent violence and strengthen the rule of law. Article 140 of the 2005 constitution required a referendum on Kirkuk's status by 31 December 2007, but the referendum was delayed twice and never held.

Najmaldin Karim was not a partisan or a dogmatic party man. As a Kurdish nationalist, Karim accepted Iraqi Kurdistan as a region in Iraq—if Iraq truly became a federal, democratic republic. As governor, Karim did not demand immediate implementation of Article 140. Rushing to hold a referendum would be divisive and could lead to violence. Believing that "the rising tide lifts all boats," he focused on providing services to all of Kirkuk's residents as a way to foster a sense of community among Kurds, Arabs, Turkmen and others. Karim gained more than 150,000 votes from a broad cross-section of Kirkukis in the national elections of 2014. For every school built in Kurdish neighborhoods, he insisted that one would be built in Arab, Turkmen and Christian neighborhoods as well. Patient and conciliatory, Karim recognized that confidence-building is a process.

The Kurds ended up in full control of Kirkuk after ISIS attacked in 2014. Major General Mohammed Khalaf al-Fahdawi, commander of the ISF's

Twelfth Division, visited Karim on 10 June 2014. ISIS had just taken Mosul, and Fahdawi wanted to assure Karim that the ISF would defend Kirkuk. Fahdawi returned 24 hours later in a panic. He and other ISF commanders had abandoned their troops to save themselves. Fahdawi asked Karim for civilian clothes and safe passage to Baghdad. Unlike the ISF, the Peshmerga fought on to prevent ISIS from entering the city.

Iraq was on the verge of fragmenting. With ISIS occupying about a third of the country, Iraq was increasingly fragile and a borderline failed state. When Karim raised the Kurdistan flag over the governor's office and other official buildings in March 2017, the Iraqi parliament criticized him for "an illegal decision." Karim gave legislators a lesson on Iraq's constitution, which permits flying the Kurdistan flag at a lesser or equal height to the Iraqi flag. Prime Minister Heider al-Abadi and the Iraqi parliament condemned Karim, angling for his removal, but Karim was unfazed, replying that it was "an honor for me" to be labeled a Kurdish nationalist.[2]

Disunity

Karim was outspoken, a lightning rod for controversy and became a marked man in Baghdad for advocating Kurdish national rights. Iranian-backed militias as well as rival Kurdish politicians wanted to get rid of him.

On 26 May 2017, the US-led coalition sent a written warning to the PUK and KDP intelligence agencies. A violent and radical Shi'ite militia group, Asa'ib Ahl al-Haq, had deployed an assassination team to kill Karim. Its ruthless commander, Qais Khazali, was notorious for planning the 2007 execution of four US soldiers in Karbala. The CIA warned that other Iranian-backed militias, including the Badr Organization led by Abu Mahdi al-Muhandis, were also planning "unspecified sabotage operations." Both Khazali and Muhandis are "bad actors" on the terrorist watch list of the United States.[3]

When Karim visited Washington in July 2017, he met Brett McGurk and members of the Iraqi National Security Council at the residence of the Iraqi ambassador to the United States. They had a wide-ranging conversation, covering the situation in Syria as well as Kurdistan's referendum. McGurk tried to persuade Karim to cancel the referendum, or at least postpone it until after Iraqi elections in May 2018 and the formation of a new Iraqi government, which could take several months. McGurk feared that the referendum would discredit Abadi, boosting the prospects of more radical

Shi'ites. According to Sierwan Karim, the governor's son and head of his security detail, "Brett McGurk and my father had a good relationship. My dad always said Brett was a good guy. But what Brett offered was not on par with a referendum for Kurdistan's independence."[4] McGurk asked Karim, "What can we do to get you to delay the referendum?" He offered US support for implementation of Article 140, but was vague on timing and terms. Karim, however, was not interested in McGurk's proposal. The time to implement Article 140 had passed. The crisis could have been avoided if Baghdad had implemented federalism and fulfilled its constitutional commitments. Masrour Barzani, Chancellor of the Kurdistan Region Security Council (KRSC), believes that "The referendum gave them an excuse to use force."[5]

Baghdad's decisions were strongly influenced by Iran. According to a senior US official, "Iran took advantage of the situation in Iraq." It was "opportunistic."[6] With Jalal indisposed from the stroke he suffered in 2012, Tehran consolidated its influence over the Patriotic Union of Kurdistan (PUK). Even incapacitated, Jalal stood in Iran's way. He was the only person who could control his family members and keep the PUK factions together. Unable to walk and barely able to speak, Jalal was still a potent symbol of Kurdish nationalism and resistance to foreign interference.

Domestic politics and economic interests motivated Iran's opposition to Iraqi Kurdistan's independence. About $20 billion of annual cross-border trade went through the Bashmagh border crossing between Iraqi Kurdistan and Iran alone.[7] In addition, at least 50,000 barrels of oil per day were transported by lorry from Iraqi Kurdistan to Iran. Araz Talabani, Jalal's nephew, is a businessman who sought to capitalize on the oil trade. He visited Karim with a former Ukrainian minister and energy tycoon who proposed a pipeline from Kirkuk to Kermanshah in Iran. Karim was open to the idea, but advised that the project needed authorization from the KRG since the pipeline would traverse KRG territory. The pipeline project would also require approval from Baghdad and the Kirkuk Provincial Council. Araz declined to pursue the project based on his strong personal antipathy towards Barzani and the KDP. He gave a full report on discussions with Karim to his Iranian sponsors.[8] "Although Karim was PUK," Masrour explains, "he was not willing to hand over the petrodollars."[9]

Tehran wanted Jalal out of the way. His demise would set back the pro-independence movement and undermine its backers, including Karim. Kurdistan's independence not only threatened Iraqi unity, it also threatened Iran's influence over Iraq, its vassal state, as well as Iran's hegemony in the region. On 10 July 2017, Jalal was taken to Tehran by his son Bafel, his nephew Araz and Qasem Soleimani. With his health deteriorating, Jalal was confined to a wheelchair and unable to speak, and his condition worsened under Iranian care. Upon his return to Suleimani, Jalal's lungs were drained of fluid. He developed advanced pneumonia and was rushed to a hospital in Berlin with multi-organ failure.

Jalal passed away on 3 October 2017, a week after the independence referendum. He was buried three days later in Suleimani, his coffin draped with the Kurdistan flag. Jalal's wife, Hero, and sons, Bafel and Qubad, were present. So were Lahur, Araz and other members of the extended Talabani family. The United States was represented by Ambassador Douglas Silliman, its envoy to Iraq. Foreign Minister Mohammad Javad Zarif also attended the funeral.

Even though Jalal had served as president of Iraq, many Iraqi officials protested the recent independence referendum by refusing to attend. Some walked out when they saw the Kurdistan flag over Jalal's coffin. But the funeral was an occasion for adversaries to come together. According to Masrour, "Mourning ceremonies in Suleimani on October 3 and Baghdad on October 7 gave Iran and the PUK a chance to discuss things and work more closely together.".[10] Iranian and US officials shared a common goal: to prevent Iraqi Kurdistan's independence.

PUK Opposition

Iraqi officials issued an ultimatum to the Talabani family members, demanding that the Kurds hand over the K-1 base, oil fields and areas that the Peshmerga had seized after the ISF fled. They also demanded that the PUK make a clear public statement annulling the results of the referendum. The IRGC General Qais Khazali attended the mourning ceremony in Suleimani and warned, "There will be conflict [if the PUK fails to comply]".[11]

Between 8 and 10 October, Baghdad issued a series of ominous written and video statements about Kirkuk. On the 11th, the ISF commander presented Wasta Rasool, head of PUK forces in Kirkuk with a letter enumerating Baghdad's demands. The letter demanded that the Kurdish authorities:

- hand over control of the K1 base to the ISF;
- remove all Kurdish Security Forces from Kirkuk, including areas taken after the arrival of ISIS;

- relinquish control of all oil fields in the Kirkuk governorate;
- surrender all international border crossings to the Federal authority;
- deliver Najmaldin Karim for arrest.

Abadi spoke to the Iraqi people on television. While extolling his duty to preserve the unity and integrity of Iraq, he vowed that Iraqi forces would not fight the Kurds. "We will not use our army against our people or fight a war against our Kurdish and other citizens."[12]

Despite his assurances, plans were well under way for a military operation against Kirkuk and other disputed territories. According to an Iraqi general, "Iraqi armed forces are advancing to retake the military positions that were taken over during the events of June 2014." Abadi denied that the movements were preparation for an attack. He called it "fake news".[13]

McGurk corroborated Abadi's position, tweeting that Iraqi forces were heading to Anbar to attack ISIS militants near the Syrian border. "Iraqi forces today shifting [en masse] from the Hawija front to west Anbar to liberate Rawa, Qaim and secure Iraq's borders with Syria."[14] He was ill-informed, however. Karim agrees with Masrour that Baghdad used the referendum as a pretext to seize Kurdish-held territory. "Their goal wasn't implementing the constitution but breaking the will of the people of Kurdistan."[15]

The ISF, Federal Police, Iraqi Counter-Terrorism Services (ICTS), PMUs and Iranian "advisors" moved into positions near Tuz Khurmatu, a 45-minute drive from Kirkuk, just 55 miles south, on the morning of 12 October. The ISF were on their way to Hawija, an ISIS stronghold, but they pivoted away from Hawija towards Kirkuk, poised to attack. According to Qubad, "There was panic and complete chaos. Nobody knew what to do."[16]

The PUK contacted Abadi and asked for a 48-hour reprieve, postponing the threat of military action. With McGurk's mediation, Abadi agreed to wait and KDP and PUK leaders agreed to meet in Dokan on 15 October to develop a consensus position.

Bafel Talabani gave a televised address on the afternoon of 12 October, in which he proposed to dissolve the Kurdish-led Kirkuk Provincial Council, remove Governor Karim and enter into negotiations with Baghdad to resolve tensions over the referendum in accordance with the Iraqi constitution. Bafel condemned "the specter of war. A war we do not need, a war we do not want." Kurdistan, he said, was acting against the will of its neighbors and its Iraqi brothers. According to Bafel, "This is not the Mam Jalal way."[17] His cousin, Lahur, criticized the KRG for holding the independence referendum against the advice of countries in the region and of the international community.

Hero Talabani seconded the position of her son Bafel, issuing a statement that questioned the timing of the referendum.

> The phase of the referendum and its results has passed. Let's begin a new phase for the sake of our land and our people, and this could be done in dialogue with Baghdad to solve all the problems between Baghdad and the Region in accordance to the [Iraqi] constitution and its results.[18]

Prime Minister Nechirvan Barzani called Qubad to inquire about his mother's change of heart. Qubad told Nechirvan that he did not have prior knowledge of Hero's statement, and that Hero was ill and did not have the capacity to issue statements on her own. Her sister, Shanaz, had prepared the statement in Hero's name. Qubad angrily confronted Shanaz and accused her of "dirty work."[19] According to Masrour, "Every single member of the Talabani family was involved. They wanted to control the oil from Kirkuk and gain personally."[20]

Qasem Soleimani was the puppeteer, manipulating events. Representatives of the PUK, IRGC and PMU met at Zaba Airport in the Rashad District of Kirkuk Province on 13 October. The Iranians discussed details of the operation to seize Kirkuk, "arrest or kill" Karim, and punish the pro-independence clique, unless there was a breakthrough at the Dokan meeting. On the 14th, Soleimani visited Jalal's grave site in Suleimani and then convened his PUK compatriots at Jalal's home in Dabashan. Soleimani was joined by IRGC Commander Mizgirian from the Quds Force. Hero, Bafel, Lahur, Araz and Qubad all attended. Soleimani indicated the operation would regain everything that Baghdad lost when ISIS attacked in 2014—the Avana and Bai Hassan oil fields, the K1 military base and the Kirkuk airport. He identified PUK positions that would be abandoned and where Shi'ite militias working in tandem with the IRGC would move in. Soleimani affirmed that the Kirkuk operation was supported by Ayatollah Khamenei and Iran's Guardian Council. He thanked Bafel for his public remarks on the 12th, and commended Araz and Lahur. Soleimani told them, "Either give up your positions or we will attack you. You need to distance yourself from the KDP or you will suffer with them."[21]

According to Qubad, there were two sets of negotiations under way. One involved the PUK, McGurk, Silliman and Abadi. The other was between the

PUK, Tehran and the Hashd. A compromise was proposed: the Peshmerga would withdraw from K1 and the Presidential Guard, a predominantly Kurdish unit, would have joint administration of the base with Iraqi forces. Other issues would be addressed after K1. Iran made it clear: "This is your last chance to avoid clashes."[22]

Members of the PUK and KDP politburo met in Dokan outside Suleimani on the morning of 15 October. Notable attendees included Masoud, Masrour, Nechirvan and the PUK's Fuad Masum, the nondescript president of Iraq. Hero, Bafel and other Talabanis were also present. Masrour described efforts to establish a joint committee comprising the Iraqis, the Kurds and the Americans about K1 and to allow the Kurdish presidential guards to come to Kirkuk. He asked Bafel, "Is there already an agreement to let the Iraqi armed forces come in?" Bafel responded, "No, we have not reached an agreement. This is a matter for discussion." Apparently, though, they had already made a deal with the PMU and Iranians, allowing them into Kirkuk.[23] A senior KDP official pulled Bafel into a separate room so they could speak privately about his recent television address, opposing the referendum, which was inconsistent with the position of the Kurdish leadership. The KDP official did not know that "There was a separate deal to let the Iraqi troops into Kirkuk to get rid of Kosrat and Najmaldin, the two main rivals of the Talabani family."[24]

Concurrent with discussions in Dokan, Araz met IRGC and PMU leaders to assure them that the meeting was underway and going well. Araz told them to expect a positive outcome and asked for another 24 hours to finalize an agreement. The Iraqis and Iranians agreed in principle to a short delay but insisted that the Kurds issue an unequivocal statement. Masrour maintains that Bafel, Lahur and Araz agreed to "let them in the back door to Kirkuk."[25]

The Dokan meeting was a disaster. Masoud and Masrour did not take Iraqi and Iranian threats seriously, believing that the Iraqis and Iranians were saber-rattling, and that there would be no military action if the Kurds were unified and ready to fight. Bafel warned Masoud that the troop build-up was not just for show and that the IRGC had orders to move if the Dokan meeting ended in failure. He pointed out that the array of forces facing the Peshmerga significantly outweighed Kurdish defenses. A confrontation would end badly for the Kurds. Instead of a message about national unity, the KDP issued a defiant statement affirming the referendum's result and practically inviting an attack.

Long Night

Karim was receiving worrisome reports about troop movements. He was alarmed about the build-up of Hashd al-Shaabi in Taz Khurmatu and Bashir, a Turkmen village south of Kirkuk. The opposing forces had tanks, heavy artillery, Humvees and mortars just three kilometers from Peshmerga frontline positions. Karim warned that war was not in the interest of anyone, but that Kirkukis "have the right to defend themselves if attacked." KRG Vice President Kosrat Rasool, a PUK member, said that they would be "All on the front lines, ready to defend Kirkuk" and to "respond to any possible attacks." Karim addressed civil defense volunteers, including Arabs who were ready to defend the city and "fight alongside the Peshmerga forces."[26]

Karim was at home on the evening of 15 October when Sierwan received a text just before midnight from "Andy", a US Marine stationed at K1, who warned that the governor's life was in danger and urged that they should leave immediately.[27] Masrour indicated that

PMU militias such as Asaeb al-Haq, Kata'ib Hezbollah, Kata'ib Nujaba and Khorosanis were involved in the attack. These groups are directly supported by Iran and on the US list of terrorist organizations. We were surprised the US did not stop them or even condemn their aggressive actions.[28]

All the checkpoints into Kirkuk were under PUK control. According to Sierwan,

Any infiltration by the CTS [counter-terrorism service], Hashd, or the Iraqi army into Kirkuk meant that PUK members who were trusted to protect Kirkuk had colluded with Baghdad. A few people who were not a part of the PUK leadership sold out Kirkuk.[29]

Members of the IRGC and Araz were just 40 meters away from the Karim residence when Andy's text arrived. Sierwan reflected, "If that text didn't come, we would have stayed in the house and been captured or even killed."

Karim and Sierwan got in their vehicle with the intention to visit the Kurdish neighborhoods of Shorija and Rahimawa. Civilian volunteers had taken to the streets, vowing to defend Kirkuk. According to an armed volunteer, "Every member of Kirkuk's ethnic and religious community has been living in peace under the protection of Peshmerga Forces since mid-2014. We have to help them by protecting this land."[30]

Two minutes after leaving the house, Karim's phone rang, the caller ID indicating that it was Bafel who was calling. But after Bafel's television address on the 12th, Karim was suspicious. Bafel asked, "Where are you?"

Karim replied vaguely, "I'm in Kirkuk."

Bafel queried, "Where in Kirkuk?"

Karim answered, "I'm driving around the city to see and support my people."

Bafel said, "You should be at home. You're the governor."

Sensing a trap, Governor Karim told Bafel, "You're not going to give me orders on where I can and can't go in my city while you're holed up in Suleimani. Fuck you," he added, and hung up the phone.[31]

Social media was reporting that Karim had left the city. Returning to his home, he took steps to address the rumors. His team contacted three television networks: Rudaw, Kurdistan 24 and Rega. Only Rega, a small network, showed up on such short notice. They conducted an interview using an iPhone 5. Karim briefed the public about events. He told them to "stay strong and stay vigilant."[32] Sierwan was tipped off that the Iranians and Araz were across the street from the governor's residence and had bad intentions.

By now, the Kirkuk military operation was under way. Karim hurriedly left his home for a second time.[33] At one o'clock in the morning on 16 October, reports indicated that Iraqi CTS, federal police forces and Hashd al-Shaabi had launched an attack. Hashd were dominant. Many federal police were actually Shi'ite militias who changed uniform. The Kurdistan Region Security Council (KRSC) issued a statement that Iraqi forces and Iranian-backed PMUs had advanced from Taza Khurmatu in a "major, multi-pronged operation." At about 2.30am, "They attacked Peshmerga Forces from two fronts in the Taz-Kirkuk intersection and the Maryam Bag bridge south of Kirkuk, using US military equipment, including Abrams tanks and Humvees." The statement indicated that "significant forces" were also present in Maktab Khalid in southwest Kirkuk.[34] They took control of several oil fields, including Baba Gur, as well as K1. The PUK Peshmerga disappeared when it was time to fight. Masrour reports that "Some PUK forces fought but were betrayed by troops loyal to the Talabani family who completely evacuated their positions. This caused a domino effect as the Peshmerga lines collapsed."[35] According to Qubad, "Our poor soldiers were on the front line with no weapons and no capabilities. The KDP didn't fire a single bullet. They withdrew all the way to the boundaries of Dohuk and Erbil."[36] A senior US official indicated, "The KDP units just evaporated."[37] Sierwan called it a tactical withdrawal from KDP Peshmerga who were left to defend Kirkuk on their own. Lightly armed local Kurds tried to resist, but they had no military training and were quickly overwhelmed. Within 48 hours, the Peshmerga abandoned other disputed territories: Sinjar, Bashiqa, Makhmour and more—all told thousands of square kilometers.[38] As many as 180,000 Kurds were streaming out of Kirkuk by 10am on 16 October.

Karim visited different Kurdish neighborhoods in the city before the sun came up. Armed civilians waved machine guns and rocket-propelled grenades (RPGs), vowing to defend Kirkuk. Some Arabs also joined in, pledging support. But Karim was being tailed. After each of his stops, the head of the PUK in Kirkuk appeared, interviewed on television and posting messages on Facebook which refuted Karim's warnings. He told civilians to go home, that the city was safe. Kirkuk's PUK police were nowhere to be found. The streets were empty.

Karim drove through Turkmen and Arab neighborhoods further south via the Baghdad road before passing by the Kirkuk governorate. Shi'ite Turkmen, many of whom had joined the Hashd, were especially vicious towards civilians in Bashir, killing hundreds of Kurds and burning Kurdish homes and stores.

He went to the heavily fortified base of Hama Haji Mahmoud, who was the head of the Kurdish Socialist Party and a Peshmerga general. There were many Peshmerga at Mahmoud's compound who welcomed Karim's arrival. Karim and Mahmoud drank tea and discussed the night's events. Without disclosing his whereabouts, Karim sent a message to his wife, Zozan, who was already out of Kirkuk. Zozan is the daughter of General Abdul Rahman Qazi, a famous Peshmerga commander who served with Mulla Mustafa Barzani in the 1960s and 1970s. She was relieved to hear from her husband that he was safe, but knew he was not out of harm's way. She nervously watched an interview with Karim on television, during which he offered reassurances that everything would be alright.

After leaving Mahmoud's compound at 4am, Karim was met by a well-armed force. They formed a convoy of Humvees and armored vehicles and headed north. The convoy arrived at the checkpoint between Kirkuk and Erbil shortly after sunrise. Karim wanted to turn the convoy around and go home. According to Sierwan, "We can go and hit them right now and destroy their plans. But the security team said their mission was to protect the Governor and see that he gets out of here safely."[39]

Back in Kirkuk, Muhandis and Hadi al-Ameri of the Badr Movement organized a ceremony at the Governor's office. They lowered the Kurdistan flag to the pavement and replaced it with an Iraqi flag so that there were two Iraqi flags flying side by side. The blue and white crescent flag of the Iraqi Turkmen Front was also draped on the façade of the Kirkuk citadel. The Turkish Foreign Ministry issued an official statement, noting that Turkey had been closely monitoring Iraq's steps to "restore its constitutional sovereignty over Kirkuk, a homeland for Turkmens for centuries, after the illegitimate referendum conducted by the KRG."[40] Photos on social media depicted Hashd al-Shaabi at Karim's desk in the governor's office. Abadi installed Karim's deputy, Rakan Said, a Sunni Arab from Hawija, as governor.

On 20 October, Iraqi forces advanced on Pirde, a majority Kurdish town north of Kirkuk on the Little Zab River. Peshmerga from the KDP and Iranian Peshmerga fighters from the Parti Azadi Kurdistan (PJAK) successfully defended Altun Kupri, the last Kurdish-controlled city in Kirkuk province. Iraqi forces advancing towards Dohuk were defeated by Peshmerga in Zummar and Rabia, west of the Tigris River, and in Telesquf, north of Mosul, on 26 October. At least 38 heavy armored vehicles and another M1 Abrams tank were destroyed, and KRG officials feared that the Iraqi armed forces wanted to occupy all of Kurdistan. According to Masrour, "If we did not defeat them, they would not have stopped."[41]

Abadi reveled in his military success. Iranian officials made no effort to conceal their role. Iran's army chief of staff, Mohamadi Gulpaigani, announced, "The instructions of the Supreme Leader and the sacrifices of General Soleimani spoiled their [i.e. US and Israel] plots [to divide Iraq], and Kirkuk was liberated."[42]

US Response

United States officials tried to minimize the significance of Iraqi and Kurdish forces, its two US allies in Iraq, fighting each other. The initial statement indicated, "[We are] aware of reports of a limited exchange of fire." They called it "a misunderstanding."[43] Masrour retorts, "We were surprised by statements coming from the State Department. They tried to cover up that militias were using American weapons and downplayed the role of Iranians and their Shi'ite militias in attacking Kirkuk."[44]

President Donald J. Trump addressed the Kirkuk crisis during a press conference a few days later. Trump said, "We don't like the fact that they're clashing. We're not taking sides, but we don't like the fact that they're clashing." He added,

> Let me tell you, we've had, for many years, very good relationship with the Kurds, as you know. And we've also been on the side of Iraq, even though we should have never been in there in the first place.

"We should have never been there," Trump repeated. "But we're not taking sides in that battle."[45] Moral equivalency clouded his response. Either Trump had a short memory or was unaware that 1,700 Peshmerga had been killed and more than 10,000 wounded between 2014 and 2017, acting at America's behest fighting ISIS.

Karim's friends and family were concerned for his safety. Even after his dramatic extraction to Erbil, Hashd al-Shaabi and Iranian intelligence agents were still hunting for him. Stanley G. Salett, a former Maryland public office holder, reached out to both Maryland US Senators to discuss protection for Karim and arrangements for a Congressional hearing on the events in Kirkuk. Karim, a US citizen, was a resident of Maryland and well known to Senator Ben Cardin, ranking minority member of the Senate Foreign Relations Committee, as well as Chris van Hollen, chair of the Democratic Senatorial Campaign Committee. Senator Bob Corker, Chairman of the Senate Foreign Relations Committee (SFRC), was very responsive to Salett's concerns. After years of building a network in Washington, Karim still had many friends on Capitol Hill.

Karim was in contact with Senator John McCain during the crisis. McCain understood Iraq and was a stalwart friend of the Kurds. In an article for the *New York Times*, he wrote:

> Clashes this month between elements of the Iraqi security forces and Kurdish fighters around Kirkuk are deeply troubling, in particular because of the United States' long-standing friendship with the Kurdish people. These clashes are also emblematic of a broader, more troubling reality: Beyond our tactical successes in the fight against the Islamic State, the

United States is still dangerously lacking a comprehensive strategy toward the rest of the Middle East in all of its complexity.

McCain confirmed that Qasem Soleimani was in Kirkuk orchestrating Iranian-backed Iraqi militias fighting alongside the ISF. McCain stated emphatically,

> Let me be clear: if Baghdad cannot guarantee the Kurdish people in Iraq the security, freedom and opportunities they desire, and if the United States is forced to choose between Iranian-backed militias and our long-standing Kurdish partners, I choose the Kurds.[46]

A senior SFRC staff member responded to Salett's query on 30 October.

> Thanks for taking the time to walk me through the details of Gov Karim's case. I have made contact with the State Department. According to our consulate in Erbil, Karim let them know of his presence but did not specifically request assistance as a US citizen. He needs to do this. Can you please ask him to ask the US Government for assistance? Secondly, the State Department cannot share any more details with me absent Gov Karim signing a privacy waiver. He can do this at the consulate in front of a witness—is he able to get to the consulate?[47]

McGurk adhered to his mandate as Special Envoy. The coalition fighting ISIS was made up of states, with the occasional participation of militias in Syria. After the Battle for Mosul, the Iraqi government became the primary partner for combating ISIS in Iraq. McGurk may have been angry with the Kurds for conducting the referendum against his wishes, but the Kurds were simply collateral damage in pursuit of a greater goal: to defeat ISIS.

The Trump administration announced a get-tough approach to Iran. Trump had recently decertified the Iran nuclear deal based on several factors, including "the regime's destabilizing activity and support for terrorist proxies in the region." But getting tough on Iran did not include preventing its plans for Kirkuk. By selling out the Kurds, US officials unwittingly created an opportunity for Iran to increase its influence in Iraq. According to a senior US official, "The Kurds set themselves back at least a decade."

Qubad maintained that

The US had full visibility of the operation. US officials were fully briefed on discussions with the Iranians and the Iraqis. They never once said something contrary to what actually happened and warned us before the referendum that this would be an unavoidable and regrettable consequence.[48]

According to Qubad, "Brett was honest with us from the beginning."[49] The fact that Baghdad acted against the wishes of Washington is a measure of how America's influence has diminished. There is no masterplan guiding US actions in Iraq and the region. Lack of a strategy for Iraq is symptomatic of problems with US foreign policy worldwide, which is incoherent and lacks principle.

With ISIS on the brink of military defeat, Washington's commitment to the anti-ISIS coalition wavered. Rumors of McGurk's dismissal raised concerns about a diplomatic vacuum in Iraq during the run-up to national elections. It also came at a time when Syria's President Bashar al-Assad was intensifying attacks against civilians as part of a final push to defeat ISIS in Syria. According to State Department Spokesperson, Heather Nauert, "ISIS remains a lethal threat and a top priority of Secretary Tillerson and this Administration. We will continue to ensure the effort receives the high-level attention and necessary resources required to achieve the enduring defeat of ISIS."[50] Meanwhile, ISIS pockets in Hawija were resurgent. Beginning in February 2018, suicide attacks in Kirkuk killed 27 members of the Hashd.[51]

Iraqi Kurds learned self-reliance the hard way. The events in Kirkuk represent just another chapter in their sad saga of betrayal by Great Powers. But Kurds have a long memory and are resilient. Today Kirkuk may be occupied by Iraqi and Shi'ite forces. However, the fight is not finished. Through their underground networks, the Kurds have undertaken insurgency. They are well armed with RPGs, heavy weapons and 50-caliber automatic weapons. Resistance is spontaneous—and determined. Attacks against Saraya Alsalam, a Shi'ite militia led by Muqtada al-Sadr, were launched on 5 November 2017, and are ongoing.

The strength of Iranian-backed political parties and militias is growing in Iraq. Hashd al-Shaabi areas are transforming themselves from militias into a political movement. Abadi faces challenges from within the Dawa Party while the Badr Organization enjoys increasing sway. Elections will reveal Iraq's true national character. After undermining Iraqi Kurdistan's independence movement, Iran believed its position as kingmaker was assured.

10 ELECTIONS

"I will not take part in an election held in an occupied city, void of freedom."

GOVERNOR NAJMALDIN KARIM[1]

US Interests

President George W. Bush justified the 2003 US invasion of Iraq by suggesting it would bring democracy to a failed state and end dictatorship in the Middle East. Arabists in the State Department understood that democracy for Iraq would empower the country's Shi'ite majority, creating an opening for Iran to exert greater influence. However, neoconservatives in the Bush administration were driven by ideology rather than pragmatism. They thought that toppling Saddam Hussein would reshape Iraq and initiate political transformation of the broader Middle East. The Bush administration believed that democracy was both a reflection of American values and in America's strategic interests. It would create an enabling environment to advance US commercial and security goals in Iraq and the region.[2]

Democracies are indeed more benign. Democracies typically do not fight wars against each other. Nor do they engage in terrorism or produce refugees. They make more reliable allies and better trading partners. Bush believed that democracy was the best system of governance to realize universal human aspirations for freedom and human development. Democracy and the rule of law go hand in hand, stimulating competition, innovation and progress while providing the necessary legal framework to establish free markets. Democracy also fosters an ethos of self-reliance and entrepreneurship that is better suited to economic growth than authoritarianism. Bush pursued Iraq's democratic development because he believed it was in in the interests of both Iraq and the United States.[3]

Iraq was completely incapacitated by violent conflict, which intensified after the US intervention. Decrees banning the Baath Party and the Iraqi army, instruments of Saddam's terror state, eliminated the only institutions with the capacity to manage Iraq's political transition. Fear and tyranny were the hallmarks of Saddam's rule, and Iraqis had little experience with self-rule or democratic governance. Establishing a secure environment for basic services and the functioning of government was a major challenge. Holding elections was also a daunting task.

Elections are often viewed as the yardstick for measuring a country's democratic development. But elections alone do not make a democracy. Elections are part of the democratization process, which occurs over time. Democratic institutions and an active civil society are essential to holding government accountable and consolidating democratic government. Constitutions enshrine the rule of law, checks and balances, and power-sharing principles.

Ravaged Iraq suffered a trust deficit after decades of abuse. Freed from Saddam's restraints, Iraqis engaged in widespread recrimination and revenge-taking. Displacement and population transfers exacerbated the difficulties, and cultural attitudes presented an additional problem; the spirit of compromise and reconciliation does not exist in Iraqi society. Many Iraqis viewed democracy as a zero-sum game.

In 2003, when Saddam was deposed, Iraqi Kurdistan was more democratically developed than the rest of Iraq. The Kurds had a head start, enjoying self-rule since 1991, when Iraqi forces fled and the US imposed a no-fly zone giving Kurds control over their territory. The PUK and KDP had an extensive infrastructure for local administration and security. Kurds are pro-American and, more than any people in the Middle East except Israel, Kurds share values with the United States. However, the Kurdish civil war in the 1990s showed that Kurds lacked the skills and temperament for power-sharing. Party divisions based on a tribal mentality were still strong.

While the rest of Iraq was still gripped by Saddam's tyrannical rule, the Kurdistan Regional Government (KRG) held a series of elections beginning in the 1990s. However, holding an election is different than consolidating democratic government. The democratization cycle starts with an electoral law, conducting a ballot and electing leaders to negotiate a constitution. In both Kurdistan and Baghdad, the Electoral Management Body had the potential to play a role greater than merely registering voters, printing and distributing ballots. Elections can also serve as a forum for adjudicating disputes between Arabs and Kurds, as well as Shi'ites and Sunnis. Resolving differences peacefully at the ballot box can be an effective method of conflict resolution.

Iraq—a post-conflict and post-authoritarian country—lacks both the institutions to address competing claims as well as a culture of peaceful dispute resolution. Iraqis were used to strict social control enforced through coercion and repression and Iraq experienced additional stress under occupation by the US military. Meddlesome neighbors sought to establish spheres of influence, which further affected Iraq's democratic development. Inter-ethnic and sectarian strife created a challenging climate during the period prior to elections in 2018. Prior to this election, post-sectarian elections were a worthy yet unrealistic goal.

Elections in Iraqi Kurdistan

The IHERC did a stellar job organizing the Iraqi Kurdistan referendum on 25 September 2017. It printed, distributed and counted ballots with little lead time and a meager budget. The referendum was a transparent process; local and international election monitors were allowed to work unhindered. But to many Arab Sunnis and Shi'ites, the Kurdish referendum was an act of sedition. The fact that 92.7 percent of voters chose independence in a free and fair election was irrelevant to Prime Minister Heider al-Abadi, who rejected the popular will of the Kurds—and attacked Kurdistan.

The KRG envisioned the referendum as part of an electoral process, culminating in the election of a leader and legislators to conduct negotiations with Baghdad and ready the country for independence. Kurdistan's presidential and parliamentary elections were originally planned for 1 November 2017, just five weeks after the independence referendum. It was thought that elections would strengthen Masoud Barzani's position in the negotiations with Baghdad. Iraq's military intervention in Kirkuk, which precipitated Masoud's decision to step down, changed everything.

Kurds were shell-shocked by Iraq's attack on Kirkuk, supported by Hashd al-Shaabi and masterminded by Iran's Revolutionary Guard Corps. With so much uncertainty about the future, Kurdistan's Assembly was unable to discuss the Presidency Law in the immediate aftermath of Iraq's attack. The Kurds did, however, debate the sequence of events. Some, mainly opposition parties, argued that Kurdistan should elect a new parliament first, which would revise the Presidency Law. The new parliament would be responsible for drafting a constitution to define the balance of powers between new structures of the KRG. Fundamental issues had to be addressed. Kurds differed on whether Iraqi Kurdistan should be a parliamentary or a presidential system. They were accustomed to Masoud as a strong leader, managing crises during the 12 years of his tenure. With Masoud's resignation, Kurds faced a dilemma as to the president's role. They also had to decide how the president would be elected, by the parliament or directly by the people, and between a party list proportional system or direct election for deputies representing specific districts. The Kurds chose the party list.

Prime Minister Nechirvan Barzani facilitated dialogue between the political parties. With his constructive mediation, they decided to hold elections for both president and parliament in the spring of 2018. The IHERC said it would need 105 days from the date that elections were announced to conduct the technical tasks associated with a general election. The KRG appropriated $19.3 million, and the IHERC went to work. It consulted with various KRG agencies, such as the Health Department, to organize voter rolls, eliminating duplicates and striking out the names of the deceased.[4] Given uncertainties, however, elections were postponed until the fall of 2018.

As we have seen, Kurdish politics is historically a balance between two dominant parties, the KDP and PUK. The emergence of Gorran, which gained popular support in Sulemani at the PUK's expense, shifted this balance between the two major parties. Jalal Talabani's death, combined with the Talabani faction's role in enabling Baghdad to take Kirkuk, had a profound effect on the psyche of Kurdish voters. Many lost confidence in the PUK's integrity and leadership.

The PUK had been in decline long before the Kirkuk fiasco. Since Jalal's stroke in 2012, the PUK had been unable to resolve the question of leadership. Nepotism further alienated the PUK from its base. Hero Ibrahim and other members of the Talabani family felt entitled to power. They marginalized patriots like Kosrat Rasoul Ali and Barham Salih. Given widespread disaffection with the PUK, the KDP and Gorran gained support at the PUK's expense in the elections of 2014.

The KDP was the first party in Kurdistani politics. Many voters have entrenched loyalty to the KDP because of Mulla Mustafa Barzani's historic role, as well as Masoud's long-term leadership and crisis management. Masoud's son, Masrour, is a political force with strong ties to the Peshmerga and the security establishment. Masoud's nephew, Nechirvan, has broad political appeal.

Governor Najmaldin Karim was also a factor. Though Kirkuk was his home city and electoral base, Karim's resolute nationalism was supported across Kurdistan. Kurds in Kirkuk handed out his photograph and clamored for his return. Karim threatened legal action against critics who alleged corruption.

Karim initially said he would not stand in the upcoming Iraqi elections, refusing to run in an "occupied city." He called on political parties to boycott the elections in Kirkuk and the other occupied territories. Of the 200,000 people who fled Kirkuk after the invasion, 60,000 were eligible to vote but would not go back to cast their ballots. People who had fled Kirkuk before 2003 also refused to go back because of security conditions. Karim queried, "Why should you participate in an election while even the Kurds remaining in Kirkuk might not vote because of losing faith?" He warned, "Taking part in these elections will give legitimacy to the elections themselves." He also called for an investigation into the PUK's involvement in the invasion. "I believe the PUK should investigate the October 16 events, find the culprits, and hold those accountable for losing 50 percent of Kurdish territory."[5] He called for the KRG and Kurdish parliament to investigate the Peshmerga commanders who had abandoned their positions.

Kurdistan's political landscape was also affected when Barham Salih defected from the PUK. In October 2017, he set up a new political entity called the Coalition for Democracy and Justice, with a platform focused on fighting corruption and good governance.[6] The PUK, however, did not tolerate dissent and it abruptly fired Barham from its politiburo. Karim was also removed.

Iraq's national elections were held on 12 May 2018, and the formation of a new government in Baghdad provided an opportunity for the Kurds to negotiate a new modus vivendi that would preserve their national rights, without relinquishing the possibility of independence in the future. According to Fuad Hussein, chief of staff of the KRG presidency:

> We must be in the government, not in opposition. It will be better to be part of the decision-making process. There are many issues to address such as the administration and security of disputed areas, as well as their future status. Peshmerga, oil, and the future of the political process in Iraq itself.[7]

After Kirkuk, the Kurds believed that Iran would control the outcome of Iraq's national elections. Fuad believes that, "Whichever Shi'ite lists win, the incoming Prime Minister will need a green light from the religious authorities in Najaf"[8] and the religious authorities will not act without consulting Tehran. Iraq had become an increasingly theocratic and autocratic state. However, the Kurds underestimated the extent to which populism and nationalism would replace sectarianism as the driving force in Iraqi politics.

Elections in Iraq

Initially Kurdish and Sunni MPs rejected the proposal for elections on 12 May 2018. They wanted to delay the ballot to give displaced Iraqis more time to resettle and return home. According to the International Organization for Migration, about 3.1 million Iraqis were internally displaced after years of sectarian strife and ISIS subjugation.[9] About half of the displaced people were located in Kurdistan, including Sunni Arabs. The US Government strongly opposed postponing the election. According to the US Embassy in Baghdad, "Postponing the elections would set a dangerous precedent, undermining the constitution and damaging Iraq's long-term democratic development."[10] Iraq's highest court ruled against postponing the election, finding that postponement would contravene the country's constitution.

Abadi was the incumbent and frontrunner, according to the polls. He was counting on a boost from Shi'ite voters for defeating ISIS and restoring Iraqi sovereignty over a third of the country. Abadi's hard line towards the Kurds also ingratiated him with Iraqi nationalists who strongly opposed Kurdistan's independence. The US discreetly supported Abadi. However, Washington's support was a double-edged sword. The US invasion of Iraq removed Saddam and created an opportunity for Shi'ites to lead the political process. However, Shi'ites deeply resented America's occupation of Iraq and resisted its influence over domestic politics. Being too closely identified with the United States was a poison pill for any Iraqi politician.

Abadi believed he could capture enough support from hardline Shi'ites to form a government without the Kurdish bloc. Qasem Soleimani had delivered a military victory to Abadi in Kirkuk and he was counting on Iran's political support in forming a government after elections on 12 May. However, Iran hedged its bets, supporting several Shi'ite parties including the Islamic Dawa Party as well as parties associated with different Shi'ite militias.

Iraqis were consumed by the country's profound challenges of reconstruction and corruption. According to the UN, Iraq needed $88 billion to rebuild its shattered infrastructure and provide humanitarian assistance. Until conditions were achieved for their sustainable return, the IDP crisis would continue. In the meantime, endemic corruption limited Iraq's political and economic development. According to Transparency International, Iraq is the tenth most corrupt country worldwide and suffers from an oil curse with its energy wealth giving rise to a kleptocracy and ineffective governance.

Nouri al-Maliki deeply resented Abadi for colluding with the United States to remove him from power in 2014. Maliki declined to endorse Abadi, working to position his State of Law Coalition for a political comeback from the day he was ousted. Maliki did not run on his record as prime minister, which was disastrous. Instead he positioned himself as the anti-establishment candidate, blaming Abadi for the country's lackluster economic performance, and the United States for fomenting Kurdish separatism.

Hadi al-Ameri was a former transportation minister who gained popular support during the fight against ISIS. He led the Badr Organization, the largest and most effective member of the Popular Mobilization Forces, and was a leader of the Hashd al-Shaabi. Ameri's Fatih ("Conquest") movement was detested by both Sunnis and Kurds. Iraq's Shi'ites are Arab, whereas Iranians are Persian. Iraqi nationalists resented Ameri for his ties to Iran and fraternity with Soleimani.

Muqtada al-Sadr, the firebrand Shi'ite cleric from Najaf, is known for his vitriol and resistance towards the US occupation. He played an important role in the Shi'ite rebellion against the US, which killed hundreds of US Marines beginning in 2004. His Mahdi Army was a major actor in Iraq's sectarian civil war, which killed thousands of Sunnis in 2006 and 2007. Sadr led the Sa'iroun Alliance ("Moving Forward"), which championed the fight against corruption, demanding public services and good governance. From firebrand cleric, Sadr evolved into a national statesman, building bridges to the Sunni community and even visiting Saudi Arabia in 2017 to meet Crown Prince Mohammed bin Salman. The Sa'iroun coalition included Sadr's Instigama Party ("Integrity"), Iraq's Communist Party, Sunni business and other small secular parties. Sadr's support has a loyal base, which includes young, poor, and dispossessed Iraqis concentrated in places like Baghdad's Sadr City. Sadr is an ardent nationalist who rejects foreign interference by both the United States and Iran. He derives significant standing from his family's reputation. His father, Grand Ayatollah Mohammed Sadeq al-Sadr, was murdered in 1999 for defying Saddam Hussein.

Election Results

Iraq held its fifth parliamentary election since Saddam's overthrow on 12 May 2018. According to Iraq's electoral law, parliamentary seats are divided by governorate, proportionate to each province's population. The fewer people turn out in one particular governorate, the fewer votes a seat will require. Ethnic minorities are allocated a quota of seats.

According to official results of the Independent High Electoral Commission of Iraq (IHEC), Sadr's Sa'iroun Alliance was the leading vote getter, running strongly in Baghdad and gaining 54 seats nationwide. Ameri's Fatih Movement won 47 seats and Abadi's Naser Coalition earned 42 seats. Voters recalled sectarian conflict during Maliki's mandate, awarding his State of Law Coalition only 26 seats.

Sadr gained support by running as a nationalist. He rejected foreign interference in Iraq's internal affairs, condemning both the United States and Iran. Sadr successfully mobilized a protest vote against the political elite's systematic patronage, riding a wave of populism. Sadr himself is more symbol than substance. He has no experience with governance and, since his name did not appear on his party list, he cannot serve as prime minister. Iraq's constitution allows 90 days from the date of an election for the formation of a coalition government. As we have seen after the 2010 election, negotiations on government formation can be contentious and protracted; Iraq has many political actors with entrenched interests.

Sadr wasted no time in exerting influence, reaching out to potential coalition partners within days of the vote. He emphasized cooperation based on three principles: no corruption, ending the practice of awarding ministries on sectarian quotas, and promoting technocrats to head government departments. Iraq faces daunting challenges with up to three million people internally displaced. The reconstruction of Mosul will be costly. Enmity between Kurds and Arabs, as well as distrust between Shi'ites and Sunnis, is deeply rooted.

Foreign powers are nervous about Sadr's strong showing, which upended Iraqi politics. Seventy-two hours after the election, Brett McGurk visited Baghdad to discuss government formation with Iraqi factions. Qasem Soleimani also went to Baghdad to facilitate negotiations between Shi'ite parties. Though he came in third place, Abadi is experienced at political jockeying and could emerge as premier with international backing.

Iraq's election was marred by widespread apathy. Only 44.52 percent of more than 24 million eligible voters went to the polls. The low turnout contrasted with more than 62 percent in the elections of 2014 and 2010, demonstrating how deeply Iraqis are disillusioned. Despite the country's vast oil wealth, poverty is widespread, services are lacking and Iraq is one of the most corrupt countries in the world.

The 2018 national election was considered a success, however. Iraq has held many elections in the post-Saddam period, in which widespread violence was always a risk. Over time, however, elections became embedded in the new Iraq, and an election without fraud or violence was considered a step forward.

Kurds participated in national elections, still smarting from their failed referendum on independence. Fuad emphasized the KRG's commitment to political dialogue. "We will participate in elections, negotiate and form a coalition in order to protect what we have. We believe in negotiations."[11]

In Iraqi Kurdistan, the KDP won 25 seats followed by the PUK with 18. Gorran earned only five seats. Gorran and other alternative parties had expected voters to hand the KDP and PUK a punishing defeat for mishandling the referendum and abandoning Kirkuk. Glitches in Iraqi Kurdistan's new electronic voting system led to allegations of fraud; the alternative parties said the voting system was hacked and filed a lawsuit with the IHEC demanding a new vote in the Kurdistan Region, Kirkuk and Diyala governorates and other disputed territories. Within a week of the vote, the IHEC registered 1,400 complains. In Suleimani, six parties accused the PUK of vote rigging. In Kirkuk, Arabs and Turkmen accused the IHEC of bias towards the PUK. The PUK ran strongly in Kirkuk because the KDP did not field candidates there. Voters reported that they were skeptical of alternative parties, which said they would form a coalition in disputed areas but kept campaigning individually. Confused about their intentions, voters were doubtful that the alternative parties would in fact unite later on. Moreover, the PUK historically has a large voter base in Kirkuk and Diyala governorates.

A gun battle erupted between PUK and Gorran supporters in Suleimani. An Iranian delegation went to Suleimani to mediate differences between the PUK and Gorran, demonstrating Iran's extraordinary influence over the PUK.[12] Tensions remained high until Kurdistan's elections on 30 September 2018.

Part IV

The Region

11 SYRIA STRUGGLES

"We do not consider the YPG as an ally to the US. Our ally is Turkey. The United States made clear from the beginning our military cooperation with the YPG [...] was a temporary, tactical arrangement aimed entirely at combating [IS]."

SENIOR US OFFICIAL IN ANKARA[1]

Thousands of Kurds were killed and wounded in Iraq and Syria, fighting ISIS at America's behest. Kurds expected support for their rights and national aspirations in return for such sacrifice. However, the Trump administration sold them out, ceding leadership in Syria to Iran, Russia and Turkey. Forsaking the Kurds accelerated the demise of America's moral standing and political influence, and undermined regional security.

Kurdish Factions

Syrian Kurds have suffered a century of betrayal and abuse beginning with the Lausanne Treaty of 1923 and extending to the present. Syria's current civil war represents another tragic chapter for Kurds, victimized by Great Powers and brutalized by Turkey, which targets them for being secular and pro-western. The struggle of Syrian Kurds and their brethren in Turkey dates back to February 1925 when Sheikh Said Piran launched an armed rebellion and established Azadi, the Kurdish Independence Society. His rebellion was brutally put down by Turkish forces; Piran was hanged in the central square of Diyarbakir and thousands of his followers were killed or arrested. Many Kurds relocated from Turkey to Syria after Sheikh Said's failed rebellion, where they joined the struggle for independence against the French administration. Kurds from Turkey and Syria formed the pan-Kurdish Xoybun League on 5 October 1927. In Kurmanji, the dialect spoken by Kurds in Turkey and Syria, Xoybun means "one who controls his own destiny."[2]

The Kurdistan Workers' Party (PKK) was founded in 1978, in response to Turkey's violent crackdown against Kurdish rights and national aspirations. Turkish leaders banned use of the Kurdish language and prohibited Kurdish geographic and place names. Kurdish identity was denied; Kurds were called "Mountain Turks." Abdullah Ocalan, who founded the PKK, espoused an ideology of the struggle for liberation. The PKK was a Marxist–Leninist group, advocating a proletarian revolution; its charter called for a "worker–peasant alliance." Ocalan's egalitarian worldview challenged Turkish nationalism, enshrined in Turkey's constitution following the military coup of 12 September 1980. The PKK was born out of the Turkish left as an anti-colonial and pan-Kurdish movement; Ocalan aspired to establish greater Kurdistan encompassing Kurds in Turkey (North Kurdistan), Syria (West Kurdistan), Iraq (South Kurdistan) and Iran (East Kurdistan).

The PKK was under constant pressure from Turkey's extensive security apparatus. Syria's President Hafez al-Assad offered territory along the Turkish–Syrian border as a safe haven for them. Hafez al-Assad was no friend of the Kurds; he was motivated by a desire to weaken Turkey. Syria and Turkey resolved their differences, signing the Adana Agreement on 20 October 1998. Expelled from Syria, Ocalan was captured in Nairobi in a joint US–Turkish and Israeli operation, then imprisoned on Imrali Island in 1999. Even from his jail cell, Ocalan remained the PKK's de facto ideological and operational head. The PKK evolved from an armed struggle for independence into a movement seeking greater political and cultural rights for Kurds in Turkey.

After the outbreak of Syria's civil war in 2011, Assad's forces pulled out of the north, leaving a vacuum that was filled by the People's Protection Units (YPG) of the Kurdish Democratic Union Party (PYD). Syrian Kurds achieved a degree of autonomy as the Syrian state collapsed and Ocalan's egalitarian ideals enjoyed widespread support in "Rojava," a de facto self-governing territory in Afrin, Jazira and Kobani provinces along the border with Turkey. The PYD institutionalized grass-roots democratic governance and gender equality. Men and women co-chair all agencies and government committees, while environmental sustainability and religious freedom are core principles: the PYD views secularism as an antidote to militant Islamism. Rojava has low levels of mismanagement and corruption, unlike other countries in the region where criminality and nepotism are widespread. The PYD and PKK share Ocalan's values, including a streak of intolerance towards dissenting views. While operationally and legally distinct, the PYD and PKK have strong ideological, spiritual and historic ties.

Ocalan's ideals also resonated with Kurdish communities in Iraq and Iran. Jalal Talabani and the PUK adopted Ocalan's ideology, which gained traction in disputed areas, like Kirkuk, and areas with minority groups, such as the Yazidis in Sinjar. The PKK established its headquarters in the Qandil Mountains of Iraqi Kurdistan. The PKK's presence represented a direct challenge to the authority of Masoud Barzani, head of the Kurdistan Democratic Party (KDP) and President of the Kurdistan Regional Government (KRG).

Ideological differences between the KDP and the PKK mirror the personal and political rivalry between Ocalan and Barzani. The KDP is the oldest Kurdish political party, the creation of Mulla Mustafa Barzani, the iconic Kurdish patriarch who founded the KDP as a classic nationalist party, reflecting the conservatism inherent in Kurdish society. The KDP is dominant among Kurmanji speakers. It is, however, simplistic to conclude that only Kurmanji speakers constitute its base. Nor is the KDP defined geographically. Its affiliate, the Kurdistan Democratic Party of Syria (KDPS), enjoys strong support in Syrian cities such as Qamishli.

Barzani established the Kurdish National Council (KNC) as a bulwark against the growing influence of the PYD in Syria. Competition between the KDP and Ocalan's supporters is intense. The KNC collapsed when the PYD accused it of allying with Sunni rebels, attacking Kurdish communities in Syria. The Movement for a Democratic Society emerged as an inclusive, multi-ethnic and multi-sectarian alternative to Barzani's centralized and conservative approach.

The split between the KDP and PUK represents another division in Kurdish society. The PUK was founded in 1975, when it separated from the KDP. In addition to personalities, the rift occurred because of divergent values and commercial interests. Violence between the KDP and PUK erupted in the mid 1990s, dramatizing their differences. The PUK areas in Iraqi Kurdistan include Suleimani province and, until recently, Kurdish areas of the ethnically mixed provinces of Kirkuk and Diyala. The KDP area consists of Dohuk province and Erbil province, which was formerly divided between KDP and PUK supporters. Both parties rely on patronage systems, driven by local branch officials, but the KDP and PUK are experiencing internal dissent. Following Talabani's death and the events in Kirkuk, PUK supporters are disaffected while KDP supporters are second-guessing Barzani's judgment about the timing and political preparation of Iraqi Kurdistan's independence referendum. There is also a growing generational divide in both parties; Kurdish youth are disappointed and unsure of their future.

Kurdish divisions are exacerbated by other states in the region, which play one Kurdish group against another to advance their national agendas. Turkey's President Recep Tayyip Erdoğan and Barzani established mutually expedient relations based on commercial, security and energy interests. Barzani was a willing partner in Turkey's efforts to eliminate the PKK in Qandil. Barzani's tense relations with the PYD also suited Turkey. To Erdoğan, the PKK and PYD are one and the same: both are terror groups aiming to destabilize Turkey. Conflating the PKK and PYD gave license to Turkey's campaign against the PYD.

Ally or Partner?

The YPG was the point of the spear for US-led operations against ISIS in Syria. Beginning in 2015, the YPG, a major component of the Syrian Democratic Forces (SDF), functioned as America's boots on the ground. Syrian Kurds had a self-interest in fighting ISIS, which targeted Kurds in Rojava and Sinjar, a Yazidi center near the border in Iraqi Kurdistan. The YPG was also fighting at the behest of the United States. After what happened to the Iraqi Peshmerga, Syrian Kurds grew increasingly wary of Washington. Were they an ally or just a partner, to be jettisoned when less useful?

Attitudes in the US towards the Syrian Kurds evolved. President Barack Obama adamantly resisted US military involvement in Syria. However, he drew a red line when US intelligence observed Syrian forces moving chemical weapons (CW) and readying CW-tipped artillery. On 21 August 2013, Syrian rocket launchers delivered a barrage of artillery tipped with the deadly nerve agent sarin on Ghouta, a Damascus suburb controlled by Sunni Arab opposition. According to a US intelligence report, 1,429 people, including at least 426 children, were killed in the attack. A US official described Ghouta as an "indiscriminate, inconceivable horror."[3]

Determined to avoid military intervention, Obama turned to the United Nations to disarm Syria of its weapons of mass destruction (WMD). Obama's effort to walk back from the red line was seen as a sign of weakness by Syrians. It was also a strategic mistake. Putting the UN in the lead sub-contracted Syria's disarmament to Russia. President Vladimir Putin seized the opportunity to deepen cooperation with Syria's President Bashar al-Assad and reassert Russia's interests in the Middle East. Russia fortified its naval air station in Tartous and its air base in Lattakia, while Obama's reluctance also signaled to ISIS that it could commit atrocities with impunity, consolidating its caliphate.

Subsequently ISIS attacked Kobani, a medium-sized Kurdish city on the border with Turkey, in the autumn of 2015. Kobani's surrounding villages were quickly overrun; ISIS committed atrocities, beheading civilians and raping women, and used suicide bombers and vehicle-borne IEDs to attack Kobani's urban center. The YPG was joined by Kurdish female fighters, the YPJ, in a heroic defense of Kobani. With their backs to the Turkish border, Kurds fought valiantly against overwhelming odds. International media observed the onslaught from the hills above Kobani on the Turkish side of the border. Prominent Americans like Hamdi Ulukaya, a Turkish Kurd who is the founder and owner of the yogurt maker Chobani, called for action. On the other side of the debate, Ryan Crocker, former US Ambassador to Iraq, cautioned against intervention, maintaining that Kobani had no strategic value. Pentagon spokesman John Kirby called for "strategic patience."[4]

Beginning in 1997, the PKK was designated a Foreign Terrorist Organization (FTO) by the United States and European countries based on its history of violence both against the Turkish military and against Kurds accused of collaborating with official security structures. In the 1990s, the PKK conducted bombings, suicide attacks and kidnappings, while the military targeted civilians to drain the swamp of support for the PKK. The Turkish military and the PKK fought a civil war for 30 years, leading to the deaths of at least 40,000 and the displacement of several million.

The Obama administration wanted Turkey, with the second largest army among NATO members, to join the fight against ISIS. However, Erdoğan was ambivalent about the anti-ISIS campaign, and initially refused to join the international coalition. Erdoğan prevaricated when the Pentagon asked to use Incirlik Air Force Base in southeast Turkey as a staging ground for humanitarian and military operations. After delaying his decision for almost a year, Erdoğan finally agreed. His reluctance reflected the historical animosity of Turkey towards Kurds in the region.

In Erdoğan's worldview, every adversary is a terrorist. Not only did he equate the PKK and the YPG, he also equated the Kurds of Kobani with ISIS, calling both terrorists. "It is wrong to view them differently," he said. "We need to deal with them jointly."[5] Meanwhile, eyewitness evidence mounted that Turkey was materially supporting ISIS. Can Dündar, the

editor-in-chief of the newspaper *Cumhuriyet*, reported that weapons used
by ISIS were transported from Turkey; he was arrested and imprisoned for
supporting terrorism. ISIS fighters staged operations against Kobani from
the Turkish territory north of the city. Columbia University's Institute for
the Study of Human Rights compiled overwhelming evidence of complicity between Turkey's National Intelligence Agency (MIT) and jihadis,
complicity that was confirmed at the highest levels of the US Government.
Vice President Joe Biden said,

> Our biggest problem was our allies. The Turks... the Saudis, the Emirates,
> etc, what were they doing? They were so determined to take down Assad
> and essentially have a proxy Sunni–Shi'a war, what did they do? They
> poured hundreds of millions of dollars and tens, thousands of tons of
> weapons into anyone who would fight against Assad.[6]

Turkish tanks were perched on the hills in Suruc above Kobani, watching
the battle unfold. International media gave a blow-by-blow account and
Erdoğan issued a series of statements extolling the YPG's imminent demise.
According to a Syrian Kurd, "ISIS is inhuman. They are the terrorists. The
YPG is fighting not only for the Kurds and their land, but for all of humanity.
We're protecting Turkey too. Why can't they see that?[7]

Though Erdoğan conflated the YPG and PKK, US officials disagreed.
The State Department was aware that "many of the PKK militants joined
the YPG, [but there has] always been a clear separation between the
two." According to Major General James B. Jarrard, Special Operations
Commander for Iraq and Syria, "There's a lot of people that do equate them
with the PKK, but I have not seen any indication of that in my dealings
with them."[8] But Erdoğan scorned the distinction. When Turkish Kurds
sought to reinforce the YPG, Turkish security blocked their path. Iranian
Kurdish fighters with the Party for a Free Life in Kurdistan (PJAK) also
tried to reach Kobani. Across Turkey, Kurds protested Erdoğan's complicity but were confronted by riot police with truncheons, tear gas and water
cannon. Scores of Kurds were killed for simply expressing solidarity with
their brethren in Syria.

The Obama administration was concerned by Turkey's inaction against
ISIS and its heavy-handed crackdown on domestic dissent. According to
a US official, "There's growing angst about Turkey dragging its feet. This
isn't how a NATO ally acts while hell is unfolding a stone's throw from

its border."[9] Kobani marked the beginning of a dramatic downturn in US–Turkey relations as Washington grew increasingly concerned about Erdoğan's demeanor—authoritarian, anti-democratic and hostile to the United States.

Eighty percent of Kobani was under ISIS control and the city was on the verge of collapse when the Obama administration reconsidered its reluctance to engage militarily. Now US officials concluded that Kobani's fall would lead to the violent execution of its defenders, both men and women, and that ISIS would broadcast their execution on its website and use it to recruit foreign fighters from around the world. Kobani would be a public relations and recruitment bonanza. The beheadings of American journalists, James Foley and Steven Sotloff, broadcast on ISIS media, contributed to the shift in US policy.

Beginning on 5 October 2015, the US launched almost 200 sorties involving F-22 Raptors, F-15 and F-16 strike aircraft, B-1 bombers and drones against ISIS in Kobani, and this US air power successfully arrested the ISIS advance. On 19 October, US Air Force C-130 transport planes dropped 27 bundles of weapons, ammunition and medical supplies to the YPG, which came from the Peshmerga in Iraqi Kurdistan. All but one bundle reached the intended beneficiary. According to US Central Command, "This assistance is another example of US resolve to deny ISIL key terrain and safe haven as well as our commitment to assist those forces who oppose ISIL."[10]

Erdoğan succumbed to intense pressure from the United States, allowing US logistical support to reach the Kurds and US warplanes to operate in Turkish airspace. Turkey allowed 150 Iraqi Peshmerga to cross through Turkish territory and enter Kobani. Peshmerga flew to Urfa and entered Kobani from the north, armed with automatic weapons, mortars and rocket launchers. Their participation in the fight was symbolic, playing only a support role. However, their arrival coincided with US engagement, which helped turn the tide. After months of siege, ISIS withdrew and Kobani was saved.

Kobani became a symbol of resistance. The Kurds had fought valiantly in brutal urban warfare; approximately 40 percent of Kobani's defenders were women, while ISIS lost up to 25 percent of its forces.[11] General Lloyd J. Austin, commander of US Central Command, called the defense of Kobani "very impressive".[12] Military historians likened it to the Russian victory over Germany's Sixth Army, which overcame overwhelming odds to defend Stalingrad in 1943.

The Obama administration understood the limits of air power and that foot soldiers were needed to kill ISIS fighters. However, Obama strongly resisted sending US troops. Instead, the CIA undertook covert efforts to train and equip Arab fighters, such as Hay'at Tahrir al-Sham, which included the al-Qaeda affiliate Jabhat al-Nusra, Ahrar al-Sham and the Nour al-Din al-Zenki Movement. The US spent $500 million to provide training and weapons. However, the train-and-equip program was grossly ineffective. In a Congressional testimony, General Lloyd Austin, head of Central Command, said only a handful of fighters were combat-ready. The Pentagon expected to have trained a force of 500, but working with Sunni Arabs was a fiasco. Moderate fighters either were defeated or defected, giving up their weapons to Salafist and other radical groups. As Syria's conflict continued, many Arabs were radicalized and joined ISIS. Kurds proved to be the most committed and capable fighters.[13]

In May 2015, the YPG attacked Tal Abyad, a strategic border crossing between Turkey and Syria in Hassakah province and a trans-shipment point for weapons and fighters to ISIS. By this time, the YPG had 40,000 men and women under arms. With US firepower, they were a formidable force. The Kurds had two strategic objectives: first, to isolate ISIS by blocking the supply of Turkish weapons and the flow of foreign fighters from Urfa to Raqqa, capital of the self-declared ISIS caliphate. The second goal was to link lands under YPG control in Jazira and Kobani provinces, thereby extending the contiguous territory in Rojava.

The fight to liberate Tal Abyad lasted from May to July 2015. Erdoğan called the YPG in Tal Abyad a "direct threat" to Turkey and accused the YPG of committing atrocities against local Arabs. Human Rights Watch also alleged ethnic cleansing of Arabs and Turkmen by the YPG. The PYD insisted, but there was no systematic effort to change the province's ethnography. Militants from ISIS crossed the border into Turkey so they could surrender to more friendly Turkish forces.[14]

NATO Ally

The Obama administration tried to maintain the difficult balance between its loyalty to Turkey, a NATO ally, and cooperation with the YPG, its partner in Syria; US officials told the Turks what they wanted to hear, while intensifying security cooperation on the ground with the YPG. This approach allowed deniability for both sides. Ambiguity worked until Special

Presidential Envoy for the Global Coalition to Counter ISIL, Ambassador Brett McGurk, visited Kobani in January 2016. It was the first declared trip by a US official in three years. McGurk was received by Senior YPG Commander Palat Jan and given a plaque with the YPG emblem. McGurk posted images of the trip on his Twitter feed, including a photo of his visit to a Kurdish cemetery where he "paid respects to over 1,000 Kurdish martyrs." McGurk met senior SDF commanders to discuss the battle plan for Raqqa, but, to emphasize neutrality, he also met with an array of Arab, Kurdish, Christian and Turkmen representatives.

McGurk's high-profile visit to Rojava was intended to mollify the PYD, which was upset that the US had succumbed to Turkish pressure and excluded their representatives from UN-sponsored peace talks in Geneva. US Deputy Secretary of State Antony A. Blinken also called PYD vice-chair Saleh Muslim, to assuage Kurdish concerns about their exclusion from the Geneva talks. Blinken reiterated the importance of an inclusive process to achieve a unified, multi-ethnic, multi-sectarian Syria, but his assurances fell on deaf ears. Though Saleh Muslim applied for a visa to visit the United States in 2013, the State Department has still not responded to his visa application.

While mollifying the Kurds, McGurk's visit outraged Turkish officials. Foreign Minister Mevlüt Çavuşoğlu expressed outrage, demanding McGurk's dismissal, and his bellicose rhetoric further strained US–Turkey relations. Turks responded with vitriol when McGurk alleged that Turkey was cooperating with al-Qaeda affiliated groups in Idlib province, blasting McGurk for making "baseless, unacceptable [and] provocative" statements. McGurk was merely stating the obvious. Intelligence agencies knew that Turkey had been working with jihadi groups since 2013.[15]

McGurk became persona non grata in Turkey for his alleged bias toward the Kurds. The banner headline of *Yeni Shafak*, a pro-government newspaper, declared: "US envoy murders 46,000 civilians in Iraq, Syria." But Erdoğan did not leave the job of attacking McGurk to his lackeys and propagandists. He blamed the United States for causing a "sea of blood" by backing the YPG, and accused the US of ignorance. He slammed America for supporting the YPG militarily and for its refusal to brand them as terrorists. "I told you many times: Are you with us or with this terrorist organization?"[16] Erdoğan pushed the US to make a choice between Turkey and the YPG, but was rebuffed.

Biden went to Ankara on 24 August 2016 in order to repair frayed relations. Upon his arrival, he learned that Turkish Special Forces, tanks, and fighters with the Free Syrian Army (FSA) had invaded Jarablus in Syria near the Turkish border. Erdoğan said the primary purpose of "Operation Euphrates Shield" was to fight ISIS. However, Turkish forces and their Islamist militias never engaged ISIS. Ankara made a deal before going in. Rather than resist, ISIS forces simply changed into FSA uniforms. Jarablus was "liberated" from ISIS without a shot.

The FSA includes jihadists and al-Qaeda remnants. They are an unsavory lot. On 3 February 2018, a video surfaced of the FSA removing the clothes of a YPJ member and mutilating her body. Another video showed the FSA forcing a 12-year old child to chop off the head of a Syrian soldier.[17] An FSA commander threatened to behead Kurdish fighters unless they adhered to a radical form of Islam practiced by ISIS and al-Qaeda. Calling the Kurds in Afrin infidels, an FSA member said: "By Allah, if you repent and come back to Allah, then know that you are our brothers. But if you refuse, then we see that your heads are ripe, and that it's time for us to pluck them."[18]

According to Erdoğan, Euphrates Shield was aimed at the YPG and "terror groups that threaten our country." Turkey would "do what is necessary" to keep Kurdish fighters to the east of the Euphrates River. Turkey announced plans for a safe zone from Jarablus to Marea, 90 kilometers long and 40 kilometers wide, stretching deep into Kurdish-controlled territory; its real goal was to prevent the YPG from establishing a contiguous Kurdish territory. McGurk called Turkey's targeting of the PYD "unacceptable and a source of deep concern."[19]

Raqqa

Depriving ISIS of territory and driving ISIS fighters out of Raqqa were the Pentagon's top priorities. The SDF launched the "Great Battle" to liberate Raqqa on 6 June 2017. Seven months prior, Iraqi Peshmerga had opened another front targeting ISIS in Mosul. The Raqqa battle drew on lessons learned in Mosul regarding urban warfare and ISIS strategy.

The Pentagon created the SDF to address Turkey's concerns about direct US security assistance to the Kurds. The SDF started as a fig leaf so the US could claim it was working with a multi-ethnic force; YPG fighters were battle-hardened and more effective. Their command and control were better than the Arabs in the SDF. After Raqqa, however, the SDF evolved into a majority Arab force, which helped wean the local Arab population from

ISIS. Joint Arab and Kurdish administration in Rojava brought stability, services and security.

At least 500 US Special Forces joined the SDF in "Operation Euphrates Wrath." The SDF advanced through Raqqa governorate, taking the city of al-Thawrah and the Tabqa and Baath dams. It advanced slowly to the outskirts of Raqqa, defended by die-hard ISIS fighters. A network of booby traps and IEDs was planted at key portals into the city. Snipers operated from a clandestine network of tunnels, inflicting significant casualties.

The SDF fought street by street in Raqqa's old city and finally took the Grand Mosque and seized the Raqqa clock tower, which ISIS used for public executions. The US air power was indispensable; sometimes whole buildings were bombed to rubble because they sheltered a single ISIS fighter. Monitoring groups suggest that more than 1,000 civilians died in Raqqa and at least 270,000 people fled the city. Eighty percent of Raqqa was flattened, its water supply and electricity grid destroyed. Brigadier General Jonathan Braga, the coalition's director of operations, commended the YPG. "They fought tenaciously and with courage against an unprincipled enemy, taking great care to move the population trapped by Daesh [ISIS] away from the battle area and minimize civilian casualties."[20]

Raqqa was liberated on 1 October 2017. Operation Euphrates Wrath took about 4,500 square miles from the control of ISIS and freed tens of thousands of people. ISIS lost 1,367 fighters while about 650 YPG and YPJ fighters died; thousands were injured. Kurds celebrated their hard-fought victory, singing and dancing. To the consternation of SDF members and Raqqa's local Arab residents, they hoisted a giant banner of Abdullah Ocalan.[21]

Appeasement

Syrian Kurds hoped that their sacrifice would translate into long-term military or diplomatic backing by the United States. It did not. In November 2017, President Donald J. Trump suggested that the United States might end military support to the YPG. Trump and Erdoğan had a phone conversation on 24 January 2018. Çavuşoğlu told reporters, "Mr. Trump clearly stated that he had given clear instructions that the YPG won't be given arms and that this nonsense should have ended a long time ago."[22] Trump's national security team was surprised by Çavuşoğlu's statement, which differed from their understanding of the discussion. The White House belatedly issued a statement:

> Consistent with our previous policy, President Trump also informed President Erdoğan of pending adjustments to the military support provided to our partners on the ground in Syria, now that the battle of Raqqa is complete and we are progressing into a stabilization phase to ensure that ISIS cannot return.[23]

The Trump administration either did not have a policy or was unsure of what to do. Eighteen days after offering assurances to Erdoğan during their phone call, Trump agreed to provide security assistance worth $393 million to the SDF, including heavy weapons and armored vehicles destined for the YPG.

On 13 January 2018, the US announced that it would establish a 30,000-strong YPG-led Border Security Force (BSF) to stave off a "resurgence" of the Islamic State, as "operations against ISIS draw to a close."[24] Under normal circumstances, the announcement would be thoroughly vetted within the administration and carefully communicated to Turkish officials but news of the BSF took Turkey by surprise. Erdoğan called the BSF an "army of terror" and promised to "strangle it before it is born." He was furious that the US did not consult before announcing the BSF, angrily accusing Trump of breaking his promise to discontinue assistance to the YPG. A disagreement between allies would typically be handled discreetly before exploding in public view.[25]

Further inflaming the situation, Erdoğan said he would attack the Kurdish enclave of Afrin in Syria's northwest, then Turkish forces would pivot east, liberating Manbij from Kurdish occupiers, and continue all the way to the Syria–Iraq border. Erdoğan affirmed,

> Beginning from the west, we will annihilate the terror corridor up to the Iraqi border. No one can say a word. Whatever happens we do not care anymore at all. Now we only care about what happens on the ground.[26]

According to Erdoğan, "We will crush anyone who opposes our national struggle."[27] Deputy Prime Minister Bekir Bozdağ justified Turkey's invasion: "People there are asking Turkey to cleanse the region and save them."[28]

On 17 January, US Secretary of State Rex W. Tillerson tried to tamp down tensions. "That entire situation has been mis-portrayed, mis-described, some people misspoke," he said. "We are not creating a Border Security Force at all." Referring to the YPG in Afrin, the Pentagon said: "We don't consider them as part of our 'Defeat ISIS' operations, which is what we are doing there and we do not support them. We are not involved with them at all."[29]

Turkey attacked Afrin on 20 January. About 25,000 FSA fighters joined the Afrin operation on the Turkish side. Turkey called its military operation "Operation Olive Branch" and the campaign sought to create a 30-kilometer-deep "security zone" inside the Syrian border. Erdoğan claimed divine inspiration, proclaiming: "We are not alone. Allah is with us."[30]

According to US Defense Secretary James N. Mattis, "They warned us before they launched the aircraft that they were going to do it." The warning came via a telephone call between high-level Turkish and US military officials. Mattis did not say whether US officials cautioned Turkey against the strikes.[31] A senior YPG commander responded, "Mattis' remarks only serve to encourage Turkey in its attacks. What we expect from the United States is to tell Turkey to stop the attacks immediately."[32]

Erdoğan maintained, "We have no intention of getting permission from anyone for this." However, the MIT head and the army's chief of staff went to Moscow days before the attack to secure Russia's acquiescence for attacking Afrin. According to Erdoğan, they discussed the operation "with our Russian friends. We have an agreement with them."[33] Turkey's operation could not occur without Moscow's consent, as Afrin lies in Russia's zone of influence; Russia has six bases in Afrin and controls the airspace. Russia pulled back when Turkish troops and the FSA came in, to avoid accidental clashes, and allowed Turkish planes to fly unfettered. Russian officials kept quiet when Hayat Tahrir al-Sham, a component of the FSA, used a Man-Portable Air-Defense (MANPAD) system it had received from Turkey to shoot down a Russian plane over Idlib province on 3 February 2018.

Calls by the Trump administration for restraint were a charade. Erdoğan indicated that he was operating with Washington's consent and committed to an open-ended operation. According to Erdoğan, "I asked the United States: Did you have any specific time duration in Afghanistan?" Erdoğan pledged to deploy Turkish troops until "the work is finished." [34]

While Mattis opposed Turkey's aggression, the administration sent mixed messages. Tillerson indicated, "Turkey is a NATO ally. It's the only NATO country with an active insurgency inside its borders. And Turkey has legitimate security concerns. We'll sort this out." Tillerson told Çavuşoğlu,

"Let us see if we can work with you to create the kind of security zone you might need."[35]

Erdoğan warned the US to withdraw from Manbij, suggesting in a veiled threat that Americans might get caught in the middle. Lieutenant General Paul E. Funk, the top US commander of the anti-ISIS coalition, warned Turkey of a sharp response if it struck Manbij. Erdoğan responded, "Those who say they will give a sharp response if hit, have clearly never got the 'Ottoman slap' in their lives."[36] Images of Erdoğan giving the Ottoman slap went viral on social media.

Kurds in Afrin had never attacked Turkey and posed no threat. Before Turkey's attack, about 600,000 civilians lived in Afrin, including many internally displaced persons (IDPs) from other parts of Syria. Most of these IDPs were Arabs from Idlib, Aleppo, Maa're and the Shahba region. Outnumbered and outgunned, about 10,000 YPG hunkered down to defend Afrin, highly motivated to defend their homeland. Afrin was an oasis of peace in war-torn Syria—until it was invaded by Turkey with Russia's acquiescence.

On 20 February, Syria announced it would send militias, including Iranian-controlled irregular forces and Shi'ite Afghans, to help defend Afrin. According to the YPG, the Syrian government "answered our call."[37] Though popular forces were not a part of the Syrian army, they came with Syrian government flags, assuming positions along the Turkey–Syria border to prevent Erdoğan from re-supplying the FSA. However, militias had no effect on the battle for Afrin.

Abandoned by Assad, Kurdish leaders practically begged the United States for help. Their pleas were ignored. The YPG had a choice: defend Afrin or stay with the anti-ISIS coalition, which included 2,000 US troops spread across northeast Syria. On 5 March 2018, the YPG announced that it was redeploying forces from Deir el-Zour, where senior ISIS commanders from Mosul and Raqqa were putting up a final fight. The YPG expressed "regret" about the "painful decision" to redeploy forces as a result of the West's failure "to curb the Turkish aggression and put real pressure" on Erdoğan to "stop its madness within our Syrian borders." Kurds lamented,

> The international coalition let us down. They did not do what we expected them to do for us after a very long partnership. We are allies. The Americans should have helped us. For one and a half months we have been under attack by Turkey. Turkey is using NATO weapons

to attack an American ally. We were partners in the fight against [the Islamic State], and they did not do anything to help us.[38]

Some SDF stayed in Deir el-Zour, but without the YPG the diluted force was ineffective. A YPG commander warned, "There is a danger this will give ISIS a chance to revive, to come back to life, and they might even expand their territory again."[39]

The Kurds invoked memory of the Mahabad Republic. "Do not forget Mahabad. Resistance will be our slogan which will lead us to victory. We call on all the Kurds, the international community to support Afrin resistance."[40] They rallied to support Afrin. A tearful woman protesting in front of the Iraqi Kurdistan parliament declared, "Long live the resistance of Afrin." A young man with the Kurdistan flag wrapped over his shoulders called for Kurdish unity: "Nobody can defeat Afrin." A PUK member offered to send Peshmerga to help fellow Kurds in their "sacred resistance." "If we can, we will help Afrin now. But before deploying forces, we will send a delegation to Ankara for dialogue."[41] Erdoğan warned Kurds away from Afrin. He admonished that anyone joining pro-Kurdish protests in Turkey would pay a "heavy price".[42]

Turkey's command of the skies and relentless bombing took its toll. As of 1 May 2018, more than 1,000 YPG fighters and at least 300 Kurdish civilians had been killed.[43] The YPG made an orderly retreat from Afrin, and civilians vacated the city. On 5 June 2018, US Secretary of State Mike Pompeo and Çavuşoğlu announced a plan for the YPG to withdraw from Manbij and for joint patrols by US and Turkish forces. The deal was done over objections by Mattis and US commanders on the ground. It marked the acquiescence of Washington to Erdoğan's demand for a security buffer in northern Syria from Afrin to the Euphrates. Moreover, Erdoğan intimated plans to deploy Turkish troops and their FSA proxies to the Iraqi border, spanning all of Rojava. The Manbij deal ended the Pentagon's partnership with the YPG, signaling the further erosion of US influence in Syria.

Syria's grinding civil war continued with no end in sight as UN-sponsored peace talks in Geneva continued to exclude the Kurds. Geneva became increasingly irrelevant as Turkey, Iran and Russia developed alternative mediation through the "Astana process." Political dialogue has no chance to succeed when the Kurds, who represent more than 10 percent of the population and control 30 percent of Syria's territory, are not at the table.

Assad Entrenched

Bashar al-Assad kept his grip on power through the indiscriminate use of force. He took a page from his father's playbook, called "Hama rules." Facing an insurgency from the Muslim Brotherhood in Hama from 1976 to 1982, Hafez al-Assad responded with brutal, overwhelming force. He shelled Hama, leveling the city and killing more than 20,000 people. Bashar applied the same tactic to Sunni Arab pockets of resistance, such as Aleppo and the Damascus suburb of Ghouta. In early 2018, Syrian forces attacked eastern Ghouta with both conventional weapons and chlorine bombs.

Assad was able to stay in power by stifling all forms of dissent. Freedom of thought and expression was denied. Thousands were arrested and disappeared, tortured in detention. Assad could not have survived on his own, however. Russian Special Forces and air power shaped the battlefield, rescuing Assad when it appeared his regime would be overrun by Sunni Arabs. Assad also cooperated extensively with Iranian-backed groups. Assad and his ruling clique are Alawites, who have strong similarities to Shi'ism. Despite the Baathist tradition of secularism, Iranian IRGC defended the Assad regime and protected Shi'ite sacred sites in Syria. It was joined by Hezbollah and other radicals. Assad offered no future to the country's Sunni Arab majority. Assad's Baathist state subjugated Sunni Arabs and Kurds alike.

Turkey's intervention further confused the situation. Assad was on the verge of seizing eastern Ghouta, the last pocket of rebel resistance near Damascus, and entering the final phase of the war when Turkey invaded Afrin. Assad threatened to shoot down Turkish planes violating Syria's airspace and counterattack if Turkish forces struck Manbij.[44] Assad condemned "brutal Turkish aggression," accusing Turkey of systematic "support for terrorism."[45] He linked the Afrin operation to Turkey's support to terrorism since the beginning of the conflict. "[It] cannot be separated from the policy used by the Turkish regime since day one of the Syrian crisis that is basically founded on helping terrorism and terrorist groups regardless of their names."[46]

Like many dictators, Erdoğan believed his own propaganda. He thought Afrin would fall without much of a fight and that Turkish armed forces would quickly establish a security belt along Turkey's border with Syria. He successfully convinced the United States to abandon its support for the YPG. However, Erdoğan did not accurately account for the YPG's battlefield prowess. Turkish officials asked the US to prevent the YPG from leaving Deir el-Zour and reinforcing their comrades in Afrin. The request was a sign of weakness as the casualty count of Turkish troops continued to climb. The Trump administration warned Erdoğan not to invade Afrin city, fearing a slaughter and humanitarian emergency. It is a measure of America's diminished influence that Erdoğan ignored US pleas and occupied Afrin.

Turkey's relationship with Russia is transactional. Putin could turn on Erdoğan in a "Moscow minute." Public opinion in Turkey could be affected if Turkish troops get bogged down in Syria. Turkey's conflict with the YPG risked becoming Erdoğan's Waterloo.

12 IRAN WINS

"If you resist, we will crush you and you will lose everything."

IRGC COMMANDER EQBALPOUR[1]

Iran turned the conflicts in Iraq and Syria to its advantage. Unlike America's mercurial support, Iran was in for the long haul. Iran's actions were guided by a strategy to promote the ideals of the Iranian revolution and consolidate a Shi'ite crescent from Basra to Baghdad, Damascus and Beirut. A land corridor through these countries was used to supply rockets to Hezbollah, thereby increasing pressure on Israel. As the US stepped back, Iran stepped up its nefarious activities in Iraq and Syria.

Rebellion

Iran purported to be friends with the Kurds. However, it was not sincere. Iran was solely focused on advancing its national interests and used the Kurds when expedient, undermining them when it suited their broader goal to diminish the United States. Iraqi Kurds tried to balance Turkey's influence through cooperation with Iran. However, neither Turkey nor Iran proved to be reliable. Tehran's disingenuous approach to the Kurds dates back to 1975 when Shah Reza Pahlevi betrayed Mulla Mustafa Barzani by conspiring with Iraq to normalize Iran–Iraq relations. The Algiers Accord signed in that year marked the end of the Mahabad Republic.

Disappointed by the Shah, Kurds joined Ayatollah Ruhollah Khomeini's Islamic revolution in February 1979. Despite their Muslim identity and conservative values, most Kurds are Sunnis and were excluded from negotiations over the Iranian constitution. The Kurdistan Democratic Party of Iran (KDPI) demanded autonomy for Kurds in the Iranian provinces of Kordestan, Kermanshah and West Azerbaijan. When their demands were ignored, Kurds rebelled in March 1979. The Iranian Revolutionary Guard Corps (IRGC) launched a counter-insurgency operation in the spring, crushing the independence movement. Thousands of Kurds were killed and many executed in the final phase of the rebellion, which ended in 1983.

A guerilla movement emerged from the Kurdish rebellion. The Party for a Free Life in Kurdistan (PJAK) was founded in 1984 at the same time as Abdullah Ocalan established the Kurdistan Workers' Party (PKK) in Turkey, and the two organizations share an ideology and common struggle on behalf of Kurdish rights. Both have a leftist orientation and are committed to peasants' and workers' rights. They espouse land reform and changes to the feudal system to emancipate Kurdish communities. Likewise, Jalal Talabani's Patriotic Union of Kurdistan (PUK) broke from the more conservative KDP in Iraqi Kurdistan to establish a progressive political movement.

The antipathy between Kurds and Iranians is far less than that between Kurds and Arabs or between Kurds and Turks. Kurds are ethnically closer to Persians, and have a shared history spanning thousands of years. Sorani, the Kurdish dialect spoken by Kurds residing near Iran, is similar to Farsi, the language of most Iranians. Like Persians, Kurds celebrate Newroz as their most important cultural holiday. Iraqi Kurds frequently visit Iran and tune into Iranian media. Unlike the governments of Iraq and Syria, the Iranian government has made an effort to have constructive relations with its Kurdish minority.

The Kurds were caught in the middle of the Iran–Iraq war, which pitted Khomeini's Islamic revolution against Saddam Hussein's Arab nationalist secularism. According to the Statistics and Information Department at the Islamic Revolution Martyrs Foundation, 204,795 Iranians lost their lives in the Iran–Iraq war between 1980 and 1990, including 188,015 military and 16,780 civilians.[2] According to Iranian health officials, about 60,000 Iranians were exposed to Iraqi chemical weapon attacks during the war.[3] Saddam believed that Iraqi Kurds were aiding the IRGC and established a security buffer on Kurdish lands to prevent Iranian incursions. Saddam's cousin, Ali Hassan al-Masjid, brutally cleansed the border area. As we have seen, a defining moment in the Anfal campaign occurred just a few months before the end of the Iran–Iraq war when, on 16 March 1988, chemical weapons killed at least 5,000 Kurdish civilians.

Iran rushed to help the Kurds after Halabja, dispatching doctors, setting up field hospitals and documenting atrocities. They also evacuated victims to Tehran for treatment of serious respiratory ailments resulting from exposure to sarin and mustard gas. Iran called on the UN Security Council (UNSC) to investigate the use of chemical weapons against Kurdish civilians and demanded that the world body hold Baghdad accountable. The US looked away. Not only was the US aligned with Iraq in the Iran–Iraq war but US and western companies had provided the chemical precursors that Iraq used for its weapons of mass destruction.

Iran also aided the Kurds after the Gulf War. Encouraged by President George H.W. Bush, Iraqi Kurds launched an insurgency in 1991 to overthrow the Baathist regime. Reprisals by Saddam drove more than one million Kurds from their homes. Fearing another chemical weapon attack, Kurds scrambled across the mountains to seek sanctuary in Iran and Turkey. Iran welcomed them and provided facilities for their relief and resettlement. Many leaders of the Iraqi opposition had homes and headquarters in Tehran. Iran assisted the Kurds despite its view that Iraqi Kurdistan was a pro-western democracy, sympathetic to Israel.

Since the 1979 Islamic Revolution, Iran has been obsessed by the United States—"The Great Satan." Iran feared that it would be the next target for America's regime-change agenda. Security was of paramount importance to Iran, which viewed regional and international relations through the prism of its anti-American and anti-Zionist agenda. When Syria's civil war broke out in 2011, Iran backed President Bashar al-Assad, while the US supported the Sunni opposition.

Iran's primary strategic objective was the creation of a land corridor via Iraqi Kurdistan to Syria and Lebanon through which it could supply rockets and other weapons to Hezbollah and Hamas. Iran's restive Kurdish minority stood in the way of securing the corridor. The Iranian government denounced PJAK as a terrorist group funded by the United States and condoned by Iraqi and Syrian Kurds. It took steps to destroy PJAK as a revolutionary force, while limiting Kurdish rights in Iran.

Party for a Free Life in Kurdistan

The PJAK base in Iraqi Kurdistan's rugged Qandil Mountains borders Iran, Iraq and Turkey. Qandil has long been a stronghold for Kurdish revolutionary movements, including PJAK and the PKK. No motorized vehicle can access the deeper recesses of Qandil. Only pack animals, namely mules, can deliver supplies. So much snow accumulates in the winter that Qandil becomes totally inaccessible. Saddam's Republican Guard tried to capture Qandil on several occasions but was defeated. Iraqi forces were joined by battle-hardened Peshmerga of the KDP, but they too were repelled.

There are many similarities between PJAK and the PKK. Both are Marxist–Leninist organizations inspired by the political ideology of Abdullah Ocalan. After Ocalan's arrest in 1999, Kurds took steps to export his movement to other Kurdish territories. This led to the creation of the PKK-affiliated Kurdistan Democratic Solution Party in Iraq in 2002, the Democratic Union Party (PYD) in Syria in 2003 and the expansion of PJAK in 2004. Although PJAK's political activities focus on Iran, it is part of a region-wide struggle for Kurdish rights. According to PJAK spokesman, Commander Shirzad Kamanger, "We do not recognize artificial borders drawn by the forces of imperialism and colonialism and countries hostile to the Kurdish people."[4]

Soon after the US attacked Iraq in March 2003, PJAK expanded its cross-border strikes, targeting Iranian regime facilities. It claimed to have 3,000 armed fighters, half of whom were women.[5] The Iranian government confirmed that 120 Iranian soldiers were killed by PJAK in 2005, and an equal number in 2006; PJAK continued its attacks in early 2007, launching three raids that killed 24 soldiers in March 2007. After President George W. Bush included Iran in his 2002 "axis of evil" speech, Iran was convinced that the United States was behind PJAK's operations.

The Pentagon allegedly provided financial, logistical and intelligence assistance to minority groups in Iran—Azeris in the north, Baluchis in the southeast and Kurds in the northeast, although the US predictably denied any covert activities.[6] Fueling speculation, PJAK's leader, Rahman Haj-Ahmadi, a German citizen based in Berlin, traveled to Washington in the summer of 2007, seeking financial and military support. Neoconservatives arranged his visit, which included meetings on Capitol Hill. Polite and well-spoken, Ahmadi found a receptive audience in Washington. Iran denounced the DC trip and launched a cross-border operation, seizing a strip of land five kilometers from Iraqi territory.

Turkey aligned itself with Iran, condemning PJAK and its sister organization, the PKK. Turkish officials claimed that the US was sponsoring them. In response, Graham Fuller, Deputy Director of the CIA's National Intelligence Council, said: "The US does not have contact with and does not support the PKK. It's a terrorist organization. It's treated as such. The only thing we want to see from it is to have it go out of business." The US military spokesman in Baghdad insisted, "US forces are not working with or advising the PJAK."[7] Anti-American feelings spiked in Turkey, despite assurances from US officials. Many Turks believed that the US had a hidden agenda to nurture the establishment of an independent state in Iraqi Kurdistan, and to support the PKK and PJAK.

Kamanger denied that PJAK was the Iranian wing of the PKK.

> We adopt the philosophy, ideas, and approach of [Abdullah Ocalan], but we are not a wing or a part of the PKK. We are linked to the PKK in terms of our shared struggle, as we are with other Kurdish parties. We are also prepared to defend this party, or any part of greater Kurdistan, if it is subject to threat or danger, but we are now concentrating our operations in the eastern part of Kurdistan, which is the Iranian part.

He continued,

> If the interests of the Kurdish people in any other part of Kurdistan were under threat or in danger, we would not hesitate to defend them. Do you think we would accept another Halabja to take place in Iraqi Kurdistan? Should we accept new crimes of genocide being committed against our people in any other part of Kurdistan? Of course this is unacceptable, because we—in principle—do not accept artificial borders, and we consider the Kurdish people to be one. Accordingly, we have repeatedly called for the unification of the Kurdish people, and we will continue to call for this unity to confront the regimes that seek to eliminate our national existence.[8]

The Bush and Obama administrations tried to assuage Turkish concerns. They provided intelligence on PKK bases and operations which Turkey used for air strikes. The US imposed sanctions on PJAK, designating it as a Foreign Terrorist Organization on 4 February 2009. Stuart Levey, the Treasury Department's Undersecretary for Terrorism and Financial Intelligence, announced, "With today's action, we are exposing PJAK's terrorist ties to Kongra-Gel (KGK) and supporting Turkey's efforts to protect its citizens from attack." According to the Treasury,

> The PKK/KGK leadership authorized certain Iranian Kurdish PKK/KGK members to create a KGK splinter group that would portray itself as independent from but allied with PKK/KGK. PJAK was created to appeal to Iranian Kurds. KGK formally institutionalized PJAK in 2004

and selected five PKK/KGK members to serve as PJAK leaders, including Hajji Ahmadi, a KGK affiliate who became PJAK's General Secretary. PKK/KGK leaders also selected the members of PJAK's 40-person central committee.[9]

However, PJAK denied the Treasury Department's conclusions. It believed that Iran was propagating rumors of its ties to the PKK in an effort to divide Turkey from the United States.

After PJAK and the Iranian government signed a ceasefire in 2011, Iran pledged to stop executing Kurdish political prisoners if PJAK suspended its military operations. Peace was short-lived, however, as Iran continued its crackdown on Kurdish political and cultural rights. Two Kurdish activists were hanged on 25 October 2014, including a senior leader of PJAK. In retaliation, PJAK killed ten members of the IRGC. A third Kurdish activist was hanged on 4 November. Iranian authorities executed six Sunni Kurds in May 2015, a day after the United Nations expressed concern about Tehran's treatment of religious minorities.[10] In August 2015, Iran charged Sirvan Nezhavi with PJAK-related terrorist activities and executed him. A few days later, PJAK attacked the IRGC base in Kamyaran, killing 12 soldiers. Later that month, Iran executed Behrouz Alkhani, a PJAK member accused of killing a public prosecutor in West Azerbaijan. Amnesty International said the trial was "grossly unfair" and called it a "denigration" of both Iranian and international law.[11] In 2016, the Iranian Human Rights Association reported that 138 Kurds had been sentenced to death by hanging for a range of offenses including drug trafficking.

After signing the Joint Cooperative Plan of Action (JCPOA) on 18 October 2015, Iran intensified its use of force against PJAK and sought to signal that accommodating the international community did not mean a softer stance towards the Kurds. It also intended to dissuade PJAK from finding common cause with progressive Persian organizations. A statement on PJAK's official website read:

> The protests that have spread throughout the whole Iranian landscape, starting with Mashhad and Kermanshah, have the potential to lead to great changes. They could lead to a democratic transformation for the whole of Iran […] As PJAK, we are calling on the Kurdish people and all the peoples of Iran to the ranks of the struggle for freedom.[12]

However, PJAK consistently refused to work with other opposition groups. It did not endorse the 2009 Green Movement of Mir Hussein Mousavi and Mehdi Karroubi because PJAK viewed them as part of the regime. According to Kamanger, "The problem of this movement was the lack of a unified and qualified leadership. This is why we called for a large national front to be formed that includes all Iranian political forces."[13]

Iranian Kurds were absent on 28 October 2016, when thousands of Iranians protested at the tomb of Cyrus the Great, and when riots erupted across the country in January 2018, which killed 21 people and injured 450. The January riots were fueled by the collapse of the rial, which precipitously lost 30 percent of its value against the dollar. Non-performing loans and the government's inability to inject money into the economy led to the rial's devaluation. Iran's economic crisis was exacerbated by the low cost of oil in global markets, driving Iranians to seek security for their savings by purchasing dollars. The budget bill lifted subsidies on the price of fuel as well as other household goods. Rising costs and high unemployment fueled popular protests.[14] Though Kurds were affected by Iran's economic crisis, few joined the protests that swept across the country.

Penetrating Iraqi Kurdistan

Iran used security, commercial and diplomatic levers to coerce the KRG into depriving PJAK of sanctuary along its 400-mile border with Iraqi Kurdistan. The rise of ISIS in 2014 threatened both Iran and the KRG. Iran filled a gap left by the United States, which refused to provide heavy weapons to Peshmerga, fearing they would be used against Iraq's armed forces. In May 2015, KRG President Masoud Barzani acknowledged Iran's support: "Iran was the first state to help us; it provided us with weapons and equipment. We have no problems with Iran [...] we are neighbors."[15] Hassan Rouhani was also explicit during a speech in Sanandaj in June 2015: "Iran protects Erbil and Baghdad the same as it protects Iranian Kurdistan. Without Iran's help Erbil and Baghdad would be in the hands of terrorist groups right now. The way we protect Sanandaj we also protect Suleimani and Duhok."[16] Beyond sending weapons, the IRGC joined the Peshmerga on the battlefield. Soldiers from Iran's 81st Armored Division helped PUK and PKK fighters expel ISIS from Khanaqin near the Iranian border in Diyala province.

Iran's overarching strategy linked its security and economic interests. Iran was indispensable to Iraqi Kurdistan's economy, acting as a counterweight to both Iraq and Turkey. Economic relations boomed between Iran and Iraqi Kurdistan, expanding from $100 million/year in 2000 to $4 billion in 2013.[17] In August 2014, the two sides agreed to further increase trade and energy ties during a meeting between Kurdish Prime Minister Nechirvan Barzani and a visiting Iranian trade delegation. While Turkey remained Kurdistan's leading trading partner, Iranian goods dominated PUK areas close to the Iran–Iraq border.[18] Iran provided access to key goods and investment; it supplied commodities and foodstuffs. After Turkey, Iran was the second largest customer of Kurdish oil.

Iraqi Kurdistan's oil industry was a major factor behind Iran's involvement in the Kirkuk operation of 16 October 2017. IRGC Commander Qasem Soleimani took a personal interest in Iraqi Kurdistan's energy sector. Iran and Iraq agreed to transport up to 60,000 barrels per day (bpd) via tanker to a refinery in the Iranian city of Kermanshah. Plans were made for a pipeline to carry 650,000 bpd from Iraq's Kirkuk fields to refineries in central Iran and onwards to the Persian Gulf.

The attack on Kirkuk affirmed the IRGC's critical role and strengthened Iran's influence over Prime Minister Heider al-Abadi. Antipathy between Iran and the KDP goes back to the 1975 Algiers Accord when Iran betrayed Mulla Mustafa Barzani. During the Kurdish conflict in the mid-1990s, Tehran backed the PUK while the KDP looked to Turkey for support. After the 2010 Iraqi elections, Iran worked with both the KDP and PUK to renew Nouri al-Maliki's mandate as prime minister. The agreement enshrined the Erbil principles on power-sharing and returned Jalal as president of Iraq. Iran's influence continued to grow after the last US combat brigade left Iraq on 19 August 2010.

Masoud met former Iranian President Mahmoud Ahmadinejad in 2011, after which Nechirvan brokered a ceasefire between Iran and PJAK. Nechirvan attended Rouhani's presidential inauguration in 2013, as Iranian–KRG relations continued to warm. Cooperation between Iran and the KRG was affirmed during the KRG's presidency crisis. In August 2015, Iranian leaders, including Qasem Soleimani, supported Masoud to stay in office after his constitutional term expired. Iran was acting in its own national interest, rather than out of loyalty to Masoud, and IRGC commanders met the PUK on October 15, describing its plan to attack Peshmerga at three locations in Kirkuk the following morning. Commander

Eqbalpour warned, "If you resist, we will crush you and you will lose everything."[19]

Iran closed its airspace to Iraqi Kurdistan immediately after the independence referendum. Rather than seal its border crossings, however, Iran sought to repair ties. When an Iranian delegation visited Erbil in November 2017, Nechirvan talked about opening a new chapter and normalizing relations. On 21 November, Nechirvan indicated that the KRG would respect a ruling by an Iraqi court that the referendum violated the constitution, which sent a conciliatory signal to both Baghdad and Tehran. He affirmed, "Iran is our neighbor. The Kurdistan Region shares a long border with Iran and we obviously want to have a good relationship."[20]

Humbled by the collapse of its independence agenda, the KRG accommodated Iranian concerns. According to Najmaldin Karim, "Iran was no longer the kingmaker. It was the king."[21] The KRG assured Iran that it would not interfere with the corridor through Iraqi Kurdistan. Iranian–KRG cooperation isolated PJAK. After Kirkuk, the US and Israel lost their foothold long the Iran–Iraq border. Not only did Iran succeed in challenging the United States in Iraq. It also challenged US interests in Syria, forming an alliance with Russia and Turkey to defend the regime of Bashar al-Assad.

Syria's Civil War

Iran rescued Assad when Damascus was almost overrun by Sunni rebels, providing weapons and deploying the IRGC and Hezbollah. Tehran viewed Syria as a vital frontier in the struggle between Shi'ites and Sunnis. The Sunni-led governments of Saudi Arabia, the United Arab Emirates, Qatar, and Turkey were pouring money and weapons into Syria to support the rebels. For Syria to become a Salafist dominion was abhorrent to Iran. Syria's fall to Sunni insurgents would set back Iran's sectarian agenda in the Middle East and be a sign of weakness to the broader Muslim community.

Iran found common cause with Russia in Syria, overcoming bilateral problems that go back centuries. After the Russian Empire defeated the Safavid Empire in the Russo-Persian War of 1722–3, the Safavids reluctantly ceded Dagestan, eastern Georgia, modern-day Armenia, the southern parts of current-day Azerbaijan, including Nakhchivan, and Igdir province, now part of Turkey. Khomeini abhorred the Soviet Union's atheist philosophy. In 1965, he called it "filthier" than Britain and the

United States. Iran resented the Soviet Union for providing weapons to Iraq during the Iran–Iraq war, and for delaying completion of the Bushehr nuclear power plant and the delivery of S-300 missiles that Iran had bought and paid for.

Iran and Russia are engaged in Syria for different reasons. Russia wants to project power in the Middle East, expanding its naval air station in Tartous and the Latakia air field. Syria offers a warm water port in the Mediterranean. For Iran, Syria is the front line in its sectarian struggle with Sunnis and a launch point for attacks on Israel. The IRGC sees an economic opportunity to rebuild Syria when the war was over.

The instruments of Iranian and Russian security assistance also differed. Iran deployed about 60,000 IRGC members and imported thousands of Shi'ite militias from Afghanistan, Pakistan, and elsewhere around the world.[22] Iran provided the boots on the ground, while Russia provided air power. As a permanent member of the UNSC, Russia was also able to give Syria diplomatic cover, vetoing UNSC resolutions aimed at ratcheting up pressure on Damascus and blocking investigations into its use of chemical weapons.

Iran and Russia had a transactional relationship, which inevitably led to a dispute over the spoils of war. According to an editorial in *Tabnak*, a news outlet with close ties to the IRGC:

> Based on an agreement between Russia and Syria, Iran and Iranian companies have been partly put aside from the process of reconstruction and investment in Syria, and consortiums have even been established between Syria and Russia in a number of sectors, and if Iran wants to join the reconstruction process, it should [first] talk to the Russians. This is not speculation but rather an issue that has been discussed in the government, and the Iranian government is deeply worried about this.

The editorial continued, "The Russians left us when UN resolutions against Iran were passed and didn't deliver the defense systems when we needed them, and are now harvesting the [fruit of the] efforts of Iranians in Syria and are accompanying Saudi Arabia in Yemen."[23] *Qanoon* reported that Rouhani sensed Iran was losing the Syrian market to Russia and contacted Assad:

> The Islamic Republic of Iran is ready for an active participation in the reconstruction process. We shouldn't allow Bashar Assad or any other

person who is trying to stop Iran from [having a role in] the reconstruction and post-IS era to reach their goal. This is because a part of the national interest is tied to economic and financial issues. That a [country] pays the price of fighting, and after the end of the conflict, [some] others come there [to harvest the fruits of Iran's labor], is not an appropriate and honorable measure.[24]

Iranian officials felt that Russia was benefiting at Iran's expense. They believed that the deal between Assad and Russia, providing a 49-year lease for military bases as well as other political and economic concessions, was one-sided.[25] At a minimum, Tehran wanted to be reimbursed for Iran's costs in Syria through in-kind payments of oil, gas and phosphate. According to the UN, Iran spent $36 billion in Syria between 2013 and 2017. It supports foreign fighters from Pakistan and Afghanistan at a cost of $100 million each year. In addition, the International Monetary Fund (IMF) says that Iran's Trade Development Organization provided Syria with a line of credit of $5.87 billion from 2011 to 2015. Iran also provided $2.8 billion in humanitarian aid.[26]

Israel

Iran is harshly critical of Israel and works towards its extinction. While the declared policy of the Iranian government accepts any outcome that is acceptable to the Palestinians, Iranian officials advance Iran's national interests by acting as an outspoken opponent of Israel. Despite this, Israel sold weapons to Iran even after the revolution. Israel's primary concern was to keep Iraq distracted or facing away from Israel.

Iran's hostility towards Iraqi Kurdistan was in response to Israel's early support for Iraqi Kurdistan. Israeli officials were the first to openly endorse its independence. Though KRG leaders were discreet, extensive security and economic cooperation existed between Israel and Iraqi Kurdistan.

Israel and Iraqi Kurdistan share a kinship born from suffering. Both are surrounded by hostile neighbors and are constantly at risk of attack. Iraqi Kurdistan was a buffer for Israel against Iran, Iraq and Turkey. Israel was a large buyer of oil from Iraqi Kurdistan, when other countries were reluctant to disobey Baghdad's edicts forbidding its sale. Israeli politicians endorsed Kurdistan's independence. In June 2014, Israeli President Shimon Peres indicated that the Kurds had created their own de facto state, which was democratic. Foreign Minister Avigdor Lieberman said that an independent Iraqi Kurdistan was a "foregone conclusion." Prime Minister Benjamin Netanyahu declared that Israel "should support the Kurdish aspiration for independence, because the Kurds are a fighting people that has proved its political commitment, political moderation, and deserves political independence."[27]

Israel provided weapons to the KRG, including drones for intelligence and air combat operations. The possibility of US military bases in Iraqi Kurdistan, institutionalizing the Kurdish–American and Kurdish–Israeli alliances, was a major concern for Iran. Israel allegedly assisted Iranian insurgent and anti-government groups, such as the People's Mujahadeen, to infiltrate Iran along its winding border with Iraq. Iraqi Kurdistan also served as a buffer between Israel and hostile countries such as Iran, Iraq and Turkey. When other countries refused to buy Kurdish oil, Israel imported up to three-quarters of its oil from Iraqi Kurdistan at preferential rates.[28]

After 9/11, the United States eliminated Iran's two great enemies—the Taliban in Afghanistan and Saddam in Iraq—which advanced Iran's regional hegemony. The corridor from the Gulf to the Mediterranean threatens Israel, supporting strategic fronts in Syria, Lebanon and Gaza by way of Hamas. Despite Syria's strategic and security cooperation with Iran, Assad tried to tamp down tensions with Israel. He adhered to the 1974 disengagement agreement to avoid provocations that would distract from Syria's civil war.

Hezbollah

Hezbollah was a potent force in the Syrian conflict, capturing Qusair and preventing Sunni opposition fighters from seizing Damascus in 2013. Hezbollah and Iranian-backed Shi'ite militias—Kata'ib Hezbollah, Asaib Ahl al-Haq and Harakat al-Nujabaa—played a critical role in capturing Aleppo in December 2016. They led the fight in Homs and the Damascus suburbs like Ghouta.[29]

From its base in Lebanon, Hezbollah is a constant threat to Israel. Hezbollah and Israel fought to a stalemate in 2006, resulting in the deaths of several hundred people. Hezbollah killed Israelis on a bus in Bulgaria in 2013. As Iran expanded its operations on Syrian soil, Israel bombed at least 100 Iranian convoys delivering weapons to Hezbollah in Lebanon between 2016 and March 2018.[30]

Shi'ite militias in Syria and Iraq replicated Hezbollah's model of establishing a state within a state. Beyond the battlefield, they provide humanitarian, reconstruction and other social services, gaining legitimacy and support from local communities. Their work is amplified by social media, which extols the role of Shi'ite militias in society. These non-state actors seek to translate their grass-roots popularity into political gains and control over state institutions. Shi'ite groups make a long-term commitment, not only to local security but to human development, becoming entrenched in the social fabric and political systems of Iraq and Syria.

United States officials turned a blind eye to Hezbollah's role in Syria. It did not want to expose Hezbollah at a sensitive stage in negotiations with Iran over its nuclear program. The Obama administration allegedly suppressed an investigation of Hezbollah's drug dealing and transnational crime networks. According to former US officials, the Drug Enforcement Agency had "amassed evidence that Hezbollah had transformed itself" into a global crime syndicate "that some investigators believed was collecting $1 billion a year from drug and weapons trafficking and money laundering." Obama Treasury official Katherine Bauer told the House Foreign Affairs Committee that under the Obama administration Hezbollah-related investigations "were tamped down for fear of rocking the boat with Iran and jeopardizing the nuclear deal." Her claim was corroborated by an unidentified former CIA officer working on Iran. The CIA official recounted discussions with Iranians who said, "We need you to lay off Hezbollah, to tamp down the pressure on them, and the Obama administration acquiesced to that request. It was a strategic decision to show good faith toward the Iranians."[31]

Iran tried to create controlled tensions with Israel. This high-risk policy inevitably led to violent conflict. An Israeli Apache helicopter shot down an Iranian drone, launched from the Tiyas air base (T4) in Homs province. A barrage of Syrian surface-to-air missiles downed an Israeli F-16 attacking T4. The shadow war risked spiraling into a full-blown confrontation, with serious ramifications in Syria and the region.[32] Israel has stated repeatedly that it would not tolerate the growing Iranian military presence in Syria so close to its border, or the deployment of increasingly sophisticated missile technology capable of overwhelming Israel's iron dome missile defense system.

On 9 April 2018, Israeli fighter jets entered Lebanese airspace and fired missiles at T4 in response to the chemical weapon attack on Dhouma. The

Israeli strike devastated a portion of the base used by the IRGC and its Quds Force and reflected the increasing intensity of Israel's concerns about Iran's presence in Syria. It also sent a message to Iran and Russia, as well as the United States. Israel will not tolerate Iran's control of chemical weapons so close to its border with Syria.

Conflict between Israel and Iran came out of the shadows on 10 May 2018. The proxy war had become a direct kinetic engagement when Iran fired 20 Grad and Fajr 5 ground-to-ground rockets against Israeli targets in the Golan Heights. The strikes represented Iran's first direct attack against Israel, which responded by putting its forces on "high alert", warning that Iran's actions represented a dangerous escalation.

Prior to 10 May, Russia had given Iran extraordinary latitude to pursue its strategic interests from Syrian soil. The day before, on 9 May, Prime Minister Benjamin Netanyahu met Putin in Moscow to ask him to keep Syria and Iran at bay. On 8 May, the US announced it was withdrawing from the Joint Cooperative Plan of Action (JCPOA), a comprehensive and verifiable agreement limiting Iran's nuclear program.

Iran was at the center of disputes between the US and the international community over the Iran nuclear accord. The interests of Russia and Iran in Syria were also diverging. Russia wanted a strong secular government in Damascus as a security partner whereas Iran preferred a weaker government that would allow Iranian-backed militias free rein.

US–Iran Relations

The JCPOA was the defining issue in relations between the US and Iran. The Obama administration was able to overcome decades of distrust to finalize the JCPOA, which represented a milestone in US–Iranian relations and Iran's relations with the international community. The JCPOA was a bet that, having benefited politically and economically from integration into the international system, Iran would choose not to resume nuclear enrichment when the deal expired in 10 to 15 years.

The Obama administration was so intent on sealing the deal, it conceded important points to Iran, allowing Iran to retain its nuclear infrastructure in what is called "nuclear latency," with the ban on building new heavy water reactors and plutonium reprocessing plants becoming voluntary after 15 years. Iran was allowed to retain its infrastructure for enriching uranium, which can be expanded during the term of the deal for research and development.

Natanz centrifuges can restart spinning highly enriched uranium between 2025 and 2030. According to the JCPOA, all constraints on enrichment will be lifted by 2030.

When the International Atomic Energy Agency certified Iran's compliance with the JCPOA requirements, Iran received a variety of benefits from the international community, including the termination of an oil embargo, sanctions relief and political re-engagement with the United States and the global community. Between $100 and $150 billion in frozen Iranian assets were released.

President Donald J. Trump strongly opposed the JCPOA. He called it "a stupid, loser deal" and "a horrible embarrassment to our country, and we did it out of weakness." Former Secretary of State Rex W. Tillerson said Iran's positive contribution to regional peace and security was "implied" in the JCPOA. Trump condemned Iran for betraying the "spirit" of the deal, bemoaning Iran's threats against Israel and its backing of Hezbollah, as well as Iran's role in destabilizing the Middle East through its support for Shi'ite militias in Syria, Yemen and Iraq.[33] Even though missile tests were not covered by the accord, the US objected when Iran tested a Khorramshar missile in violation of a UNSC resolution.

On 15 October 2017, Trump refused to certify that Iran was complying with deal terms, arguing that the accord is not in America's national security interest. The next day the IRGC was actively involved in attacking Kirkuk. Turning a blind eye to Iran's role in Kirkuk and its influence over Iraqi politics was inconsistent with Trump's pledge to get tough on Iran's regional meddling.

The Trump administration insisted on upgrading the JCPOA, threatening to pull out of the accord unless annexes were finalized by 12 May 2018. One of the annexes was intended to prevent and, if necessary, punish Iran for its aggressiveness in the Middle East. The other was intended to limit Iran's missile program, imposing sanctions if Iran tested any type of missile. Sanctions would also be imposed if Iran impeded access to its nuclear facilities by international inspectors or if Iran expanded its nuclear program sufficiently to be able to break out and develop a nuclear weapon in less than one year.

During an official visit to Washington in April 2018, France's President Emmanuelle Macron warned Trump not to push too hard. He asked, "What do you have as a better option? I don't have any Plan B for nuclear against Iran." Germany's Chancellor Angela Merkel followed Macron with a visit to DC and Britain's Foreign Secretary Boris Johnson weighed in to support fixing the deal rather than nixing it.

The JCPOA was an accord between Iran and six countries; Russia and China strongly opposed changes to an agreement that had been enshrined by the UNSC. Iran's Foreign Minister Mohammad Javad Zarif cautioned the US to abide by its international commitments. Citing US negotiations with North Korea, he warned: "Who would, in their right mind, deal with the US anymore?" Zarif admonished the US for bad faith. "Now the United States is saying, 'What's mine is mine and what's yours is negotiable. But whatever I gave you, now I want it back.'"[34]

On 8 May 2018, the Trump administration withdrew its support for the JCPOA and immediately took steps to impose new sanctions on Iran. Israel's Benjamin Netanyahu was one of the few international figures to praise the decision. Other signatories to the JCPOA scrambled to keep Iran in the deal, over which Iran has several options. It could simply withdraw from the JCPOA and restart enrichment activities. It could become more active in Iraq and Syria, activating proxies to target US interests. It could resume cyberattacks against US banks, financial institutions and critical infrastructure in multiple industries. President Rouhani succeeded in turning the tables on Trump, making Iran look like the rational actor, abiding by international agreements, while Trump seemed impulsive and emotional. Transatlantic cooperation broke down across the board, not only on Iran, but on trade, climate change, migration and an approach to Russia, as US foreign policy became a toxic mix of isolationism and unilateralism. Italian politician Federica Mogherini blamed the transatlantic schism on an "impulse to destroy." She bemoaned the "screaming, shouting, insulting, bullying, systematically destroying and dismantling everything that is already in place."[35] The European Union's Donald Tusk said that Trump had "rid Europe of all illusions" with his "capricious assertiveness." He queried, "With friends like Trump, who needs enemies?"[36] Trump's approach to Iran was emblematic of a broader problem: the lack of strategic coherence in US foreign policy, which led to a breakdown in multilateral cooperation.

13 RUSSIA RISES

"We think it is an enormous mistake to refuse to cooperate with the Syrian government and its armed forces, who are valiantly fighting terrorism face to face."

RUSSIAN PRESIDENT VLADIMIR V. PUTIN[1]

The US invasion and occupation of Iraq displaced Russia as Baghdad's protector in the international community. Moscow played a long game waiting for the US to lose interest. Meanwhile, Russia pursued two tracks, broadening its energy cooperation with the Iraqi Kurds and deepening security cooperation with Assad in Syria. Putin's willingness to use his money and military strength advanced Russia's strategic interests, while further marginalizing the United States.

Russia's Intervention

Commander Qasem Soleimani secretly visited Moscow on 24 July 2015. Sunni rebels had seized Syria's Idlib province during the first half of 2015, leaving Syrian government forces in control of only 20 percent of Syria's territory. Panicked by insurgent gains, the situation was becoming critical to President Bashar al-Assad's survival. Rebels were on the verge of occupying the country, overrunning Damascus and slaughtering their Alawite adversaries. Soleimani went to Moscow to work out the details of a joint Iranian–Russian intervention aimed at turning the tide of Syria's civil war.[2]

High-level talks involving Russia's Foreign Minister Sergei Lavrov and Ayatollah Khamenei were held in Tehran prior to Soleimani's trip. They discussed a political agreement between Iran and Russia, with the military deployment details to be worked out later. In July, Assad met Iranian and Russian officials to underscore the urgency of security assistance and describe Syria's manpower problem. Insurgents were advancing towards the coast, capturing Jisr al-Shughour and other strategically important towns. Rebel gains threatened the Alawite heartland and could potentially represent a risk to Tartous, Russia's only Mediterranean base.

Assad formally invited the participation of Iranian and Russian forces, which initiated the phase of military planning. During Soleimani's trip to Moscow, which violated a travel ban and personal sanctions, he met Putin and Russian Defense Minister Sergei Shoygu. According to reports,

> Soleimani put the map of Syria on the table. The Russians were very alarmed, and felt matters were in steep decline and that there were real dangers to the regime. The Iranians assured them there is still the possibility to reclaim the initiative.

Soleimani assured them, "We haven't lost all the cards." They agreed that Russian air strikes would support ground operations by Iranian, Syrian and Hezbollah forces.[3] In May 2015, Soleimani traveled to Syria to "organize the entry of Iranian officials to supervise and aid Iranian proxy forces."[4]

Russia's engagement involved different components. Russia expanded its military facilities at Tartous and Latakia, which enabled it to more effectively project power into the Mediterranean. It established a process for intelligence sharing with Iran and Syria. Russia also announced a flight corridor agreement with Iran and Iraq, allowing access to Syrian airspace. In addition to warplanes, the flight corridor could also be used to fire cruise missiles from Russian destroyers in the Caspian Sea at targets in Syria.

Russia and Syria had been allies since the Cold War. Russia's decision to deploy forces reflected historical amity between the countries, as well as the strategic decision to ensure the survival of Assad's regime. Russia was also motivated to fight ISIS in Syria. It was concerned about so-called Black Russians, Muslims in the southern Caucusus who had joined ISIS and could return to Russia with enhanced terror skills. The intelligence-sharing and air-corridor agreements allowed Russia to deepen its security and military cooperation with Iraq. Though Russia and Iraq were aligned during the Cold War, Iraq has been dominated by the US since the Iraq War of 2003. Putin was consumed with countering America's unipolar powers, which came to a head in 1999 with the US-led bombing campaign of Serbia and Washington's subsequent coordination of Kosovo's independence declaration.

Iran's alliance with Russia advanced multifaceted cooperation between the two countries. Iran sought Russian S-300 surface-to-air missiles as deterrence against Israeli air strikes, as well as help from Russia in building the Bushehr nuclear power plant in order to mitigate international sanctions that affected the cost and supply of energy. To end its international isolation, Iran hoped to deepen cooperation with Russia and China by joining the Shanghai Cooperation Organization (SCO). When Iran signed the JCPOA, which limited Iran's nuclear program, Lavrov immediately called for Iran's membership in the SCO.

Iran was transparent about preserving Assad's regime and countering the influence of Saudi Arabia, its chief regional rival. Russia was less honest about its intentions, justifying its intervention in Syria by claiming its forces were fighting ISIS. However, Russia's air strikes mostly neglected ISIS-controlled territory. Russia targeted Syria's northwest, rather than ISIS strongholds in the east of Syria. Russia attacked groups backed by the United States and coalition countries, including Turkey and the Gulf States.

Putin addressed the situation in Syria during his speech to the UN General Assembly on 27 September 2015. He compared Russia's leadership role countering ISIS to the Yalta Conference.

> In 1945, the countries that defeated Nazism joined their efforts to lay solid foundations for the postwar world order. I remind you that the key decisions on the principles guiding the cooperation among states, as well as on the establishment of the United Nations, were made in our country, in Yalta, at the meeting of the anti-Hitler coalition leaders.

He likened Russia's role fighting ISIS to the "anti-Hitler coalition [...] resisting those who, just like the Nazis, sow evil and hatred of humankind" and admonished the US for "playing games with terrorists." Invoking the specter of US assistance to the Taliban, he warned against arming Syrian rebels, a policy which is "short-sighted [and] hazardous." Putin warned, "This may result in the global terrorist threat increasing dramatically and engulfing new regions, especially given that Islamic State camps train militants from many countries, including the European countries." He continued,

> We cannot allow these criminals who already tasted blood to return back home and continue their evil doings [...] We think it is an enormous mistake to refuse to cooperate with the Syrian government and its armed forces, who are valiantly fighting terrorism face to face.[5]

In September 2015, satellite imagery confirmed that Russia was engaged in a massive military build-up, upgrading Bassel al-Assad international airport in Latakia with runway improvements, two additional helicopter pads, a new taxiway and a new air traffic control station. It delivered state-of-the-art weaponry to Latakia, including T-90 tanks, deploying special forces and building mobile housing for up to 1,500 soldiers and their families.

Despite irrefutable evidence that Russia was establishing a base of operations, Russian and Syrian officials denied the obvious. Lavrov said that the transfer of military equipment and advisors was part of a pre-existing arms deals and not an expeditionary force. "Our soldiers and military specialists are located there to service Russian equipment, cooperate with the Syrian army in using this equipment."[6] Ambassador Riad Haddad, Syria's envoy in Moscow, denied extraordinary Russian military activities in Syria. He said that Syria was receiving arms under existing defense contracts. "We have been cooperating with Russia for 30 to 40 years in various areas, including the military sphere. Yes, we receive arms, military equipment, all this is done in line with agreements sealed between our countries." Haddad denied a military build-up, calling it "a lie spread by western countries, the United States."[7]

Russian warplanes—Sukhoi-25, Sukhoi 24-M and Sukhoi-34—focused their attacks on insurgents in northwestern Syria, not on ISIS. The coalition, which included the United States, major European powers, Arab states and Turkey, issued a statement:

> We express our deep concern with regard to the Russian military build-up in Syria and especially the attacks by the Russian Air Force on Hama, Homs and Idlib since yesterday which led to civilian casualties and did not target Daesh. We call on the Russian Federation to immediately cease its attacks on the Syrian opposition and civilians and to focus its efforts on fighting ISIL.[8]

According to Jeff Davis, a Pentagon spokesman, Washington welcomed Moscow's contributions to the effort against ISIS, but military assistance to Assad could "risk adding greater instability to an already unstable situation."[9]

Putin visited Paris days after his address to the United Nations. France's President François Hollande described conditions for France to support Russia's intervention: Russia must stop strikes on groups other than ISIS and al-Qaeda; ensure the protections of civilians; and commit to removing

Assad as part of Syria's political transition.[10] British Prime Minister David Cameron said, "They are backing the butcher Assad, which is a terrible mistake, for them and the world."[11] His political recommendations were echoed by President Barack Obama, who insisted, "Assad must go."[12] Putin dismissed demands from the international community and denied Russia's combat operations.

Obstructionism

Syria used chemical weapons to attack the Damascus suburb of Ghouta on 21 August 2013. The official UN report called it "The most significant confirmed use of chemical weapons against civilians since Saddam Hussein used them in Halabja in 1988." The sarin gas nerve agent was delivered by Soviet-era 140 mm surface-to-surface artillery rockets, known as the M-14, each with a chemical weapons payload of 2.2 kilograms. According to a US Government assessment, the Ghouta attack killed 1,429 people, including 426 children.[13]

Little doubt existed about the Syrian government's responsibility. The Syrian military was believed to have more than 1,000 tons of chemical agents and precursor materials, hundreds of tons of sarin, as well as the necessary expertise to load and deliver. Missile trajectory analysis identified launch points, which targeted rebel-controlled suburbs. Damascus used chemical weapons to dislodge insurgents who were stubbornly resisting Syrian conventional forces.

When US intelligence observed Syrian armed forces loading the missiles with sarin, Obama warned that the use of use of chemical agents would be a "red line." The red line was, however, more a deterrent than a commitment to military action. Syrian officials ignored his warning and went ahead with the attack.

According to the US Government's after-action report, "We intercepted communications involving a senior official intimately familiar with the offensive who confirmed that chemical weapons were used by the regime on 21 August and was concerned with the UN inspectors obtaining evidence." The assessment continued, "The regime intensified the artillery barrage targeting many of the neighborhoods where chemical attacks occurred."[14]

The Syrian government's responsibility should have been straightforward. However, its culpability was clouded by claims that the rebels fired chemical weapons at their own positions in order to provoke international military intervention. Putin rallied to Assad's defense, describing reports of the Syrian government's involvement as "utter nonsense."[15]

When Obama refused to take military action, the US sub-contracted the task of disarming Assad. It turned to the UN Security Council (UNSC), where Russia and the US, as veto-wielding permanent members, were equal actors. By giving the UNSC a leading voice on disarmament, the US opened the door for Russia to expand its role in Syria.

The US and Russia jointly sponsored UNSC Resolution 2118 on 27 September 2013. The Resolution condemned the use of chemical weapons anywhere and endorsed the scheduled destruction of Syria's chemical weapons program, with inspections to begin within 96 hours. The resolution, which was passed unanimously, prohibited Syria from using, developing, producing, otherwise acquiring, stockpiling or retaining chemical weapons, or transferring them to other states or non-state actors. It mandated the Organization for the Prohibition of Chemical Weapons (OPCW) to carry out the work of disarming Syria. The UNSC had learned from Saddam's "cheat and retreat" strategy in the 1990s and demanded that Syria provide all OPCW personnel with immediate unfettered access to any site suspected of manufacturing or storing chemical weapons. The OPCW, through the UN Secretary General (UNSG), was required to report on progress within 30 days and every month thereafter, and UNSG Ban Ki-moon hailed the resolution's passage as "the first hopeful news on Syria in a long time." He urged, "We must capitalize on the new-found unity of the Council by focusing on the two other equally crucial dimensions of the conflict: the dire humanitarian situation and the political crisis."[16]

Lavrov heralded the resolution, which required the OPCW to "act impartially in Syria in full respect of its sovereignty." Furthermore, the resolution absolved Syria of sole responsibility. It stipulated that "Violations of its requirements and use of chemical weapons by anyone must be carefully investigated." The resolution required compliance by non-state actors, a code word for Sunni insurgents, thereby leveling the field and asserting moral equivalency. The text was not passed as a coercive Chapter VII resolution, mandating "all necessary measures" to enforce Syria's compliance. If Syria obstructed the OPCW or failed to comply with any of resolution's terms, the Council would debate and potentially impose Chapter VII measures.

The resolution also gave Russia a leading role in negotiations over a political settlement. The resolution set up a framework for the political settlement of the conflict by backing the convening of an international conference, which would take place by mid-November, involving both the Syrian state and opposition. The resolution explicitly assigned a lead role to the Russian Federation, which "would participate in implementing the chemical disarmament program and in preparing for the Geneva II conference." According to US Secretary of State John Kerry, "The Council had shown that when we put aside politics for the common good, we are still capable of great things."[17] The resolution was a diplomatic victory for Russia, which succeeded in putting itself at the center of all international efforts concerning Syria.

Russia wielded its veto as a permanent member of the UNSC to prevent any additional pressure on Syria. Ban Ki-Moon warned, "We must never forget that the catalog of horrors in Syria continues with bombs and tanks, grenades and guns." The plan to eliminate Syria's chemical weapons was "not a license to kill with conventional weapons."[18] As violence continued to escalate, however, Russia used its veto to shield Syria from international pressure. It was often joined by China, an unflinching champion of state sovereignty, vetoing resolutions that enjoyed broad support with other members of the UNSC as well as the UN General Assembly.

The following sample of UNSC resolutions and the reasons Russia offered for vetoing them demonstrate how useless the UN system can be.

Russia vetoed Resolution S/2011/162 on 4 October 2011. The resolution "Condemns the continued grave and systematic human rights violations and the use of force against civilians by the Syrian authorities, and expresses profound regret at the deaths of thousands of people including women and children." Vitaly Churkin, Russia's Permanent Representative to the UN, explained: "The Russian Federation could not agree with the accusatory tone against Damascus, nor the ultimatum of sanctions against peaceful crisis settlement. The Russian Federation's proposals on the non-acceptability of military intervention, among others, had not been taken into account."

Russia and China vetoed S/2014/548 on 19 July 2012. The resolution called on Damascus to "cease troop movements towards population centres, and all use of heavy weapons in such centres." Furthermore,

If the Syrian authorities have not fully complied within ten days, then it shall impose immediately measures under Article 41 of the UN Charter (complete or partial interruption of economic relations and of rail, sea, air, postal, telegraphic, radio, and other means of communication, and the severance of diplomatic relations).

Churkin responded,

> Instead of levelling insinuations against the Russian Federation, which
> throughout the conflict had provided key support for the Annan mission,
> those members had today made unacceptable statements. They could
> have done something to promote dialogue with their Syrian counterparts,
> rather than fan the flames of conflict, including of Syrian terrorist groups,
> as they furthered their own "geopolitical designs".

Russia and China vetoed S/2014/348 on 22 May 2014. The resolution

> Reaffirms strong condemnation of the widespread violations of human
> rights and international humanitarian law by the Syrian authorities
> and pro-government militias, as well as the human rights abuses and
> violations of international humanitarian law by non-State armed groups.
> [It] refers the situation in the Syrian Arab Republic described in para-
> graph 1 above since March 2011 to the Prosecutor of the International
> Criminal Court.

Churkin responded,

> Although the motivations of delegations supporting the draft resolution
> and their emotions are understandable, it was difficult to understand
> France's motivation since that delegation had been fully aware of the
> end result of tabling the text draft. "P5" [i.e. the five permanent members
> of the UNSC] unity had been demonstrated through concrete positive
> results like resolutions 2118 on the destruction of Syria's chemical
> weapons, or resolution 2139 on humanitarian issues. Why deal a blow
> to the P5 in this case?

Russia vetoed S/2016/846 on 8 October 2016. According to Churkin,

> The text of the document, which was obviously drawn up with
> Washington's encouragement directly after the United States refused to
> observe the Russian-US agreements on the Syrian settlement, flagrantly
> misrepresented the actual state of affairs and had a politically-charged and
> unbalanced character. The French-proposed document indiscriminately
> laid the blame for the escalation of tensions in the Syrian Arab Republic

solely on the country's authorities and plainly attempted, through a ban on military flights over the city of Aleppo, to afford protection to Jabhat al-Nusra terrorists and the militants that have merged with it, despite the UN member states' obligation to fight the terrorist threat with all available means. The draft resolution completely obscured the fact that the humanitarian crisis in Aleppo was provoked deliberately, when in August and September the militants refused to provide access to humanitarian convoys, threatening to open fire on them.[19]

International diplomacy to deter Syria's aggression was a fiasco. Likewise, the OPCW process turned out to be a sham. The Syrian government knew that Russia would shield it from opprobrium and went through the motions of partly destroying its stockpile of chemical weapons. In fact, it retained stores of chlorine-tipped missiles and phosphorus bombs, as well as other nerve agents in reserve for future use. Chlorine was not included as a banned substance, although its usage was prohibited under the Chemical Weapons Convention that Syria joined in 2014. Russia was supposed to be guarantor of Syria's chemical weapon disarmament. It either colluded with Syria to hide stockpiles of chemical agents or was willfully ignorant of Syria's continuing chemical capabilities.

On 4 April 2017, the Syrian army launched a poison gas attack from Sharyat air base on Khan Sheikhoun, killing 86 people including 27 children. The strike was met with widespread international condemnation and public revulsion. Russia blamed the opposition, claiming that Syrian forces hit a laboratory where rebels were producing chemical weapons. The UN pledged to investigate the incident, calling it a possible war crime.

United States President Donald J. Trump was appalled at the images of dying children gasping for breath as their lungs collapsed. He said, "There can be no dispute that Syria used banned chemical weapons, violated its obligations under the chemical weapons convention and ignored the urging of the UN Security Council." Trump continued, "No child of God should ever suffer such horror. It is in the vital national security interest of the United States to prevent and deter the spread and use of deadly chemical weapons."[20]

On 7 April, Trump ordered an attack on Sharyat using 59 Tomahawk cruise missiles. The strike hit Syrian planes, air defenses, aircraft, hangars and fuel. Although Sharyat is used as a base by Russian attack helicopters, no Russian equipment or personnel was affected by the strike; the Pentagon informed Russian military officials in advance. The cruise missiles cost $100 million. However, the strike caused minimal damage; Sharyat was back in operation just 24 hours later.

Russia condemned the cruise missile strike, warning that it would "inflict major damage on US–Russia ties".[21] It suspended an October 2015 memorandum of understanding (MOU) between Russia and the US aimed at minimizing the risk of in-flight incidents among coalition and Russian aircraft operating in Syrian airspace. The MOU created the de-confliction channel, a hotline between American forces at Al-Udeid Air Base outside Doha and Russian officials at Hmeymim base in Syria. The MOU did not require US–Russia cooperation on intelligence sharing or target information.

Russia vetoed Resolution S/2017/315 on 12 April 2017. The resolution called for an investigation into the use of chlorine bombs and other chemical weapons. Russian Deputy Permanent Representative Vladimir Safronkov told the Council before the vote that the resolution pre-judged the Syrian government for the attack on Khan Sheikhoun. According to Safronkov, "The primary problem was the fact that the draft resolution by the troika designated the guilty party prior to an independent and objective investigation."[22]

Britain's UN Ambassador Matthew Rycroft was incredulous. "How could anyone look at the faces of lifeless children and choose to veto a resolution condemning those deaths?"[23] The US Ambassador to the UN, Nikki Haley, told the Council,

> With its veto, Russia said no to accountability, Russia said no to cooperating with the UN investigation, Russia said no to helping keep peace in Syria. Russia chose to side with Assad, even as rest of the world, even the Arab world, comes together to condemn the murderous regime.[24]

After the vote, French President François Hollande said Russia "bears a heavy responsibility" for continuing to protect Assad and blocking a united international response.[25]

Trump's cruise missile strike was impulsive rather than strategic. It was not accompanied by an intensified diplomatic effort or additional measures to enforce the ban on chemical weapons. On 17 April 2018, a week after Trump had indicated that the US would withdraw from Syria "very soon," Syrian forces dropped barrel bombs laced with poisonous chemicals on the eastern Ghouta town of Douma, killing 150 people. A US spokesperson held Russia accountable for the strike. Trump tweeted, "President Putin, Russia and Iran are responsible for backing" Syrian President Bashar al-Assad, whom he called "Animal Assad." The Syrian government denied the incident and accused the rebels of spreading "fake news."[26]

Whether by chemical or conventional weapons, the slaughter in Syria continued during the spring of 2018. Bombing raids killed more than 500 people in eastern Ghouta, as Russia delayed a vote in the UNSC on a ceasefire to allow medical and food aid to reach civilians. Under siege since 2013, Eastern Ghouta was the last remaining rebel position near Damascus. On 24 February, the UN passed a resolution calling for a 30-day ceasefire across Syria, with the exception of military operations against "terrorist" groups. Attacks intensified after the ceasefire expired.

Russia was more than informed about these war crimes. On at least one occasion that was documented, Russian warplanes targeted civilians. Russia bombed a market in Aleppo on 22 August 2016, killing 84 people. A UN report concluded that Russian aircraft used "unguided bombs, including blast weapons, in a densely civilian populated area," which "may amount to the war crime of launching indiscriminate attacks resulting in death and injury to civilians."[27] The police station in Aleppo was not a legitimate target of war, since no rebel forces were stationed there. Its actions put Russian forces in direct conflict with the US.

In February 2018, several hundred Russian mercenaries were killed when they attacked the YPG and US warplanes retaliated. That month, the Syrian Observatory for Human Rights reported that 450,000 people have been killed in Syria since the outbreak of the conflict. The UN refugee agency (UNHCR) had registered over 5.5 million refugees from Syria and estimated that there are over 6.5 million internally displaced persons within Syria's borders. Assad and his Russian backers were not interested in a negotiated end to the conflict. Like his father in Hama in 1980, Assad wanted a military victory and total destruction of the enemy regardless of its humanitarian consequences.

Peace Talks

United Nations Security Council Resolution 2118 assigned Russia a role preparing for peace talks in Geneva. Russia undermined UN-led negotiations, launching a parallel process with Iran and Turkey under its control. While sitting at the table discussing de-confliction zones, Russia was ramping up its military presence and expanding its support for Syria's military operations. Russia's insistence that Assad remain in power, at least during a transition period, was the primary sticking point in negotiations.

The Syrian government and opposition members met in Geneva in June 2012. Former UN Secretary General Kofi Annan served as Special Envoy and chaired the conference. Secretary of State Hillary Clinton and Russian Foreign Minister Sergei Lavrov attended along with envoys from other permanent UNSC member states and Middle East countries. The Syria Action Group condemned the violence. However, Lavrov cast blame on the insurgents, insisting they were equally to blame. Challenging Clinton's emphasis on regime change, Lavrov demanded a role for Assad during the transition period.

Kofi Annan presented a six-point plan, which called for an end to the violence, a Syrian-led political process to resolve the conflict, the release of prisoners, unimpeded access for humanitarian organizations, freedom of assembly and the right to demonstrate. He envisioned a transitional government made up of the current regime and the opposition. The opposition adamantly refused to include those responsible for crimes against humanity. Assad was the perpetrator of these crimes and would be excluded from the future government. They criticized Russia's role and rejected the conference conclusions. This phase of the UN's mediation, called "Geneva I", ended in disarray with the opposition rededicated to armed struggle.

Lakhdar Brahimi, Algeria's former foreign minister and an experienced peace negotiator who helped broker peace agreements in Lebanon, Afghanistan and Iraq, replaced Kofi Annan as the UN–Arab League mediator. The upgraded format, "Geneva II," was launched at successive meetings in January and February 2014. Brahimi knew the difficulty of negotiating a political transition, so he focused on humanitarian issues—evacuating civilians from the besieged city of Homs as well as humanitarian access to more than three million people in other cities. The Syrian government delegation refused to make any concessions. The US blamed the Syrian regime for preventing progress and scolded Moscow for not making a more serious effort to push Assad. A disgruntled Brahimi apologized to the Syrian people for Geneva II's failure. He resigned in May, expressing regret for his inability to forge a coherent international response.

Staffan de Mistura replaced Brahimi as the UN Special Envoy for Intra-Syrian Negotiations in July 2014. His task was made even more difficult by the gap between Russia and the United States. Russia had proven to be

196 THE GREAT BETRAYAL

Assad's strongest supporter, while Washington supported the insurgents. Countries in the region and around the world supported different sides, turning Syria into a proxy war. The rebels themselves were hardly coherent. The Syria desk officer at the State Department had a chart on her wall identifying hundreds of different rebel groups and their connections to one another.

De Mistura brought "constructive outrage" to the task. A self-described "chronic optimist," he believed that no problem is intractable if the mediator has vision and perseverance to mobilize political will among the parties to a conflict.[28] Within a year after de Mistura took the job, Russia showed its true colors by deploying as many as 4,000 troops, and US officials questioned Putin's sincerity about diplomacy. If he really wanted peace, Putin could have pressed Assad into making more concessions. Though Iran was well placed to encourage concessions, the Obama administration was negotiating a nuclear deal with Tehran and did not want to put too much pressure on it. Turkey, a NATO ally, complicated the battlefield by supporting jihadists with weapons, money and logistics. The rise of ISIS exacerbated de Mistura's task, with Assad positioning himself as part of the anti-ISIS coalition.

Russia undermined de Mistura by launching an alternative dialogue under its control. The alternative dialogue was convened in Astana, the capital of Kazakhstan. The UN-led Geneva process was about political transition, while the so-called Astana process focused on conflict mitigation. The President of Kazakhstan, Nursultan Nazarbayev, who is close to Putin, hosted five meetings in 2017 with Russia, Iran and Turkey acting as guarantors. A low-level US official was invited as an observer to the first meeting on 23–24 January 2017, but only at the last minute. However, de Mistura was gracious, commending efforts by the troika.

At the January meeting, the guarantor states agreed on a ceasefire. The agreement was ignored by Syrians, especially Assad, who wanted to regain government control over every square inch of Syrian territory regardless of the human toll. At the second meeting on 15–16 February, the guarantors agreed to set up a monitoring group, but there was no ceasefire to monitor. An exchange of prisoners was explored at the third meeting on 14–15 March. However, no prisoners were actually exchanged. On 3–4 May, the guarantor states signed a Memorandum of Understanding on the creation of de-escalation zones in Idlib, Homs and eastern Ghouta, as well as Deraa and Al-Quneitra, over which Syrian and Russian fighter jets would not be allowed to fly. However, violence and air attacks continued unabated. The fifth meeting on 4–5 July was equally ineffectual.

In January 2018, Russia convened a conference at Sochi on Russia's Black Sea coast. Opposition leaders refused to attend. They believed the Russian-led process was undercutting de Mistura's efforts to negotiate a fair political solution.

The same week that Trump announced his intention to "get out" of Syria and withdraw the remaining 2,000 American troops "very soon," the leaders of Russia, Turkey and Iran were once again meeting to chart Syria's future.[29] No US representative was invited to the Ankara meeting on 4 April 2018. The Ankara statement supported a constitutional committee to be undertaken by the Syrian National Dialogue, as well as the "release of detainees/abductees and handover of the bodies as well as the identification of missing persons." Deepening cooperation between the Syrian, Russian and Iranian militaries and their intelligence services, the statement confirmed "trilateral coordination in all aspects of anti-terrorist activity and increase information exchange." The statement also addressed humanitarian issues, vowing to expedite the return of refugees. Russia and Turkey agreed to build a hospital in Tal Abyad in a cynical effort to deprive Kurdish militias control of the strategic border crossing between Turkey and Syria.[30]

Though Russia, Iran, and Turkey came together through the Astana process, they had fundamentally different priorities. Russia wants to consolidate its presence in Syria by expanding military facilities and demonstrating its indispensable role in diplomacy. Iran seeks the survival of Assad's regime, so that Syria can be a launch point for attacks against Israel and a safe haven for Iranian-backed Shi'ite militias. The IRGC demurred from participating in the offensive against Ghouta, which it viewed as a sideshow to its primary objectives. Turkey hopes to defeat the YPG, dismantle the PYD, and thereby increase pressure on its own restive Kurdish population.

In the Afrin operation, Turkey partnered with the Free Syrian Army, which functions like a terror group. After Afrin, Erdoğan focused on Manbij, an American training center for the YPG just west of the Euphrates. Erdoğan warned that US personnel could be collateral damage when Turkey clears Manbij of the YPG, whom he calls "terrorists." Through the Astana track, Iran, and Russia, gave Turkey a free hand in northern Syria in exchange for Turkey's blind eye to the slaughter of Sunnis in the eastern suburbs of Damascus. Rouhani was increasingly alarmed by war crimes in Afrin. He called on Erdoğan to hand over control of Afrin to Syrian armed forces, fearing the rise of Turkey's diplomatic influence and the actions of its Sunni cohorts. Russia joined Rouhani in demanding that Turkey hand over Afrin to the Syrian government. Lavrov said,

> We always proceed from the fact that the easiest way to normalize the situation in Afrin, now that Turkish representatives say that the main goals they set there have been achieved, would be to return the territory under the control of the Syrian government.

Erdoğan dismissed his demand calling it a "very wrong approach." Erdoğan added, "We will personally hand over Afrin to the people of Afrin when the time is right. But the timing of this is up to us. We will decide this, not Mr Lavrov."[31]

Cooperation between Russia, Iran and Turkey was transactional, shallow and short-lived. There have been previous disagreements and there will surely be others. For example, Russia announced a deal to use Iran's Hamadan Air Base in July 2016. It failed to coordinate the announcement with the Iranian government, and did not adequately assess attitudes towards Russian forces on Iranian soil. No foreign power has had bases in Iran since World War II, and Tehran is fiercely protective of its independence and sovereignty. Russia released videos of its planes operating from Hamadan. The announcement embarrassed Iran, which quickly revoked the deal. Iran's minister of defense, Brigadier General Hossein Dehghan, accused Russia of grandstanding. He called the Kremlin's behavior a "betrayal of trust" and "ungentlemanly."[32]

Russian–Iraqi Relations

Iraq sided with the Soviet Union during the Cold War, signing a 15-year "treaty of friendship and cooperation" in April 1972. Cooperation encompassed the security sector with the Soviet Union giving Iraq weapons to suppress Mulla Mustafa Barzani's Kurdish rebellion. Iraq's intelligence agencies, including the Mukhabarat, were trained by Soviet and East German agents. When the US refused to sell Iraq military hardware, the Soviets provided a vast arsenal including Sukhoi warplanes, attack helicopters and T-72 tanks. The Soviet Union adopted a policy of strict neutrality during the Iran–Iraq war, until 1987 when Moscow transferred a large supply of weapons to Iraq to prevent Saddam's regime from falling.

Moscow also had an interest in Iraq's energy sector. Iraq's decision to nationalize assets of the Iraq Petroleum Company (IPC) in 1972 marginalized Western oil interests and created an opening for the Soviet Union to expand its position. The Soviets assisted the Iraqis in the development of the vast Rumaila oil field, where Premier Alexei Kosygin participated in the ribbon-cutting ceremony. Ever opportunistic, Moscow took advantage of Iraq's vulnerable position to expand the volume of its oil purchase at a discounted price. The day after nationalization, an Iraqi delegation visited Moscow to seek assistance with marketing IPC assets. Nationalization occurred at a time when global demand for oil was low. Additionally, IPC oil was less profitable than oil produced in the Persian Gulf.

When Iraq invaded Kuwait in 1990, the Soviet Union sought to exert influence over Saddam Hussein by drawing on decades of cooperation. Mikhail Gorbachev sent Yevgeny Primakov, a former Russian prime minister and foreign minister, to negotiate Iraq's withdrawal from Kuwait. Primakov was an Arabist who had known Saddam for 20 years. However, the Soviet Union was weak and on the verge of collapse. Though the Soviets warned Saddam that a "very strong force" would come to Kuwait, he dismissed Primakov's warning and rejected his six-point plan. The US-led international coalition liberated Kuwait and decimated Iraq's armed forces, an outcome that further marginalized the Soviet Union's influence in Iraq.

Dimitri Trenin, a Russian analyst with the Moscow Carnegie Center, believes the Gulf War was a turning point. "This was the first time that the United States started to act as a global policeman, that there was no counterweight to the great might of the United States."[33] The US expanded its influence in Iraq between the 1991 Gulf War and the Iraq War of 2003, working with the opposition on regime change. Saddam mistakenly thought that Putin could organize diplomatic opposition at the UN to stop America's war plan.

The Russians had a source at Central Command who provided intelligence on the US invasion plan. According to a captured Iraqi document dated 5 March 2003, the Russian Ambassador to Iraq leaked information on the troop deployments, equipment, locations and attack movements to Saddam's government.[34] While the US successfully toppled Saddam, the occupation was no cakewalk. America's enormous investment of troops and treasure put it in a dominant position, pushing Russia further to the margins.

Russia was the only great power that did not criticize the KRG's independence referendum, seeking to capitalize on divisions in the international community. Days before the referendum, Russian energy company Rosneft announced an investment of $1 billion in Iraqi Kurdistan's natural gas sector. It took control of Iraqi Kurdistan's main oil pipeline, assuming a 60 percent ownership position. Though Rosneft struggled to borrow money due to US sanctions, it preyed on the KRG's fiscal crisis to acquire assets at a discount. The KRG borrowed around $4 billion from Rosneft and others, guaranteed by future oil sales. Rosneft invested $400 million in five exploration blocks, which were actually worth far more.

Rosneft's business position put Putin in a position where he could play a leading role normalizing relations between the KRG and Baghdad. Outstanding issues are oil revenue sharing, payment of Kurdistan's debts, and how much money Iraq will transfer to Kurdistan from its national budget. The KRG demands that some of the crude oil is retained for local refineries and that Baghdad must pay pumping tariffs to Rosneft. The details of a deal were planned to be hammered out after Iraqi elections on 12 May 2018, but a government report found widespread voting irregularities in several provinces, including Kirkuk. Government formation was consequently delayed as the ballots were recounted manually. Regardless, the outcome will be advantageous to Russia.

EPILOGUE

Russia, Iran and Turkey constitute the new axis of evil through their pursuit of narrow self-interests and crimes against humanity. The absence of US leadership has created a gap, allowing the expansion of their influence in Iraq and Syria. Problems in the Middle East region have been further compounded by the failure of the United States to support its long-term allies, the Kurds.

It is not too late for the US to make a strategic decision to engage more deeply. That engagement can take many forms, encompassing diplomatic, economic and security cooperation. In the short term, engagement would prevent the resurgence of ISIS while over time it would stabilize the region, create conditions for democratic and economic development and protect the Kurds. The Middle East will remain of central importance to the United States.

The collapse of Kurdistan as a political possibility was concurrent with the rise of authoritarianism in Iraq and Syria. Progressive governance died when the Kurdistan flag was replaced by the Iraqi flag in Kirkuk, when Afrin fell to Turkish-backed jihadis, and when chemical weapons decimated the civilian population of Ghouta. These events were a tragedy for people directly affected, and they also marked the marginalization of America in the Middle East. There is plenty of blame to go around, including failures by both the Obama and Trump administrations.

Trump's deference to Putin was inexplicable. Russia took responsibility for disarming Syria of its chemical weapons, but chlorine was left off the list of banned substances. Chemical weapons were used approximately 85 times in Syria between 2012 and 2018, killing thousands.[1] Russia is either guilty of inaction, making it an accomplice to Assad's crimes, or it has helped choreograph the slaughter of civilians. Putin has an overarching objective: to diminish the United States and restore Russia's influence in the Middle East.

Iran is obsessed by its conflict with Saudi Arabia, fueling proxy fights between Shi'ites and Sunnis in Iraq, Syria, Yemen and elsewhere. During

202 THE GREAT BETRAYAL

Iraqi Kurdistan's push for independence in 2017, Iran was in a unique position to facilitate a mutually beneficial agreement between Baghdad and the Kurds, which would have enhanced its influence with both. Instead Iran fomented conflict through Shi'ite militias and, drawing on the Hamas model, facilitated their transition into political parties. Iraq's elections on 12 May 2018 demonstrated the deep divisions in Iraqi society, which fuel sectarian and ethnic conflict.

Erdoğan committed crimes against the Kurds in both Turkey and Syria. In Turkey, he arrested oppositionists, including Kurdish political and civic leaders who stood against his dictatorship. In Iraq, Turkey was quick to close the border and ban flights to Iraqi Kurdistan after the referendum. In Syria, Turkey provided weapons, money and logistical support to jihadi groups. Russia allowed Turkey to invade Afrin, where Kurds were beheaded and the bodies of female fighters mutilated by Turkish proxies.

Under both the Obama and Trump administrations, US policy further marginalized America. Obama made a false choice between Iraq's stability and democracy for Iraqi Kurdistan. Supporting Kurdish national aspirations and facilitating a friendly divorce between Iraqi Kurdistan and Baghdad had the potential to stabilize Iraq. By opposing self-determination, a core principle of democracy and human rights, the US fueled Arab hard-liners and left the door open for Iran to expand its influence. The US policies had the unintended consequence of making Iraqi Kurdistan vulnerable to ISIS and Iranian infiltration.

Obama was elected on a platform to end the disastrous and expensive US engagements in Iraq and Afghanistan. Even as Syria became a slaughter-house, Obama resisted the counsel of Secretary of State Hillary Clinton and CIA Director David Petraeus to set up safe zones for civilians. Obama rejected the notion that air strikes early in the conflict could push Assad to the negotiating table. He concluded that US involvement in Syria's civil war would require a massive deployment of ground forces. The Obama administration's de-escalation policy focused on humanitarian aid, a ceasefire and political negotiations that would result in a transitional government and Assad's departure. Obama's ineffectual policy accelerated the spiral of deadly violence in Syria.

In Libya, Obama ceded political and military leadership to Britain and France. The term "leading from behind" was coined by a senior White House official. It would unfortunately characterize the Obama administration's overall approach to foreign policy. Obama allowed the Status of Forces

Agreement (SOFA) with Iraq to lapse, leading to the precipitous withdrawal of US troops. He chose not to project American power or back diplomacy with a credible threat of force in Syria. The Syrian people paid a steep price. Bill Clinton, reflecting on his own presidency, concluded that not preventing genocide in Rwanda was his biggest failure. Obama did not include Syria on his list of regrets, although he said Syria haunts him constantly. "I do ask myself. Was there something we hadn't thought of [to end the Syrian conflict]?"[2]

Obama's problem was not lack of creativity. The conflict escalated because the US failed to intervene diplomatically and politically at critical points early in the conflict when it could have made a difference. The 2013 chemical weapons attack on Ghouta was a defining moment. Establishing a red line and refusing to enforce it had repercussions beyond Syria. Senator John McCain and others argued that Russia would never have seized Crimea or attacked eastern Ukraine if it feared reprisals from the United States. Ambassador Richard C. Holbrooke was the master of backing diplomacy with a credible threat of force. One can only imagine a different course if Holbrooke were alive and in a position to influence US policy.

President Donald J. Trump scapegoated Obama for Syria's crisis, in a crass attempt to cover his own failings. For sure, Obama's decisions on Iraq and Syria were flawed. But Trump's refusal to take responsibility empowered America's enemies, sold out its friends, and changed the perception of the United States as a reliable ally and a force for good in the world.

Trump was critical of everyone during the first year of his presidency; everyone, that is, except Vladimir Putin. He refused to criticize Russia for launching cyberattacks promoting discord among Americans, compromising the US electoral system and undermining public confidence in American institutions. Trump became more critical of Putin as investigators probed Trump and his inner circle, and Trump went from being Putin's lapdog to his critic. Consistency is critical to national security policy but the Trump administration has proved to be unpredictable towards Russia, vacillating from conciliatory to confrontational.

Consistency was also lacking in US policy towards Iran. The day after Trump promised to get tough on Iran for meddling in the region, he turned a blind eye to the IRGC's role in the takeover of Kirkuk. Trump was, however, constant in criticizing the Joint Comprehensive Plan of Action (JCPOA). He sought to eliminate sunset clauses that lift restrictions on Iran's nuclear activities after 10 to 15 years; demanded tougher inspections and snap inspections; and expanded the scope of the deal to curb Iran's testing of ballistic and cruise missiles. United States officials tried to negotiate changes to the JCPOA, but Iran rejected them. The P5 (the five permanent members of the Security Council) plus Germany were also unwilling to scrap the existing agreement. He tried to get the P5 plus Germany to fix problems in the agreement. However, Trump's ability to bring other countries on board was limited by the US withdrawal from the Paris Accord on climate change, his NATO-bashing and the appointment of John Bolton—notoriously hostile to the UN and multilateral cooperation—as US National Security Advisor. After a weak effort to fix it, Trump canceled US participation in the JCPOA on 8 May 2018.

Events in Iraq and Syria further divided the US and its formerly stalwart ally, Turkey. Erdoğan squeezed Iraqi Kurdistan after the referendum, coercing the KRG to abandon its independence claim. The US acquiesced when Turkey and Iran isolated Iraqi Kurdistan and Washington was silent on the Astana process. The proposed acquisition of S-400 missiles from Russia prompted a serious debate in the US Congress on suspending all weapons transfers to Turkey. Russia succeeded in driving a wedge between the US and Turkey by offering surface-to-air missiles and allowing Turkey to use Russian-controlled airspace to attack the YPG in Afrin, putting the US in a position of having to choose between its NATO ally, Turkey and the People's Protection Units (YPG), its boots on the ground in Syria.

And what about Kurdistan? Iraqi Kurds have not abandoned their dream of independence. Despite the low points in 1975, 1988 and 1991, Kurds remain resilient. According to Fuad Hussein, chief of staff for the KRG presidency, "Struggle is part of our life. Without struggle we cannot live. I was a part of the struggle since age 17. We already lost many things."[3] Despite the recent setback, Kurds remain optimistic about the future and grateful for what has been achieved. Independence may not be at hand, but Kurds were not slaughtered or gassed. The economy is depressed, but it is in better shape than it was before 2003. Kurdistan is less isolated, with open borders and airports. Once again, Kurds have shown they are survivors. "We have experienced many ups and downs," says Fuad. "But we have always come back."[4]

Masoud Barzani resigned as KRG president under a cloud, accused of mishandling the referendum. Though he left office, Masoud continues the struggle as a Peshmerga. Fuad explains, "From my generation, no one can resign from the cause. One can resign from their job but not from the cause."[5]

Masoud remains President of the KDP, Iraqi Kurdistan's most powerful political party. In Kurdistan's elections, scheduled for 30 September 2018, the KDP is likely to gain at the expense of the PUK and Gorran. Jalal would be deeply disappointed to see how Bafel and some members of the Talabani family besmirched his name and betrayed Kurdish national aspirations. Barham Salih's Coalition for Justice and Democracy (CJD) is a new and appealing opposition party. It has the potential to gain votes from the PUK and perform strongly in disputed territories like Kirkuk and Diyala. The Erbil principles establish power-sharing, with the presidency typically reserved for a Kurd. Though Barham harshly criticized the PUK and was abruptly removed from its politburo, the CJD could establish a coalition with the PUK and Gorran that would send Barham to Baghdad. Alternatively, Barham and the KDP could find common cause. Either way, Barham is experienced in Iraqi politics and would effectively represent Kurdish interests with the Government of Iraq.

Najmaldin Karim was never formally removed from his post as Governor of Kirkuk. He merely fled before assassins could kill him. Iraqi provincial elections are planned for the last quarter of 2018, when Kirkukis will elect an entirely new Kirkuk Council. The Council could invite him back, but it is unclear whether Karim wants the job. However, this course of events would vindicate him after the PUK's betrayal. A low-intensity insurgency is under way targeting Arab administration in Kirkuk.

The shattered mosaic of Assad's Syria was held together with mass repression and the fear of an Alawite overthrow. Today, Syria is controlled by outside powers—Russia, Iran and Turkey—with other stakeholders—the United States, Israel, Saudi Arabia, France, the United Kingdom—vying for influence. Syria has become a killing ground for the settlement of old scores and the ignition of new flames.

Syrian Kurds are caught in the middle. They wanted to be left in peace, but ISIS and Turkey would not allow it. The YPG expected security assistance and political support from the United States after Raqqa; they believed the US needed them to contain Iran and pressure Russia. However, Syrian Kurds were deeply disappointed when Washington abandoned them in Afrin. Washington's reluctant engagement in Syria made the position of the Kurds even more precarious.

The YPG may have lost Afrin, but its struggle continues. The term *Berxwedan* means "resistance" in Kurdish. Berxwedan is ingrained into the psyche of Kurds who have been fighting the Turkish state for decades.

Syrian Kurds are adaptable. If America will not help them, they will find other patrons. Putin or Assad could champion their interests in the short term, but they are false friends.

All wars end, and Syria's civil war is no exception. The ultimate peace agreement will include a new constitution that devolves power to the regions and a bill of rights that protects group rights and safeguards the rights of religious minorities. A federal or confederal arrangement will establish the Democratic Federation of Northern Syria (Rojava) as a legal entity within Syria. The PYD will take care of local governance, with energy and water managed by local authorities. It will be responsible for local security. Until then, the Syrian Kurds will live in a constant state of insecurity.

Fuad reflects, "We are in a region where everything is burning. Kurds are the weakest and the first to be thrown into the fire." Under current circumstances, "Our main strategy is in the first place to survive." Battle-hardened, Fuad is resigned to reality. "You cannot always get what you want as a person or as a politician." Yet he cannot hide his disappointment. "We expected more from the US."[6]

The Kurds used to be America's good friends. United States forces and Peshmerga cooperated closely together in the aftermath of the Iraq war, providing security and stewarding Iraq's political transition. Based on shared values and common interests, the Kurds thought they were allies of the United States. However, the Kurds were never an ally of the United States. They were simply an expedient partner to advance America's agenda. The bond of friendship was broken when Washington abandoned the Peshmerga and surrendered the field to Iran and its Shi'ite proxies. Kurds are disappointed and betrayed by the events described in this book. Iraqi and Syrian Kurds both joined the fight against ISIS without assurance or promise of reward. Many were martyred. Not only does America's betrayal of the Kurds ramify across the region; allies and potential partners worldwide have also taken note. The US is a diminished power, lacking credibility. Who will fight and die for the United States the next time it asks for help?

NOTES

INTRODUCTION

1 Joseph Fitchett, "Kurds say CIA betrayed them," *Washington Post*, 19 November 1975.

2 Henry Kissinger, "Quotable Quotes," *Goodreads*, www.goodreads.com/quotes/633024-america-has-no-permanent-friends-or-enemies-only-interests (accessed 3 July 2018).

3 John McCain, "We need a strategy for the Middle East," *New York Times*, 24 October 2017, www.nytimes.com/2017/10/24/opinion/john-mccain-kurds-iraq.html (accessed 3 July 2018).

4 Dan Murphy, "The Iraqi army the US spent billions building is a disaster," *Christian Science Monitor*, 2 July 2014, www.csmonitor.com/World/Security-Watch/Backchannels/2014/0702/The-Iraqi-army-the-US-spent-billions-building-is-a-disaster (accessed 3 July 2018).

5 Email from Najmaldin Karim to the author, 23 February 2018.

6 McCain, "We need a strategy for the Middle East."

7 Dana Rohrabacher, "Rohrabacher calls for U.S. backing of Kurdistan against terrorism," *Congressman Dana Rohrabacher*, 30 November 2017, rohrabacher.house.gov/media-center/press-releases/rohrabacher-calls-for-us-backing-of-kurdistan-against-terrorism (accessed 3 July 2018).

1. SOVEREIGNTY DENIED

1 "President Wilson's address to Congress, analyzing German and Austrian Peace utterances," 11 February 1918, *World War I Document Archive*, www.gwpda.org/1918/wilpeace.html (accessed 3 July 2018).

2 Jim Muir, "Sykes–Picot: the map that spawned a century of resentment," *BBC News*, 16 May 2016, www.bbc.com/news/world-middle-east-36300224 (accessed 3 July 2018).

3 Robin Wright, "How the curse of Sykes–Picot still haunts the Middle East," *New Yorker*, 19 June 2017, www.newyorker.com/news/news-desk/how-the-curse-of-sykes-picot-still-haunts-the-middle-east (accessed 3 July 2018).

4 "Wilson's Fourteen Points, 1918," *Department of State Office of the Historian*, history.state.gov/milestones/1914-1920/fourteen-points (accessed 3 July 2018).

5 Ibid.

6 Ibid.

7 Michael Duffy, "President Wilson's addendum to the Fourteen Points," *First World War.com*, 22 August 2009, www.firstworldwar.com/source/fourteenpoints_wilson2.htm (accessed 3 July 2018).

8 The Editors of Encyclopaedia Britannica, "Armistice of Mudros," *Encyclopaedia Britannica*, www.britannica.com/event/Armistice-of-Mudros (accessed 3 July 2018).

9 Michael Alison Chandler, "A president's illness kept under wraps," *Washington Post*, 3 February 2007, www.washingtonpost.com/wp-dyn/content/article/2007/02/02/AR2007020201698_2.html (accessed 3 July 2018).

10 Ibid.

11 Ibid.

12 "On This Day: March 19," *New York Times Learning Network*, 19 March 2014, learning.blogs.nytimes.com/on-this-day/march-19 (accessed 3 July 2018).

13 *Encyclopaedia Britannica*, "Armistice of Mudros."

14 "The Grand National Assembly of Turkey," Republic of Turkey: Ministry of Culture and Tourism, www.kultur.gov.tr/EN,104186/the-grand-national-assembly-of-turkey.html (accessed 3 July 2018).

15 "Cairo Conference (1921)," *Encyclopedia of the Modern Middle East and North Africa*, Encyclopedia.com, www.encyclopedia.com/history/modern-europe/wars-and-battles/cairo-conference (accessed 3 July 2018).

16 "Crying 'wolf': why Turkish fears need not block Kurdish reform," *Europe Report No. 227*, International Crisis Group.

17 W. Rupert Hay, *Two Years in Kurdistan: Experiences of a Political Officer, 1918–1920* (London: Sidgwick & Jackson, 1921). Quotations in the following paragraphs are taken from this source.

18 Ibid.

19 Peter Sluglett, *Britain in Iraq, 1914–1932* (London: Ithaca University Press for the Middle East Centre, St. Anthony's College, Oxford, 1976).

20 The Editors of Encyclopaedia Britannica, "Treaty of Sèvres," *Encyclopaedia Britannica*, www.britannica.com/event/Treaty-of-Sevres (accessed 3 July 2018).

21 Treaty of Sèvres, 1920, Section I, Articles 1–260," *World War I Document Archive*, wwi.lib.byu.edu/index.php/Section_I,_Articles_1_-_260 (accessed 3 July 2018).

22 Ibid.

23 Ibid.

24 "The Treaty of Kars," *This Week in Armenian History*, 13 October 2016, thisweekinarmenianhistory.blogspot.com/2016/10/the-treaty-of-kars-october-13-1921.html (accessed 3 July 2018).

25 A.L. Macfie, "British intelligence and the causes of unrest in Mesopotamia, 1919–21," *Middle Eastern Studies* 35(1) (1999), pp. 165–77.

26 Azad Aslan, "Revision of the Treaty of Sèvres and incorporation of South Kurdistan into Iraq: History Revisited," *Kurdish Globe*, 4 March 2010.

27 *A Speech Delivered by Mustafa Kemal Atatürk, 1927* (Ankara: Başbakanlık Basımevi, 1981), www.scribd.com/document/359762979/A-SPEECH-delivered-by-MUSTAFA-KEMAL-ATATURK-1927-aka-NUTUK-in-English-aka-THE-GREAT-SPEECH-pdf (accessed 3 July 2018).

28 *Mesopotamia Intelligence Report, No. 4*, 31 December 1920.

29 Ibid.

30 Ibid.

31 Ibid.

32 Sluglett, *Britain in Iraq*, pp. 116–25.

33 Ibid.

34 Ibid.

35 Wright, "The Curse of Sykes–Picot."

36 Muir, "Sykes–Picot."
37 Ibid.

2. VICTIMS OF THE COLD WAR

1 Daniel Schorr, "Telling it like it is: Kissinger and the Kurds," *Christian Science Monitor*, 18 October 1996, www.csmonitor.com/1996/1018/101896.opin. column.1.html (accessed 4 July 2018).
2 "The Tehran Conference, 1943," *Department of State Office of the Historian*, history. state.gov/milestones/1937-1945/tehran-conf (accessed 4 July 2018).
3 Hakan Ozoglu and Hille Hanso, "Creating an independent Kurdistan: the history of a hundred-year-long dream," *Maydan: Politics and Society*, 19 October 2017, www. themaydan.com/2017/10/creating-independent-kurdistan-history-hundred-year-long-dream/ (accessed 4 July 2018).
4 Amir Hassanpour, "The Kurdish experience," *Middle East Research and Information Project*, Spring 2018, www.merip.org/mer/mer189/kurdish-experience (accessed 4 July 2018).
5 "The Baghdad Pact," *Department of State Office of the Historian*, https://history. state.gov/historicaldocuments/frus1958-60v12/d70 (accessed 1 August 2018).
6 *Al-Hayat* (London), 15 October 2006.
7 *Sionizm* (*Bol'shaya sovetskaya entsiklopediya*) (*Great Soviet Encyclopedia*, 3rd Edition. 1969–78) http://encycl.yandex.ru/art.xml?art=bse/00071/37300.htm (accessed 6 January 2018) (in Russian).
8 David A. Korn, "The last years of Mustafa Barzani," *Middle East Forum*, June 1994, www.meforum.org/220/the-last-years-of-mustafa-barzani (accessed 4 July 2018).
9 Sergey Minasian, "The Israeli–Kurdish relations," Noravank Foundation, Yerevan, p. 22, http://www.noravank.am/upload/pdf/256_en.pdf (accessed 4 July 2018).
10 The Editors of Encyclopaedia Britannica, "Mustafa Al-Barzani," *Encyclopaedia Britannica*, www.britannica.com/biography/Mustafa-al-Barzani (accessed 4 July 2018).
11 Gerald K. Haines, "The Pike Committee investigations and the CIA: looking for a rogue elephant," *Central Intelligence Agency*, 27 June 2008, https://www.cia.gov/library/center-for-the-study-of-intelligence/csi-publications/csi-studies/studies/winter98_99/art07.html (accessed 4 July 2018).
12 David McDowall, *A Modern History of the Kurds* (New York: I.B.Tauris, 2004), pp. 327–8.
13 "Reversing Arabization of Kirkuk," *Claims in Conflict: Reversing Ethnic Cleansing in Northern Iraq*, www.hrw.org/reports/2004/iraq0804/7.htm (accessed 4 July 2018).
14 Ibid.
15 "Iraqi–Kurdish Autonomy Agreement of 1970," *Revolvy*, www.revolvy.com/page/Iraqi–Kurdish-Autonomy-Agreement-of-1970 (accessed 4 July 2018).
16 Firas Al-Atraqchi, "What did the Arabs really win in the 1973 war with Israel?" *Huffington Post*, 5 October 2010, www.huffingtonpost.com/firas-alatraqchi/what-did-the-arabs-really_b_751263.html (accessed 4 July 2018).
17 Pierre Terzian, *OPEC: The Inside Story* (London: Zed Books, 1985).
18 Stephen McGlinchey, "How the Shah entangled America," *The National Interest*, 2 August 2013, nationalinterest.org/commentary/how-the-shah-entangled-america-8821 (accessed 4 July 2018).

19 David A. Korn, "The last years of Mustafa Barzani," *Middle East Quarterly* 1(2), June 1994, www.meforum.org/220/the-last-years-of-mustafa-barzani (accessed 4 July 2018).

20 Interview by the author with Henry Kissinger, 12 September 2016.

3. CRACKDOWN

1 Reuters, "War in the Gulf: Bush statement; excerpts from 2 statements by Bush on Iraq's proposal for ending conflict," *New York Times*, 16 February 1991, www.nytimes.com/1991/02/16/world/war-gulf-bush-statement-excerpts-2-statements-bush-iraq-s-proposal-for-ending.html (accessed 4 July 2018).

2 Thomas Friedman, "The Iraqi invasion; Bush, hinting force, declares Iraqi assault 'will not stand'; proxy in Kuwait issues threat," *New York Times*, 6 August 1990, www.nytimes.com/1990/08/06/world/iraqi-invasion-bush-hinting-force-declares-iraqi-assault-will-not-stand-proxy.html (accessed 4 July 2018).

3 Alan Taylor, "Operation Desert Storm: 25 years since the First Gulf War," *The Atlantic*, 14 January 2016, www.theatlantic.com/photo/2016/01/operation-desert-storm-25-years-since-the-first-gulf-war/424191/ (accessed 4 July 2018).

4 Christopher D. O'Sullivan, *Colin Powell: American Power and Intervention from Vietnam to Iraq* (Lanham, MD: Rowman & Littlefield, 2009), p. 90.

5 "WikiLeaks: Mubarak warned toppling Saddam would bolster Iran," *Ynetnews*, 2 October 2011, www.ynetnews.com/articles/0,7340,L-4026467,00.html (accessed 4 July 2018).

6 Ibid.

7 Robert Fisk, *Great War for Civilisation: The Conquest of the Middle East* (London: Fourth Estate, 2005), p. 646.

8 Reuters, "War in the Gulf: Bush statement."

9 George Bush, "The President's News Conference on the Persian Gulf Conflict," 1 March 1991, *The American Presidency Project*, http://www.presidency.ucsb.edu/ws/?pid=19352 (accessed 1 August 2018).

10 Judith Miller, "Iraq accused: a case of genocide," *New York Times*, 2 January 1993, www.nytimes.com/1993/01/03/magazine/iraq-accused-a-case-of-genocide.html (accessed 4 July 2018).

11 Eric Goldstein, *Endless Torment: The 1991 Uprising in Iraq and Its Aftermath* (New York: Human Rights Watch, 1992), pp. 60–8.

12 Ibid., p. vii.

13 Ibid.

14 United Nations High Commissioner for Refugees, "Refworld: chronology for Sunnis in Iraq", UNHCR, http://www.refworld.org/docid/469f38a7c.html (accessed 4 July 2018).

15 Judith Miller, "The World; displaced in the Gulf War: 5 million refugees," *New York Times*, 16 June 1991.

16 Ibid.

17 Human Rights Watch, *Human Rights Watch World Report 1992 – Iraq and Occupied Kuwait*, https://www.hrw.org/reports/1992/WR92/MEW1-02.htm (accessed 4 July 2018).

18 George Bush, "The President's news conference with Prime Minister Toshiki Kaifu of Japan in Newport Beach, California," 4 April 1991, *The American Presidency Project*, www.presidency.ucsb.edu/ws/index.php?pid=19439 (accessed 4 July 2018).

19 "Iraqi Kurds, Operation Provide Comfort, and the birth of Iraq's opposition," *Association for Diplomatic Studies and Training*, 16 February 2016, adst.org/2016/02/iraqi-kurds-operation-provide-comfort-and-the-birth-of-iraqs-opposition/ (accessed 4 July 2018).

20 Fred Kempe and Jeffrey Lightfoot, "Brent Scowcroft: An enlightened realist," *Atlantic Council*, 19 March 2015, www.atlanticcouncil.org/blogs/new-atlanticist/general-scowcrowft-at-ninety (accessed 4 July 2018).

4. SELF-RULE

1 Philip Shenon, "Two Kurd groups unite against Baghdad in pact brokered by U.S.," *New York Times*, 18 September 1998, www.nytimes.com/1998/09/18/world/two-kurd-groups-unite-against-baghdad-in-pact-brokered-by-us.html (accessed 4 July 2018).

2 Campbell MacDiarmid, "'I want to die in the shadow of the flag of an independent Kurdistan,'" *Foreign Policy*, 15 June 2017, foreignpolicy.com/2017/06/15/i-want-to-die-in-the-shadow-of-the-flag-of-an-independent-kurdistan/ (accessed 4 July 2018).

3 Ibid.

4 Wikipedia, "Iraqi Kurdistan Parliamentary Election, 1992," reproduced at www.republicofkurdistan.net/uploads/8/5/6/1/85619432/iraqi_kurdistan_parliamentary_election_1992_-_wikipedia.pdf (accessed 4 July 2018).

5 "Iraqi Kurdistan Profile – Timeline," *BBC News*, 31 October 2017, www.bbc.com/news/world-middle-east-15467672 (accessed 4 July 2018).

6 "Ex-agent says CIA dropped ball," *ABC News*, 17 January 2002, abcnews.go.com/Primetime/story?id=132147&page=1 (accessed 4 July 2018).

7 Vanora Consulting, "August 31st 1996, historical facts," *A Spotlight on Kurdish Issues*, 30 August 2016, https://menainformer.wordpress.com/2016/08/30/august-31st-1996-historical-facts/ (accessed 4 July 2018).

8 Burak Akçapar, "The Regional Imperative," in *Turkey's New European Era: Foreign Policy on the Road to EU Membership* (Lanham MD: Rowman & Littlefield, 2007), p. 84.

9 "Transcript: Albright, Talabani, Barzani remarks," USIS Washington File, Federation of American Scientists, 17 September 1998, http://www.fas.org/irp/news/1998/09/98091707_nlt.html (accessed 4 July 2018).

10 Alan Makovsky, "Kurdish agreement signals New U.S. commitment," *Washington Institute for Near East Policy*, 29 September 1998, www.washingtoninstitute.org/policy-analysis/view/kurdish-agreement-signals-new-u.s.-commitment (accessed 4 July 2018).

11 Ibid.

12 Unrepresented Nations & Peoples Organization (UNPO), "Kurdistan: Constitution of the Iraqi Kurdistan Region," 19 April 2004, www.unpo.org/article/538 (accessed 1 August 2018).

13 Ibid.

14 Ibid.

15 MacDiarmid, "'I want to die in the shadow of the flag.'"

16 Chris Kutschera, "Kurdistan Iraq: KDP and PUK have reached an agreement which would assure them prominence in any new federal Iraq," December 2002, www.chris-kutschera.com/A/reconciliation.htm (accessed 4 July 2018).

5. DYSFUNCTIONAL IRAQ

1 Thomas E. Ricks, "Ryan Crocker on Iraq," *Foreign Policy*, 26 May 2015, foreignpolicy. com/2015/05/26/ryan-crocker-on-iraq-and-on-whether-we-are-seeing-the-arab-state-system-fragment (accessed 8 August 2018).

2 Coalition Provisional Authority, "Law of Administration for the State of Iraq for the Transitional Period," 8 March 2004, http://www.cesnur.org/2004/iraq_tal.htm (accessed 1 August 2018).

3 Ibid.

4 Full text of the Iraqi Constitution, *Washington Post*, 12 October 2005.

5 Ibid.

6 Ibid.

7 Azad Berwari and Thomas Ambrosio, "The Kurdistan referendum movement: political opportunity structures and national identity," *Democratization* 15 (5) (2008), www.tandfonline.com/doi/full/10.1080/13510340802362489 (accessed 4 July 2018).

8 Press Release, Kurdistan Referendum Movement, London, 8 February 2005.

9 Zachary George Najarian-Najafi, "Once upon a time in the nepotist republic of Barzanistan," *Medium*, 28 June 2017, medium.com/@zacharygeorgenajariannajafi/once-upon-a-time-in-the-nepotist-republic-of-barzanistan-92200df8909d (accessed 4 July 2018).

10 "The 2010 Iraqi Parliamentary Elections," *New York Times*, 11 March 2010, www.nytimes.com/interactive/2010/03/11/world/middleeast/20100311-iraq-election.html (accessed 4 July 2018).

11 Christophe Ayad, "Kurdistan conflict threatens to bring new violence to Iraq," *Guardian*, 14 August 2012, www.theguardian.com/world/2012/aug/14/iraq-kurdistan-maliki-barzani (accessed 4 July 2018).

12 Ibid.

13 Hawre Hasan Hama, "The death of Jalal Talabani and the future of the PUK," *Middle East Monitor*, 3 October 2017, https://www.middleeastmonitor.com/20171003-the-death-of-jalal-talabani-and-the-future-of-the-puk/ (accessed 4 July 2018).

14 "Elections in Iraqi Kurdistan (1992 Elections)," *The Kurdish Project*, thekurdishproject. org/history-and-culture/kurdish-democracy/kurdish-elections/ (accessed 4 July 2018).

15 Joost Hiltermann and Maria Fantappie, "Twilight of the Kurds," *Foreign Policy*, 16 January 2018, foreignpolicy.com/2018/01/16/twilight-of-the-kurds-iraq-syria-kurdistan/ (accessed 4 July 2018).

6. A PERFECT STORM

1 Recounted by Qubad Talabani, Erbi, May 2014.

2 Martin Chulov, "Isis insurgents seize control of Iraqi city of Mosul," *Guardian*, 10 June 2014, www.theguardian.com/world/2014/jun/10/iraq-sunni-insurgents-islamic-militants-seize-control-mosul (accessed 4 July 2018).

3 Ibid.

4 Tim Arango, Kareem Fahim and Ben Hubbard, "Rebels' fast strike in Iraq was years in the making," *New York Times*, 14 June 2014, www.nytimes.com/2014/06/15/world/middleeast/rebels-fast-strike-in-iraq-was-years-in-the-making.html (accessed 4 July 2018).

5 "Iraq Conflict: Shia cleric Sistani issues call to arms," *BBC News*, 13 June 2014, www.bbc.com/news/world-middle-east-27834462 (accessed 4 July 2018).

6 Alissa Rubin, Suadad Al-Salhy and Rick Gladstone, "Iraqi Shiite cleric issues call to arms," *New York Times*, 13 June 2014, www.nytimes.com/2014/06/14/world/middleeast/iraq.html (accessed 4 July 2018).

7 Rowan Scarborough, "Iran responsible for deaths of 500 American service members in Iraq," *Washington Times*, 13 September 2015, www.washingtontimes.com/news/2015/sep/13/iran-responsible-for-deaths-of-500-us-service-memb/ (accessed 4 July 2018).

8 Michael Crowley, "How the fate of one holy site could plunge Iraq back into civil war," *Time*, 26 June 2014, time.com/2920692/iraq-isis-samarra-al-askari-mosque/ (accessed 4 July 2018).

9 Peter Beaumont and Fazel Hawramy, "Iraqi Kurdish forces take Kirkuk as Isis sets its sights on Baghdad," *Guardian*, 12 June 2014, www.theguardian.com/world/2014/jun/12/iraq-isis-kirkuk-baghdad-kurdish-government (accessed 4 July 2018).

10 Bill Roggio, "ISIS' advance halted at Samarra," *FDD's Long War Journal*, 12 June 2014, www.longwarjournal.org/archives/2014/06/isiss_southward_adva.php (accessed 4 July 2018).

11 Dexter Filkins, "The fight of their lives," *New Yorker*, 29 September 2014, www.newyorker.com/magazine/2014/09/29/fight-lives (accessed 4 July 2018).

12 Fernando Lujan, "Light footprints: the future of American military intervention," *Center for New American Security*, March 2013, https://www.cnas.org/publications/reports/light-footprints-the-future-of-american-military-intervention (accessed 4 July 2018); Austin Long, "Small is beautiful: the counterterrorism option in Afghanistan," *Orbis* 54(2), Spring 2010.

13 Interview by the author with Brett McGurk, Deputy Assistant Secretary of State for Iraq and Iran, on the *Charlie Rose Show*, PBS, 28 July 2015.

14 Interview by the author with Masoud Barzani, Erbil, 19 May 2015.

15 Isabel Coles, "Iran supplied weapons to Iraqi Kurds; Baghdad bomb kills 12," *Reuters*, 26 August 2014, www.reuters.com/article/us-iraq-security-kurds/iran-supplied-weapons-to-iraqi-kurds-baghdad-bomb-kills-12-idUSKBN0GQ11P20140826 (accessed 4 July 2018).

16 Lazar Berman, "The Iranian penetration of Iraqi Kurdistan," *Jerusalem Center for Public Affairs* 16 (3), 21 January 2016, jcpa.org/article/the-iranian-penetration-of-iraqi-kurdistan/ (accessed 4 July 2018).

17 Michael Gordon, "Kurdish leader agrees to accept arms on U.S. terms in fight against ISIS," *New York Times*, 9 May 2015.

18 Asitha, "Obama and Barzani discuss ISIS and independence," *The Kurdish Project*, 6 May 2015, http://thekurdishproject.org/latest-news/us-kurdish-relations/obama-and-barzani-discuss-isis-and-independence/ (accessed 4 July 2018).

19 Julian Pecquet, "Defense Bill recognizes Iraq's Kurdish, Sunni militias as a 'country,'" *Al-Monitor*, 29 April 2015.

20 Letter from Secretary of Defense Ashton Carter to John McCain, Chairman of the Committee on Armed Services, US Senate, 10 June 2015.

21 Tom McCarthy, "'Degrade and destroy': a look back at Obama's evolution on Isis," *Guardian*, 6 December 2015, www.theguardian.com/us-news/2015/dec/06/obama-statements-isis-timeline (accessed 4 July 2018).

22 Ibid.

23 Interview by the author with Pentagon officials, 22 July 2015.

24 Filkins, "Fight of their lives."

25 Ibid.

26 Interview with Najmaldin Karim.

27 *Iraq* (country report), Economist Intelligence Unit, 2018, p. 24.

28 International Organization of Migration, Displacement Tracking Matrix (DTM) 2015.

29 Karim Sinjari and David L. Phillips, "Kurdistan needs help from the US and international community to build a stable future," *The Hill*, 26 January 2018, thehill. com/opinion/international/370668-kurdistan-needs-help-from-the-us-and-international-community-to-build-a (accessed 5 July 2018).

30 "Immediate Response Plan Phase II (IRP2) for internally displaced people in the Kurdistan Region of Iraq: 15 November 2014 – 31 March 2015," UN Office for the Coordination of Humanitarian Affairs, UN Country Team in Iraq and KRG Ministry of Planning, December 2014, http://reliefweb.int/sites/reliefweb. int/files/resources/Immediate Response Plan 2 KR-I Nov-Mar.pdf (accessed 5 July 2018).

31 Impressions provided to the author by a Human Rights Watch researcher recently returned from the KRG, 14 August 2015.

32 "Iraq Health Situation Reports," World Health Organization, http://www.who. int/hac/crises/irq/sitreps/en/ (accessed 26 June 2015).

33 Email from a KRG official to the author, 5 February 2018.

34 Information provided by the Office of Iraq Affairs, Bureau of Near Eastern Affairs at the US Department of State in an email on 29 July 2015.

35 Economist Intelligence Unit, p. 40.

36 T.K. Maloy, "Infrastructure in Iraqi Kurdistan: overview," Kurdistan Region of Iraq Report, *Marcopolis*, http://www.marcopolis.net/infrastructure-in-iraqi-kurdistan-overview.htm (accessed 2 June 2015).

37 Economist Intelligence Unit, p. 46.

38 Ibid.

39 Ibid., p. 39.

40 Ibid., p. 29.

41 Ibid., p. 6.

42 "It was believed by many petroleum geologists, however, that Iraq may hold between 45 billion barrels (Gbbl) and 100 Gbbl of recoverable oil on top of the 115 Gbbl of proven reserves." Dirk Kempthorne and Mark Myers, "Iraq," in *Mineral Commodity Summaries 2008* (Washington DC: United States Government Printing Office, 2008).

43 Oil-in-place is not the same as proven recoverable reserves, which are smaller.

44 Kempthorne and Myers, *Mineral Commodity Summaries 2008*.

45 KRG Prime Minster Nerchivan Barzani, Erbil, 3 December 2012.

46 "KRG publishes the Monthly Export Report for June 2015," press release, KRG Ministry of Natural Resources, 2 July 2015, mnr.krg.org/index.php/en/press-releases/462-krg-publishes-the-monthly-export-report-for-june-2015 (accessed 5 July 2015).

47 David O'Byrne, "Kurdistan: oil pipeline to Turkey is a reality," *Financial Times*, 1 November 2013, http://blogs.ft.com/beyond-brics/2013/11/01/kurdistan-oil-pipeline-to-turkey-is-a-reality/#axzz2kq9DD0wz (accessed 5 July 2015).

48 Humeyra Pamuk and Orhan Coskun, "Exclusive: Turkey, Iraqi Kurdistan clinch major energy pipeline deals," *Reuters*, 6 November 2013, http://www.reuters.com/article/2013/11/06/us-turkey-iraq-kurdistan-idUSBRE9A50HR20131106 (accessed 5 July 2018).

49 Dorian Jones, "Turkey, Iraqi Kurdistan seal 50-year energy deal," *Voice of America*, 5 June 2014, http://www.voanews.com/content/turkey-iraqi-kurdistan-seal-50-year-energy-deal/1930721.html (accessed 5 July 2018).

50 "Turkey: input on strategy to integrate Iraq into region," *Wikileaks*, 17 March 2009, https://search.wikileaks.org/plusd/cables/09ANKARA395_a.html (accessed 5 July 2018).

51 For more on the Erbil–Baghdad dispute over hydrocarbons and the Constitution, see David Romano, "The Iraqi–Kurdish view on federalism: not just for the Kurds," in David Romano and Mehmet Gurses (eds), *Conflict, Democratization and the Kurds in the Middle East* (New York: Palgrave Macmillan, 2014), pp. 189–209.

52 Aydin Selcen, "Kurdistan region of Iraq—a friend to the North," *Oil and Gas Year* 35, p. 16.

53 "Masrour Barzani: Kurdish independence would help defeat ISIS", *Al-Monitor*, 2 July 2015, http://www.al-monitor.com/pulse/originals/2015/07/turkey-iraq-syria-kurdish-independence-help-war-against-isis.html#ixzz3f4ieYyPA (accessed 5 July 2015).

54 Cengiz Candar, "Erdoğan–Barzani 'Diyarbakir encounter' milestone," *Al-Monitor*, 20 November 2013, http://www.al-monitor.com/pulse/originals/2013/11/erdogan-barzani-kurdistan-diyarbakir-political-decision.html (accessed 5 July 2015).

55 Diyarbakir, "Iraqi Kurdish leader Barzani urges support for peace process in Diyarbakir rally with Turkish PM," *Hurriyet Daily News*, 16 November 2013, www.hurriyetdailynews.com/iraqi-kurdish-leader-barzani-urges-support-for-peace-process-in-diyarbakir-rally-with-turkish-pm-58028 (accessed 5 July 2018).

56 Interview by the author with President Barzani's chief of staff, Dr Fuad Hussein.

57 Delovan Barwari, "Barzani must remain president to lead Kurds out of crisis," *Huffington Post*, 10 August 2015, www.huffingtonpost.com/delovan-barwari/barzani-must-remain-presi_b_7963590.html (accessed 5 July 2018).

58 "Barzani's salary for one month equal to Obama's salary for the entire year!" *Ekurd Daily*, 29 June 2010, ekurd.net/mismas/articles/misc2010/6/state4002.htm (accessed 5 July 2018).

7. COUNTDOWN

1 Alexander Whitcomb, "President Barzani asks parliament to proceed with independence vote," *Rudaw*, 3 July 2014, http://www.rudaw.net/english/kurdistan/030720141 (accessed 5 July 2018).

2 Masrour Barzani, remarks made at the Atlantic Council on 6 May 2015.

3 Ibid.

4 Cited in David L. Phillips, *The Kurdish Spring: A New Map of the Middle East* (New Brunswick: Transaction Publishers, 2015), p. 108.

5 David L. Phillips, *Power-Sharing in Iraq* (New York: Council on Foreign Relations, 2005).

6 Joseph R. Biden and Leslie H. Gelb, "Unity through autonomy in Iraq," *New York Times*, 30 April 2006, www.nytimes.com/2006/05/01/opinion/01biden.html (accessed 5 July 2018).

7 Sami Moubayed, "Kirkuk, Mosul and the ever changing demographics of Iraq," *Gulf News*, 20 November 2016, gulfnews.com/news/mena/iraq/kirkuk-mosul-and-the-ever-changing-demographics-of-iraq-1.1930570 (accessed 5 July 2018).

8 Derek Stoffel, "Life under ISIS: Mosul residents reflect on a brutal occupation,"

CBC, 23 March 2017, www.cbc.ca/news/world/life-under-isis-mosul-residents-reflect-on-a-brutal-occupation-1.4034574 (accessed 5 July 2018).

9 "Is the world going to dismiss the Kurds after Mosul?" *Rudaw*, 14 July 2017, www.rudaw.net/english/kurdistan/14072017 (accessed 1 August 2018).

10 Associated Press, "Tillerson urges fractious anti-ISIS coalition to stay focused," *CBS News*, 13 February 2018, www.cbsnews.com/news/rex-tillerson-islamic-state-of-iraq-and-syria-coalition-turkey-kurds-fsa/ (accessed 1 August 2018).

11 "Baghdad, Kurds at odds over control of post-ISIL Mosul," *Al Jazeera*, 18 November 2016, www.aljazeera.com/news/2016/11/baghdad-kurds-odds-control-post-isil-mosul-161117150810662.html (accessed 1 August 2018).

12 "Iraq's PM sees Kurdish referendum as 'undisputed right,'" *Rudaw*, 26 August 2016, www.rudaw.net/english/kurdistan/26082016 (accessed 1 August 2018).

13 "Baghdad and Erbil to jointly form 'independence committees,'" *Rudaw*, 2 September 2016, www.rudaw.net/english/kurdistan/020920168 (accessed 1 August 2018).

14 AFP, "Iraqi Kurds pressure Baghdad with referendum bid," *Jordan Times*, 19 September 2017, www.jordantimes.com/news/region/iraqi-kurds-pressure-baghdad-referendum-bid (accessed 5 July 2018).

15 Rhys Dubin and Emily Tamkin, "Iraqi Kurds vote for independence over U.S. objections," *Foreign Policy*, 25 September. 2017, foreignpolicy.com/2017/09/25/iraqi-kurds-vote-for-independence-over-u-s-objections/ (accessed 5 July 2018).

16 Ibid.

17 "President Barzani meets with Kurdistan Region's Political Parties to Set the Date for the Referendum," *Kurdistan Region Presidency*, 7 June 2017, www.presidency.krd/english/articledisplay.aspx?id=E8ZKw7evZVQ= (accessed 5 July 2018).

18 "Iraqi Kurds set date for independence referendum," *Al Jazeera*, 8 June 2017, www.aljazeera.com/news/2017/06/iraqi-kurds-set-date-independence-referendum-170608044202182.html (accessed 5 July 2018).

19 Erika Solomon, "Iraq fires Kirkuk governor in Kurdish referendum stand-off," *Financial Times*, 14 September 2017, www.ft.com/content/709caa8a-9954-11e7-a652-cde3f882dd7b (accessed 1 August 2018).

20 "Iraq parliament vote to reject Kurdistan referendum," *Rudaw*, 12 September 2017, www.rudaw.net/english/middleeast/iraq/12092017 (accessed 5 July 2018).

21 Dubin and Tamkin, "Iraqi Kurds vote for independence."

22 Aram Rafaat, *Kurdistan in Iraq: The Evolution of a Quasi-State* (New York: Routledge, 2018).

23 "Rally planned for Kurdistan region's referendum in Washington on Sunday," *Rudaw*, 16 September 2017, www.rudaw.net/english/kurdistan/16092017 (accessed 5 July 2018).

24 David Zucchino, "As Kurds celebrate independence vote, neighbors threaten military action," *New York Times*, 25 September 2017, www.nytimes.com/2017/09/25/world/middleeast/kurds-referendum.html (accessed 5 July 2018).

25 Dubin and Tamkin, "Iraqi Kurds vote for independence."

8. THE REFERENDUM

1 Sangar Ali, "Commission releases sample ballot paper for Kurdistan Referendum," *Kurdistan24*, 6 September 2017, www.kurdistan24.net/en/news/434490fe-72d8-456b-83c9-ff63735b5066 (accessed 5 July 2018).

2 Interview by the author with KRG Deputy Prime Minister Qubad Talabani, 13 March 2018.

3 Interview by the author with Special Presidential Envoy Ambassador Brett McGurk, 12 March 2018.

4 Interview with Qubad Talabani.

5 Interview with Brett McGurk.

6 Ibid.

7 Ibid.

8 Interview with Qubad Talabani.

9 Ibid.

10 Bethan McKernan, "Kurdistan referendum results: 93% of Iraqi Kurds vote for independence, say reports," *Independent*, 27 September 2017, www.independent. co.uk/news/world/middle-east/kurdistan-referendum-results-vote-yes-iraqi-kurds-independence-iran-syria-a7970241.html (accessed 5 July 2018).

11 Ibid.

12 "KRG: Referendum results not issued by electoral commission 'baseless'," *Rudaw*, 27 September 2017, www.rudaw.net/english/kurdistan/270920171 (accessed 5 July 2018).

13 Interview with Brett McGurk.

14 "Iraqi Kurds decisively back independence in referendum," *BBC News*, 27 September 2017, https://www.bbc.co.uk/news/world-middle-east-41419633 (accessed 5 July 2018).

15 McKernan, "Kurdistan Referendum Results."

16 Ibid.

17 "Iraqi Kurds vote in controversial referendum," *Al Jazeera*, 25 September 2017, www.aljazeera.com/news/2017/09/iraqi-kurds-vote-independence-referendum-170925032733525.html (accessed 1 August 2018).

18 David Zucchino, "Kurds back independence by 92% in referendum; Iraq may send troops," *IdubaiNews.com*, 27 September 2017, http://idubainews.com/?p=111803 (accessed 1 August 2018).

19 Michael Georgy, "Defiant Kurds shrug off risk of trade war after independence vote," *Reuters*, 18 October 2017, www.reuters.com/article/us-mideast-crisis-iraq-kurds-economy/defiant-kurds-shrug-off-risk-of-trade-war-after-independence-vote-idUSKBN1CN0QS (accessed 5 July 2018).

20 "Vote count under way after large turnout for Kurdish independence referendum," *RadioFreeEurope / RadioLiberty*, 26 September 2017, www.rferl. org/a/kurdistan-iraq-independence-referendum/28755137.html (accessed 5 July 2018).

21 "Iraqi Kurds vote in controversial referendum," *Al Jazeera*, 25 September 2017, www.aljazeera.com/news/2017/09/iraqi-kurds-vote-independence-referendum-170925032733525.html (accessed 5 July 2018).

22 RFE/RL, "Vote count under way."

23 McKernan, "Kurdistan referendum results."

24 David Zucchino, "As Kurds celebrate independence vote, neighbors threaten military action," *New York Times*, 25 September 2017, www.nytimes.com/2017/09/25/world/middleeast/kurds-referendum.html (accessed 5 July 2018).

25 John Beck, "How a shocking reversal of fortunes unfolded in Kirkuk," *Al Jazeera*, 20 October 2017, www.aljazeera.com/news/2017/10/shocking-reversal-fortunes-unfolded-kirkuk-171020092324524.html (accessed 5 July 2018).

26 Krishnadev Calamur, "Why doesn't the U.S. support Kurdish independence?" *The Atlantic*, 20 October 2017, www.theatlantic.com/international/archive/2017/10/us-kurdish-independence/543540/ (accessed 5 July 2018).

27 Ibid.

28 RFE/RL, "Vote Count Under Way."

29 Ibid.

30 Amberin Zaman, "KRG intelligence chief: Baghdad must give us our rights," *Al-Monitor*, 25 February 2018, www.al-monitor.com/pulse/originals/2018/02/masrour-barzani-iraq-kurdistan-region-independence-baghdad.html#ixzz58AF8Bpmo (accessed 5 July 2018).

31 "Gorran says Barzani should resign after Kurdish vote," *Al Jazeera*, 23 October 2017, www.aljazeera.com/news/2017/10/gorran-barzani-resign-kurdish-vote-171023071117432.html (accessed 5 July 2018).

32 "Iraqi Kurdish party calls on Barzani to resign," *Middle East Monitor*, 22 October 2017, www.middleeastmonitor.com/20171023-iraqi-kurdish-party-calls-on-barzani-to-resign/ (accessed 5 July 2018).

33 Joseph Daher, "The Kurdish struggle and self-determination," *SocialistWorker.org*, 23 February 2018, socialistworker.org/2018/02/23/the-kurdish-struggle-and-self-determination (accessed 1 August 2018).

9. KIRKUK CRISIS

1 Peter Galbraith, "Why the Kurds are paying for Trump's gift to Iran," *New York Review of Books*, 2 November 2017, http://www.nybooks.com/daily/2017/11/02/kurds-pay-for-trumps-gift-to-iran/ (accessed 5 July 2018).

2 Kirkuk Governor Najmaldin Karim, conversation with the author.

3 Galbraith, "Why the Kurds are paying for Trump's gift to Iran."

4 Interview by the author with Sierwan Karim, 21 February 2018.

5 Interview by the author with Masrour Barzani on 16 April 2018.

6 Interview by the author with Special Envoy Ambassador Brett McGurk, 12 March 2018.

7 "Iran reopens border crossing with Iraq's Kurdish region," *RadioFreeEurope / RadioLiberty*, 26 October 2017, www.rferl.org/a/iran-reopens-border-crossing-iraqs-kurdish-region-bashmagh/28816540.html (accessed 5 July 2018).

8 Interview with Sierwan Karim.

9 Interview with Masrour Barzani.

10 Ibid.

11 Email from Qubad Talabani to the author, 14 March 2018.

12 "Erbil–Baghdad: coalition says Iraq shifts troops west of Kirkuk to Anbar," *Rudaw*, 10 December 2017, www.rudaw.net/english/middleeast/iraq/12102017 (accessed 5 July 2018).

13 Campbell MacDiarmid, "Thousands of Kurdish troops sent to Kirkuk to Face 'Iraqi threat,'" *Telegraph*, 13 October 2017, www.telegraph.co.uk/news/2017/10/13/iraq-army-launches-operation-retake-kirkuk-kurdish-authorities/ (accessed 1 August 2018).

14 Ibid.

15 David Zucchino, "Iraqi forces sweep into Kirkuk, checking Kurdish independence drive," *New York Times*, 16 October 2017, www.nytimes.com/2017/10/16/world/middleeast/kirkuk-iraq-kurds.html (accessed 5 July 2018).

16 Interview by the author with Deputy Prime Minister Qubad Talabani, 13 March 2018.

17 "Talabani's son offers to dissolve Kirkuk council, replace governor to mend ties with Baghdad," *Rudaw*, 10 December 2017, www.rudaw.net/english/kurdistan/121020176 (accessed 5 July 2018).

18 Ibid.

19 Interview with Masrour Barzani.

20 Ibid.

21 Zucchino, "Iraqi Forces Sweep Into Kirkuk."

22 Interview with Qubad Talabani.

23 Interview with Masrour Barzani.

24 Ibid.

25 Ibid.

26 Interview by the author with Sierwan Karim, 20 April 2018.

27 "Andy" is a pseudonym used to protect the informant's identity.

28 Interview with Masrour Barzani.

29 Interview with Sierwan Karim.

30 Sangar Ali, "Peshmerga, people of Kirkuk stand prepared to face Iraqi forces, Shiite Militia," *Kurdistan24*, 13 October 2017, www.kurdistan24.net/en/news/64f1ca61-0b31-437f-a3f8-4579996dc957 (accessed 5 July 2018).

31 Interview with Sierwan Karim.

32 Ibid.

33 Ibid.

34 Bridget Johnson, "U.S. weapons being used by Iraqis and Shiite militias against us in Kirkuk, say Kurds," *PJ Media*, 16 October 2017, pjmedia.com/news-and-politics/2017/10/16/u-s-weapons-used-iraqis-shiite-militias-us-kirkuk-say-kurds/ (accessed 6 July 2018).

35 Interview with Masrour Barzani.

36 Interview with Qubad Talabani.

37 Interview by the author with Special Envoy Brett McGurk, 12 March 2018.

38 John Beck, "How a shocking reversal of fortunes unfolded in Kirkuk," *Al Jazeera*, 20 October 2017, www.aljazeera.com/news/2017/10/shocking-reversal-fortunes-unfolded-kirkuk-171020092324524.html (accessed 6 July 2018).

39 Interview with Sierwan Karim.

40 "Turkey supports Iraq's moves to restore peace, order in Kirkuk, MFA says," *Daily Sabah*, 16 October 2017, www.dailysabah.com/diplomacy/2017/10/16/turkey-supports-iraqs-moves-to-restore-peace-order-in-kirkuk-mfa-says (accessed 6 July 2018).

41 Interview with Masrour Barzani.

42 David Romano, "Op-Ed: McGurk's Kurdish policy," *Rudaw*, 18 November 2017, www.rudaw.net/english/opinion/18112017 (accessed 1 August 2018).

43 Associated Press, "U.S. military says clash between Iraq, Kurdish forces is a 'misunderstanding'," *Los Angeles Times*, 16 October 2017, www.latimes.com/world/la-fg-iraq-kurds-20171015-story.html (accessed 6 July 2018).

44 Interview with Masrour Barzani.

45 Johnson, "U.S. weapons being used by Iraqis."

46 John McCain, "We need a strategy for the Middle East," *New York Times*, 24 October 2017, www.nytimes.com/2017/10/24/opinion/john-mccain-kurds-iraq.html (accessed 6 July 2018).

47 Email from the Senate Foreign Relations Committee, 30 October 2017.

48 Interview with Qubad Talabani.

49 Ibid.

50 Rhys Dubin and Dan De Luce, "Trump administration ready to scrap envoy to anti-ISIS coalition," *Foreign Policy*, 22 February 2018, foreignpolicy.com/2018/02/22/trump-administration-weighs-scrapping-envoy-to-counter-isis-coalition-iraq-syria-islamic-state-terrorism-terrorist-daesh/ (accessed 6 July 2018).

51 Information provided in an email from Shwan Karim to the author, 23 February 2018.

10. ELECTIONS

1 Hiwa Husamaddin, "Najmaldin Karim won't run for election in 'occupied city,'" *Rudaw*, 26 February 2018, www.rudaw.net/english/interview/26022018 (accessed 6 July 2018).

2 The author served as Senior Advisor to the State Department's Future of Iraq Project in 2002–3.

3 This section draws on a project involving the author and Lincoln A. Mitchell, "Enhancing Democracy Assistance," *American Foreign Policy Interests* xxx/ 3 (2008), pp. 156–75).

4 "Iraqi Kurdistan General Election, 2018," Wikipedia, 4 March 2018, https://en.wikipedia.org/wiki/Iraqi_Kurdistan_general_election,_2018.

5 Hiwa Husamaddin, "Najmaldin Karim won't run for election in 'occupied city,'" *Rudaw*, 26 February 2018, www.rudaw.net/english/interview/26022018 (accessed 6 July 2018).

6 Amberin Zaman, "KRG intelligence chief: Baghdad must give us our rights," *Al-Monitor*, 25 February 2018, www.al-monitor.com/pulse/originals/2018/02/masrour-barzani-iraq-kurdistan-region-independence-baghdad.html#ixzz58AF8Bpmo (accessed 5 July 2018).

7 Interview by the author with Fuad Hussein, 27 April 2018.

8 Ibid.

9 Sandra Black, "Reconstruction needed as displaced Iraqis continue to return: IOM Iraq," *International Organization for Migration*, 20 February 2018, www.iom.int/news/reconstruction-needed-displaced-iraqis-continue-return-iom-iraq (accessed 6 July 2018).

10 "U.S. government opposes delaying Iraqi elections: U.S. Embassy in Baghdad," *Reuters*, 18 January 2018, www.reuters.com/article/us-mideast-crisis-iraq-vote-us/u-s-government-opposes-delaying-iraqi-elections-u-s-embassy-in-baghdad-idUSKBN1F71O2 (accessed 6 July 2018).

11 Interview with Fuad Hussein.

12 Fazel Hawramy, "Violence taints election in Iraq's Kurdistan region," *Al-Monitor*, 14 May 2018, www.al-monitor.com/pulse/originals/2018/05/iraq-election-kurdistan-violence.html#ixzz5FalFj6VF (accessed 27 September 2018).

11. SYRIA STRUGGLES

1 Amberin Zaman, "Turkey moves to take key town in Afrin operation," *Al-Monitor*, 5 March 2018, www.al-monitor.com/pulse/originals/2018/03/turkey-operation-syria-afrin-jindires.html#ixzz58uzSCALQ (accessed 6 July 2018).

2 Cited by Jawad Mella, *The Colonial Policy of the Syrian Baath Party in Western Kurdistan* (London: Western Kurdistan Association, 2006), www.knc.org.uk/wp-content/uploads/2013/01/Book-of-Western-Kurdistan-in-English.pdf (accessed 6 July 2018), p. 70.

3 Joby Warrick, "More than 1,400 killed in Syrian chemical weapons attack, U.S. Says," *Washington Post*, 30 August 2013, www.washingtonpost.com/world/national-security/nearly-1500-killed-in-syrian-chemical-weapons-attack-us-says/2013/08/30/b2864662-1196-11e3-85b6-d27422650fd5_story.html (accessed 6 July 2018).

4 Brett LoGiurato and Michael B. Kelly, "The ISIS siege of Kobani exposes a critical flaw in Obama's Syria plan," *Business Insider*, 8 October 2014, www.businessinsider.com/obama-isis-strategy-kobani-kobane-syria-2014-10 (accessed 6 July 2018).

5 Kirk Semple and Tim Arango. "Kurdish rebels assail Turkish inaction on ISIS as peril to peace talks," *New York Times*, 12 October 2014, www.nytimes.com/2014/10/13/world/middleeast/kurdish-rebels-assail-turkish-inaction-on-isis-as-peril-to-peace-talks.html (accessed 1 August 2018).

6 Barbara Plett Usher, "Joe Biden apologised over IS Remarks, but was he right?" *BBC News*, 7 October 2014, www.bbc.com/news/world-us-canada-29528482 (accessed 6 July 2018).

7 Constanze Letsch and Ian Traynor, "Kobani: anger grows as Turkey stops Kurds from aiding militias in Syria," *Guardian*, 8 October 2014, www.theguardian.com/world/2014/oct/08/kobani-isis-turkey-kurds-ypg-syria-erdogan (accessed 6 July 2018).

8 Rod Nordland, "Allied with both the U.S. and a leader jailed as a terrorist," *New York Times*, 11 March 2018, p. A7.

9 Letsch and Traynor, "Kobani: anger grows."

10 Jerry Gordon, *National Security News*, 24 October 2014.

11 Interview by the author with Governor Karim, Washington Kurdish Institute, 26 November 2017.

12 Till F. Paasche, "Syrian and Iraqi Kurds: conflict and cooperation," *Middle East Policy Council* XXII (1), Spring 2014, www.mepc.org/syrian-and-iraqi-kurds-conflict-and-cooperation (accessed 6 July 2018).

13 Interview with Governor Karim.

14 "U.S. expresses concern about Kurdish offensive in Syrian Kurdistan," *Ekurd Daily*, 16 September 2015, ekurd.net/u-s-expresses-concern-about-kurdish-offensive-in-syrian-kurdistan-2015-06-13 (accessed 6 July 2018).

15 Cansu Dikme, "Turkey protests US envoy McGurk's 'provocative' remarks," *Anadolu Agency*, 30 July 2017, aa.com.tr/en/todays-headlines/turkey-protests-us-envoy-mcgurks-provocative-remarks/872834 (accessed 6 July 2018).

16 Greg Botelho, "Turkish leader: U.S. responsible for 'sea of blood' for supporting Syrian Kurds," *CNN*, 10 February 2016, www.cnn.com/2016/02/10/middleeast/turkey-erdogan-criticizes-us/index.html (accessed 6 July 2018).

17 Daniel Wagner, "The dark side of the Free Syrian Army," *Huffington Post*, 31 December 2012, www.huffingtonpost.com/daniel-wagner/dark-side-free-syrian_b_2380399.html (accessed 6 July 2018).

18 Patrick Cockburn, "Syria's war of ethnic cleansing: Kurds threatened with beheading by Turkey's allies if they don't convert to extremism," *Independent*, 12 March 2018, www.independent.co.uk/news/world/middle-east/syria-civil-war-assad-regime-turkey-afrin-kurds-eastern-ghouta-us-allies-militia-a8252456.html (accessed 6 July 2018).

19 David L. Phillips, "Erdogan's Waterloo: Turkey invades and occupies Syria," *Huffington Post*, 29 August 2016, www.huffingtonpost.com/david-l-phillips/erdogans-waterloo-turkey_b_11767934.html (accessed 6 July 2018).

20 Louisa Loveluck, "U.S.-led coalition declares ISIS forces vanquished, battle for Raqqa over," *Washington Post*, 20 Oct. 2017, www.washingtonpost.com/world/us-led-coalition-declares-isis-forces-vanquished-battle-for-raqqa-over/2017/10/20/85da033a-b4f6-11e7-9b93-b97043e57a22_story.html (accessed 6 July 2018).

21 Ibid.

22 Carol Morello and Erin Cunningham, "Trump tells Turkish president U.S. will stop arming Kurds in Syria," *Washington Post*, 24 November. 2017, www.washingtonpost.com/world/national-security/trump-tells-turkish-president-us-will-stop-arming-kurds-in-syria/2017/11/24/61548936-d148-11e7-a1a3-0d1e45a6de3d_story.html (accessed 6 July 2018).

23 Ibid.

24 "US backtracks on 'Kurdish Border Force', Turkey cites record of broken promises," *RT News*, 20 February 2018, www.rt.com/news/416256-turkey-criticize-us-syria (accessed 6 July 2018).

25 "How US went from supporting Syrian Kurds, to backing Turkey against them – in just 9 days," *RT News*, 20 February 2018, www.rt.com/news/416689-how-us-went-against-kurds/ (accessed 6 July 2018).

26 Carlotta Gall, "Turkish jets bomb Kurdish militias in Syria," *New York Times*, 21 January 2018, p. A8.

27 Kareem Shaheen, "Turkey starts ground incursion into Kurdish-controlled Afrin in Syria," *Guardian*, 21 January 2018, www.theguardian.com/world/2018/jan/21/turkey-starts-ground-incursion-into-kurdish-controlled-afrin-in-syria (accessed 6 July 2018).

28 Ibid.

29 Sune Engel Rasmussen, Nancy A. Youssef and Dion Nissenbaum, "U.S. border plan in Syria fuels tensions with Turkey," *Wall Street Journal*, 17 January 2018, www.wsj.com/articles/turkey-threatens-to-attack-kurdish-allies-of-u-s-in-syria-1516211606 (accessed 1 August 2018).

30 "Turkey continues its assault on Kurdish Afrin in Syria," *Rudaw*, 21 January 2018, www.rudaw.net/mobile/english/middleeast/syria/21012018 (accessed 6 July 2018).

31 William Gallo, "Mattis: Turkey alerted US before striking Kurds in Syria," *VOA News*, 21 January 2018, www.voanews.com/a/mattiis-says-turkey-alerted-us-before-striking-kurds-in-syria/4217562.html (accessed 6 July 2018).

32 Amberin Zaman, "KRG delegation arrives in Afrin as Turkey offensive softens Kurdish split," *Al-Monitor*, 13 February 2018, https://www.al-monitor.com/pulse/originals/2018/02/kurdish-disunity-nation.html (accessed 6 July 2018).

33 Turkish Press Office, "'Turkey is fighting against the terrorist organisation in Afrin, not the Kurds,'" *Presidency of the Republic of Turkey*, 22 January 2018, www.tccb.gov.tr/en/news/542/89167/turkey-is-fighting-against-the-terrorist-organisation-in-afrin-not-the-kurds (accessed 1 August 2018).

34 Daniel L. Davis, "Time to end America's foreign policy losing streak," *The National Interest*, 21 February 2018, nationalinterest.org/blog/the-skeptics/time-end-americas-foreign-policy-losing-streak-24589 (accessed 1 August 2018).

35 Gallo, "Mattis: Turkey Alerted US."

36 "Erdogan threatens US with 'Ottoman slap,' says all NATO countries created equal," *RT News*, 26 February 2018, www.rt.com/news/418712-ottoman-slap-erdogan-us-nato/ (accessed 6 July 2018).

37 Carlotta Gall, "Syrian militias enter Afrin, dealing a setback to Turkey," *New York Times*, 22 February 2018, www.nytimes.com/2018/02/22/world/middleeast/syria-afrin-kurds-ypg.html (accessed 6 July 2018).

38 Liz Sly, "Kurds pull back from ISIS fight in Syria, saying U.S. 'let us down,'" *Washington Post*, 6 March 2018, www.washingtonpost.com/world/kurds-pull-back-from-isis-fight-in-syria-say-they-are-let-down-by-us/2018/03/06/3fd2c2ca-2173-11e8-946c-9420060cb7bd_story.html (accessed 6 July 2018).

39 Ibid.

40 "Turkey continues its assault on Kurdish Afrin in Syria," *Rudaw*, 21 January. 2018, www.rudaw.net/mobile/english/middleeast/syria/21012018 (accessed 6 July 2018).

41 Ibid.

42 "Syria: Turkish ground troops enter Afrin enclave," *BBC News*, 21 January 2018, www.bbc.com/news/world-middle-east-42765697 (accessed 6 July 2018).

43 Ibid.

44 Simon Tisdall, "Recep Tayyip Erdoğan's risky gamble could quickly turn sour," *Guardian*, 21 January 2018, www.theguardian.com/world/2018/jan/21/recep-tayyip-erdogan-kurds-syria-risky-gamble-could-quickly-turn-sour (accessed 6 July 2018).

45 "Syria: Turkish ground troops enter Afrin enclave."

46 "Turkey continues its assault on Kurdish Afrin."

12. IRAN WINS

1 James M. Dorsey, "Kurdish battle positions Kurds as US ally against Iran," *Huffington Post*, 18 October 2017, www.huffingtonpost.com/entry/kurdish-battle-positions-kurds-as-us-ally-against-iran_us_59e70826e4b0e60c4aa3667a (accessed 6 July 2018).

2 Islamic Republic News Agency (IRNA), 23 September 2000 and *Iran Times*, 10 November 2000, p. 4.

3 Arshin Adib-Moghaddam, *The International Politics of the Persian Gulf: A Cultural Genealogy* (Abingdon: Routledge, 2006). p. 139, n. 38.

4 Conversation with the author.

5 Alexandra Di Stefano Pironti, "Iranian repression of Kurds behind rise of militant PJAK," *Rudaw*, 23 January 2014, www.rudaw.net/english/middleeast/iran/23012014 (accessed 6 July 2018).

6 Seymour M. Hersh, "Preparing the battlefield," *New Yorker*, 7 July 2008, https://www.newyorker.com/magazine/2008/07/07/preparing-the-battlefield (accessed 6 July 2018).

7 John C.K. Daly, *U.S.–Turkish Relations: A Strategic Relationship under Stress* (Washington, DC: The Jamestown Foundation, February 2008), jamestown.org/wp-content/uploads/2008/02/Jamestown-DalyUSTurkeyUpdate.pdf (accessed 6 July 2018), p. 19.

8 Sherezad Sheikhani and Asharq al-Awsat, "A visit to the PJAK, Iranian Party for Free Life in Kurdistan," *Ekurd Daily*, 7 September 2010, ekurd.net/mismas/articles/misc2010/7/irankurd631.htm (accessed 6 July 2018).

9 John Pike, "PJAK/PEJAK," *Global Security*, www.globalsecurity.org/military/world/para/pjak.htm (accessed 6 July 2018).

10 "Tehran hangs 6 Sunni Kurds, day after UN concern over Iran executions," *Rudaw*, 3 May 2015, www.rudaw.net/english/middleeast/iran/05032015 (accessed 6 July 2018).

11 Bozorgmehr Sharafedin, "Iran executes Kurdish activist, wary of Kurdish gains in Middle East," *Reuters*, 27 August 2015, www.reuters.com/article/us-iran-rights-kurds/iran-executes-kurdish-activist-wary-of-kurdish-gains-in-middle-east-idUSKCN0QW24H20150827 (accessed 3 April 2018).

12 "PJAK calls on peoples of Iran to fight and stand together," *ANF News*, 31 December 2017, anfenglish.com/news/pjak-calls-on-peoples-of-iran-to-fight-and-stand-together-23940 (accessed 6 July 2018).

13 Saudi Research and Marketing, "Asharq Al-Awsat visits the PJAK," *Asharq Al-Awsat English Archive*, 31 January 2013, eng-archive.aawsat.com/theaawsat/features/asharq-al-awsat-visits-the-pjak (accessed 1 August 2018).

14 Saeed Jalili, "Currency devaluation against US dollar rattles Iran," *Al Jazeera*, 16 February 2018, https://www.aljazeera.com/news/2018/02/currency-devaluation-dollar-rattles-iran-180216123318948.html (accessed 6 July 2018).

15 Rebecca Collard, "The enemy of my enemy: Iran arms Kurds in fight against ISIS," *Time*, 27 August 2014, time.com/3196580/iran-kurds-isis-erbil-iraq/ (accessed 1 August 2018).

16 Dr Majid Rafizadeh, "Are Kurds really treated equally in Iran?" *Al Arabiya English*, 17 June 2016, english.alarabiya.net/en/views/news/middle-east/2016/06/17/Are-Kurds-really-treated-equally-in-Iran-.html (accessed 1 August 2018).

17 George Richards, "Across the Zagros: Iranian influence in Iraqi Kurdistan," *Guardian*, 21 November 2013, www.theguardian.com/world/2013/nov/21/iran-influence-iraqi-kurdistan (accessed 6 July 2018).

18 Lazar Berman, "The Iranian penetration of Iraqi Kurdistan," *Institute for Contemporary Affairs* 16 (3), 21 January 2016, http://jcpa.org/article/the-iranian-penetration-of-iraqi-kurdistan/ (accessed 6 July 2018).

19 Dorsey, "Kurdish battle positions Kurds as US ally."

20 Fazel Hawramy, "Iran willing to normalize ties with KRG, but not without change," *Shabtabnews*, 23 December 2017, https://english.shabtabnews.com/2017/12/23/iran-willing-to-normalize-ties-with-krg-but-not-without-change/ (accessed 1 August 2018).

21 Interview by the author with Najmaldin Karim, 14 April 2018.

22 Farzin Nadimi, "Iran's Afghan and Pakistani proxies: in Syria and beyond?" *Washington Institute for Near East Policy*, 22 August 2016, www.washingtoninstitute.org/policy-analysis/view/irans-afghan-and-pakistani-proxies-in-syria-and-beyond (accessed 6 July 2018).

23 Mohsen Rezaie, *Tabnak* news site, 17 January 2018, cited in Rohollah Faghihi, "Iranian mistrust of Russia surges as Syrian war winds down," *Al-Monitor*, 12 March 2018, www.al-monitor.com/pulse/originals/2018/03/iran-syria-russia-sentiment-reconstruction-spoils-safavi.html (accessed 24 March 2018).

24 Editorial, *Al-Qanoon*, 18 January 2018.

25 Faghihi, "Iranian mistrust of Russia surges as Syrian war winds down."

26 Ali Ghadimi, "How much does the Syrian war cost Iran?" *BBC Farsi*, 26 February 2018, www.bbc.com/persian/iran-features-43157803#Anchor1 (accessed 6 July 2018) (in Farsi).

27 Jeffrey Heller, "Israel endorses independent Kurdish State," *Reuters*, 13 September 2017, https://www.reuters.com/article/us-mideast-crisis-kurds-israel/israel-endorses-independent-kurdish-state-idUSKCN1BO0QZ (accessed 6 July 2018).

28 Berman, "The Iranian Penetration of Iraqi Kurdistan."

29 Ranj Alaadin, "How Iran used the Hezbollah model for domination," *International New York Times*, 31 March 2018.

30 Ben Hubbard and David M. Halfbinger, "Strike in Syria lights up Iran–Israel shadow war," *New York Times*, 10 April 2017, p. A1.

31 "Obama's Pass for Hezbollah," *Wall Street Journal*, 21 December 2017, www.wsj. com/articles/obamas-pass-for-hezbollah-1513813424 (accessed 6 July 2018).

32 Charles Lister, "The Israeli Airstrike on Syria Monday: A Message to Iran, Russia— and Trump," *Daily Beast*, 9 April 2018, www.thedailybeast.com/the-israeli-airstrike-on-syria-monday-a-message-to-iran-russia-and-trump (accessed 6 July 2018).

33 Amanda Erickson, "Iran nuclear deal: what you need to know," *Washington Post*, 12 October 2017, www.msn.com/en-us/news/world/analysis-iran-nuclear-deal-what-you-need-to-know/ar-AAt5nUl (accessed 1 August 2018).

34 Peter Baker and Julie Hirschfeld Davis, "Europe's leaders will urge Trump to save Iran deal," *New York Times*, 24 April 2018, p. A1.

35 Quoted by Roger Cohen, "The moral rot threatening America," *New York Times*, 19 May 2018, p. A21.

36 Gabriela Baczynska, "EU's Tusk asks: 'With friends like Trump, who needs enemies?'" *Reuters*, 16 May 2018, www.reuters.com/article/us-usa-trump-eu/eus-tusk-asks-with-friends-like-trump-who-needs-enemies-idUSKCN1IH1OH (accessed 6 July 2018).

13. RUSSIA RISES

1 Address by Vladimir V. Putin, President of the Russian Federation, to the United Nations General Assembly, 27 September 2015.

2 Jay Solomon and Sam Dagher, "Russia, Iran seen coordinating on defense of Assad regime in Syria," *Wall Street Journal*, 21 September 2015, www.wsj.com/articles/russia-iran-seen-coordinating-on-defense-of-assad-regime-in-syria-1442856556 (accessed 6 July 2018).

3 Laila Bassam, "Insight – How Iranian general plotted out Syrian assault in Moscow," *Reuters*, 7 October 2015, uk.reuters.com/article/uk-mideast-crisis-syria-soleimani-insigh/insight-how-iranian-general-plotted-out-syrian-assault-in-moscow-idUKKCN0S02BX20151007 (accessed 6 July 2018).

4 Natasha Bertrand, "Israeli official: Iran's military mastermind went to Russia to talk to Putin about saving Assad," *Business Insider*, 10 September 2015, uk.businessinsider.com/israeli-official-irans-military-mastermind-went-to-russia-to-talk-to-putin-saving-assad-2015-9 (accessed 6 July 2018).

5 "Read Putin's U.N. General Assembly speech," *Washington Post*, 28 September 2015, www.washingtonpost.com/news/worldviews/wp/2015/09/28/read-putins-u-n-general-assembly-speech/?utm_term=.51556e5051c5 (accessed 6 July 2018).

6 Alec Luhn, "Russia sends artillery and tanks to Syria as part of continued military buildup," *Guardian*, 14 September 2015, www.theguardian.com/world/2015/sep/14/russia-sends-artillery-and-tanks-to-syria-as-part-of-continued-military-buildup (accessed 1 August 2018).

7 Our Foreign Staff, "Russia 'creating forward air operating base in Syria,'" *Telegraph*, 14 September 2015, www.telegraph.co.uk/news/worldnews/middleeast/syria/11864577/Russia-creating-forward-air-operating-base-in-Syria.html (accessed 1 August 2018).

8 Reuters, "US, allies ask Russia to halt strikes outside IS areas in Syria," *Dawn*, 3 October 2015, www.dawn.com/news/1210559/us-allies-ask-russia-to-halt-strikes-outside-is-areas-in-syria (accessed 6 July 2018).

9 Luhn, "Russia sends artillery and tanks to Syria."

10 Reuters, "US, allies ask Russia to halt strikes."

11 Dominic Evans and Suleiman Al-Khalidi, "Assad says Russian air campaign vital to save Middle East," *Reuters*, 4 October 2015, in.reuters.com/article/mideast-crisis-assad-iran/assad-says-russian-air-campaign-vital-to-save-middle-east-idINKCN0RY0EY20151004 (accessed 6 July 2018).

12 Scott Wilson and Joby Warrick, "Assad must go, Obama says," *Washington Post*, 18 August 2011, www.washingtonpost.com/politics/assad-must-go-obama-says/2011/08/18/gIQAelheOJ_story.htm (accessed 1 August 2018).

13 "Syria chemical attack: what we know," *BBC News*, 24 September 2013, www.bbc.com/news/world-middle-east-23927399 (accessed 6 July 2018).

14 Ibid.

15 Ibid.

16 UN Security Council, "Security Council requires scheduled destruction of Syria's chemical weapons, unanimously adopting Resolution 2118 (2013)," *United Nations*, 27 September 2013, www.un.org/press/en/2013/sc11135.doc.htm (accessed 6 July 2018).

17 "UN unanimously adopts Syria arms resolution," *Al Jazeera*, 28 September 2013, www.aljazeera.com/news/middleeast/2013/09/un-set-vote-syria-arms-resolution-20139272250595954106.html (accessed 1 August 2018).

18 Reuters, "UN Security Council votes to adopt resolution demanding destruction of Syria's chemical weapons," *Telegraph*, 28 September 2013, www.telegraph.co.uk/news/worldnews/middleeast/syria/10341131/UN-Security-Council-votes-to-adopt-resolution-demanding-destruction-of-Syrias-chemical-weapons.html (accessed 1 August 2018).

19 "Security Council – Quick Links – Veto List," *Dag Hammarskjöld Library*, United Nations, research.un.org/en/docs/sc/quick (accessed 6 July 2018).

20 "Transcript and video: Trump speaks about strikes in Syria," *New York Times*, 6 April 2017, www.nytimes.com/2017/04/06/world/middleeast/transcript-video-trump-airstrikes-syria.html (accessed 1 August 2018).

21 "US launches cruise missiles on Syrian airbase," *Al Jazeera*, 7 April 2017, www.aljazeera.com/news/2017/04/us-missiles-syria-170407013424492.html (accessed 6 July 2018).

22 "Security Council – Veto List."

23 "Russia slammed for vetoing yet another Syria resolution," *Al Jazeera*, 13 April 2017, www.aljazeera.com/news/2017/04/russia-veto-syria-resolution-170413004627326.html (accessed 1 August 2018).

24 Ibid.

25 Ibid.

26 Chris Graham *et al.*, "Russia blames Israel for attack on Syrian air base as pressure mounts over gas atrocity," *Telegraph*, 8 April 2018, www.telegraph.co.uk/news/2018/04/08/dozens-reported-dead-chemical-attack-insyria-us-blames-russia/ (accessed 6 July 2018).

27 Conor Finnegan, "Russia may have committed war crime in Syria: UN investigators," *ABC News*, 7 March 2018, abcnews.go.com/International/russia-committed-war-crime-syria-investigators/story?id=53580112 (accessed 6 July 2018).

28 Janine di Giovanni, "The man with the toughest job in the world," *Guardian*, 30 July 2015, www.theguardian.com/world/2015/jul/30/staffan-de-mistura-man-with-toughest-job-in-world-syria (accessed 6 July 2018).

29 Ryan Browne and Barbara Starr, "Trump says US will withdraw from Syria 'very soon,'" *CNN*, 29 March 2018, www.cnn.com/2018/03/29/politics/trump-withdraw-syria-pentagon/index.html (accessed 1 August 2018).

30 Kassioun, "The full text of the joint statement of Ankara," *People's Will Party*, 4 April 2018, kassioun.org/en/news-activities/item/25261-the-full-text-of-the-joint-statement-of-ankara (accessed 1 August 2018).

31 Ayla Jean Yackley, "Erdoğan rebuffs Moscow's call to hand Afrin to Syrian government," *Al-Monitor*, 10 April. 2018, www.al-monitor.com/pulse/originals/2018/04/turkey-erdogan-rebuff-call-turn-over-afrin-syria-government.html (accessed 6 July 2018).

32 Anne Barnard and Andrew E. Kramer, "Iran revokes Russia's use of air base, saying Moscow 'betrayed trust,'" *New York Times*, 22 August 2016, www.nytimes.com/2016/08/23/world/middleeast/iran-russia-syria.html (accessed 6 July 2018).

33 Jill Dougherty, "The Gulf War: Moscow's role," *CNN*, 17 January 2001, edition.cnn.com/2001/WORLD/europe/01/16/russia.iraq/index.html (accessed 7 July 2018).

34 Joel Wing, "Russia provided Iraq with details of the US's planned invasion in 2003," *Business Insider*, 15 April 2016, www.businessinsider.com/russia-provided-iraq-with-details-of-the-uss-planned-invasion-in-2003-2016-4 (accessed 7 July 2018).

EPILOGUE

1 Estimate by Human Rights Watch cited by Sarah Almukhtar, "Aid group says Syria has often used gas on civilians," *New York Times*, 14 April 2018, p. A9.

2 Kevin Liptak, "Obama says Syria war 'haunts' him," *CNN*, 23 September 2016, www.cnn.com/2016/09/22/politics/obama-syria-civil-war-haunts/index.html (accessed 1 August 2018).

3 Interview by the author with Fuad Hussein on 26 April 2018.

4 Ibid.

5 Ibid.

6 Ibid.

FURTHER READING

Cagaptay, Soner, *The New Sultan: Erdoğan and the Crisis of Modern Turkey* (London: I.B.Tauris, 2017).

Černy, Hannes, *Iraqi Kurdistan, the PKK and International Relations: Theory and Ethnic Conflict* (London: Routledge, 2018).

Fromkin, David, *A Peace to End All Peace: The Fall of the Ottoman Empire and the Creation of the Modern Middle East* (New York: H. Holt and Co., 2009).

Galbraith, Peter W., *The End of Iraq: How American Incompetence Created a War without End* (New York: Simon & Schuster, 2007).

Hopkirk, Peter, *The Great Game: The Struggle for Empire in Central Asia* (New York: Kodansha International, 1992).

Kinzer, Stephen, *All the Shah's Men: An American Coup and the Roots of Middle East Terror* (Hoboken, NJ: Wiley, 2008).

Lewis, Bernard, *The Middle East: A Brief History of the Last 2,000 Years* (New York: Scribner, 1996).

Mackey, Sandra, *The Reckoning: Iraq and the Legacy of Saddam Hussein* (New York: Norton, 2003).

Makiya, Kanan, *Republic of Fear: The Politics of Modern Iraq* (Berkeley: University of California Press, 1989).

Phillips, David L., *Losing Iraq: Inside the Postwar Reconstruction Fiasco* (New York: Basic Books, 2006).

———— *The Kurdish Spring* (New Brunswick, NJ: Transaction Publishers, 2015).

TATORT Kurdistan, *Democratic Autonomy in North Kurdistan: The Council Movement, Gender Liberation, and Ecology—in Practice: A Reconnaissance into Southeastern Turkey* (Porsgrunn, Norway: New Compass Press, 2013).

Yildiz, Kerim, *The Kurds in Iraq: The Past, Present and Future* (London: Pluto Press, 2007).

INDEX